THE
AMERICAN MUSICAL

History & Development

Peter H. Riddle, Ph.D.

Edited by
Gay Riddle

mosaic press

National Library of Canada Cataloguing in Publication

Riddle, Peter H.
    The American musical : history & development / Peter
Riddle.

Includes bibliographical references.
ISBN 0-88962-828-9

    1. Musicals—United States—History and criticism—
Textbooks.
I. Title.

ML2054.R542 2003   782.1'4'0973   C2003-906738-6

Published by Mosaic Press, offices and warehouse at 1252 Speers Road, Units 1 and 2, Oakville, Ontario, L6L 5N9, Canada and Mosaic Press, PMB 145, 4500 Witmer Industrial Estates, Niagara Falls, NY, 14305-1386, U.S.A.

Mosaic Press acknowledges the assistance of the Canada Council and the Department of Canadian Heritage, Government of Canada through the Book Publishing Industry Development Program (BPIDP) for their support of our publishing activities.

3 4873 00315 5421

Mosaic Press in Canada:
1252 Speers Road, Units 1 & 2,
Oakville, Ontario
L6L 5N9
Phone/Fax: 905-825-2130
mosaicpress@on.aibn.com

Le Conseil des Arts   The Canada Council
du Canada | for the Arts

www.mosaic-press.com

Mosaic Press in U.S.A.:
4500 Witmer Industrial Estates
PMB 145, Niagara Falls, NY
14305-1386
Phone/Fax: 1-800-387-8992
mosaicpress@on.aibn.com

Also by
Peter H. Riddle:

Fiction

Twelfth Birthday

Thirteenth Summer

Fourteenth Concerto

Running Away

Non-fiction

Trains From Grandfather's Attic

Wiring Your Lionel Layout (Three Volumes)

Greenberg's Guide To Lionel Trains 1901-1942, Vol. III

Tips & Tricks For Toy Train Operators (1st & 2nd Editions)

Easy Lionel Layouts You Can Build

America's Standard Gauge Electric Trains

Track Planning Ideas For Toy Trains

About The Author

Peter H. Riddle joined the faculty of the School of Music at Acadia University (Wolfville, Nova Scotia) in 1969 after eight years of public school teaching in the United States and Canada. He initiated that institution's instrumental music education program and currently teaches theory and history, in addition to courses in music theatre.

A prolific author, Riddle has published four novels, eleven books on the history and technology of antique model trains, and numerous articles in music and hobby periodicals. His wife, Gay, edits all of his non-fiction works.

Foreword

The chronicle of musical theatre is immense and astoundingly diverse, even when limited to the modern era, which dates from the Princess Theatre musicals of Jerome Kern early in the 20th century. I have not attempted to provide a comprehensive history of the medium, but rather to comment upon aspects of its development and high points in its repertoire that represent important trends as I see them. Critics may accuse me of leaving out their favourites, and I am no doubt guilty of this. My choices have simply been guided by my own taste, for which I take full responsibility.

I dedicate this book to the students and faculty of the School of Music of Acadia University, past, present and future, and particularly to those who are, at the time of publication, involved in our fledgling music theatre program. May your efforts continue to bear fruit, and your careers to prosper.

Contents

INTRODUCTION

The primary purpose inherent in the vast majority of dramatic works is to recount stories of characters and their lives, whether real or imaginary, ordinary or supernatural. Above all, good drama most often deals with subjects to which the audience can relate, either those events and situations they may already have experienced, or those which they can envision themselves as encountering.

This element of empathy accounts in part for the impact of such realistic works as Arthur Miller's *Death of a Salesman*, but even fantasy can be explained in these terms. The exploits of a Sir Lancelot or an Indiana Jones may seem far-fetched and implausible, yet if the audience members can imagine themselves assuming those same roles, however improbably, the performance succeeds. Even a Merlin (or a Harry Potter) is an essentially credible character, if not in reality, then in conceivable imagination.

In this context, the longstanding historical bond between drama and music would seem to be almost absurdly artificial. The insertion or imposition of songs and dances and overtures should be rejected as impossibly foreign to dramatic presentations, because music is an adjunct to everyday life, and not an element inherent in it.

Even in the blush of first love, for example, one does not suddenly burst into song in broad daylight, impelled by nothing more than being in the vicinity of the object of one's affections.[1] People don't do such things in real life, but on the stage we not only accept it, we applaud it. Why?

The answer lies in the capacity for drama to involve the audience, on a deep and emotional level, in the story, characters and sensibilities portrayed on stage. While conventional inhibitions would prevent our singing in public to express ourselves, we might *want* to do so. The character in the play is therefore doing it for us.

To cite another example, how does the average person react to sudden violence, such as a shooting where the victim lies dying in the street? By attempting to administer first aid? By calling 911? Perhaps, but one is just as likely to scream for help or to run in terror. The average person would not, however, gather the victim in close and sing tenderly of love and eternity as life ebbs away.[2] At the very least, we would try to get help instead.

Powerful emotions sometimes require the suspension of disbelief, and staged drama does not always demand our acceptance of the credibility of a character's actions. We might suspect that we would not always react wisely or effectively in a given situation, such as a shooting or a tragic accident. Whatever the reality, however, we would *prefer* to perform heroically or nobly, or especially lovingly. A tender song at such a moment might be totally inappropriate, but we would wish it to be otherwise.

And so we accept the inclusion (some would say intrusion) of music as an accessory to some types of dramatic presentation, however improbable that would be in the everyday world. But this does not explain the development of genres in which the music seems not to be appended to the drama, but vice versa. For example, the excesses of operatic performance in the Baroque period of musical history were such as to obscure the content of the plot, and even to render it superfluous, but this did not diminish the popularity of the form.[3]

To the annoyance of many, our lives are attended by music on a daily basis. Business establishments pipe it in, telephones subject us to other people's taste while we are on hold, and inconsiderate drivers broadcast it at unbearable decibel levels as they traverse the streets. Radio and television are everywhere. But this tangential music is not integrated into our lives. It surrounds us, but does not necessarily apply specifically to our activities at any given time. It may accompany us, but it has nothing really to do with us, other than to offer entertainment if we are in the appropriate mood. Were we able to choose our own background music, to have it spring forth from lush strings or inspirational brass to suit our daily deeds, our lives would likely be far more romantic, splendid and opulent.

The theatre can and does provide this kind of dedicated accompaniment. As an experiment, secure the filmed version of the final work by the team of Rodgers and Hammerstein, *The Sound of Music*. Watch the opening sequence, that magnificent sweeping panorama of mountainous serenity that culminates in a delightful image of a lovely young nun, her arms flung out to embrace the overwhelming emotion of just being alive.

But play it with the sound turned off.

It doesn't really work that way, does it? It may be simply that this scene is so familiar to most of us that it seems incomplete without the music. But to someone who has never seen it before (if indeed there is any such person in the developed world!), the image might be attractive, but devoid of strong emotional impact without the music.

Such is the power of music that we can routinely accept its improbable presence in order to indulge in emotions we cannot express for ourselves so effectively. We know there is no orchestra atop that mountain, and that not one nun in a million can sing like the incomparable Julie Andrews. So what? We can feel what she is purported to be feeling, not in spite of the music, but because of it.

To cite another example, rent the movie *Jaws* and watch the early sequence showing two young people on the beach, just prior to the first shark attack. Again, turn the sound off. The scene may be dark and even somewhat foreboding, but without a more specific context, it might be merely a midnight swim, a love tryst, even a tender romance.

Now play it again, this time with the sound on, and notice how the sense that something terrible is about to happen becomes inescapable. Those insistent low-pitched cellos, rhythmic and tuneless, are not just auxiliary to, but are an essential element of the very essence of menace and terror that the audience experiences long before the fish takes its first bite. Until then, the music has nothing to do with what we are seeing on the screen, but everything to do with what we expect (or are afraid) to see.

Similar examples abound in the theatre, and for those who have never seen the stage plays, filmed versions are available that convey the same atmosphere. The brooding "Prologue" to *West Side Story* and the opening street scene in *Guys and Dolls* both herald portraits of New York City, albeit very different ones. These two moods, one ominous and the other comic and satirical, emanate directly from the styles of the music.

While the above two examples are visual as well as musical, a setting may be primarily emotional instead, such as the opening song "Try To Remember" from *The Fantasticks*,[4] a gentle solo replete with nostalgia and tenderness. An even better known illustration is the revolutionary curtain-raiser of the best remembered musical of 1943, *Oklahoma!* To an audience accustomed to overtures, chorus lines and extravaganzas, the image of a solitary cowboy singing about the weather must have been extraordinary.[5]

However implausible music may seem to be in the context of theatrical production, it is, and may have been since the dawn of drama, one of the integral and often essential elements used to convey action and emotion. The early filmmakers realized this. Before the advent of sound motion pictures,[6] movie houses regularly employed musicians (most often a pianist or an organist) to supply an appropriate background: ballads for the love scenes, ominous tremolos to convey menace, and allegros and galops for the chase sequences. Staples of the trade for these artists were the famous Bach Toccata for horror films like *Phantom of the Opera*, and the Overture to William Tell (Rossini) for almost every motion picture with a western theme, predating its adoption by *The Lone Ranger* in the 1930s.

To say that music is essential to theatre is simplistic and incorrect. Certainly fine drama exists without it. Yet it is undeniable that music is almost universally seen to enhance some types of theatrical performance in the broadest sense, especially on film. As evidence of this, try to recall any mainstream motion picture since 1930 that is without at least some sort of background musical accompaniment. The list of such productions is amazingly short.

Stage productions without music are much more common, and yet they are often the targets of composers who see the addition of melody as an improvement. This is not necessarily a recent phenomenon. Ever since the mid 19th century, far more people are familiar with parts of Felix Mendelssohn's incidental music to *A Midsummer Night's Dream* than have ever seen Shakespeare's play.[7] Similarly, the number of stage plays that have been translated into musicals is fairly extensive,[8] while musicals that have been stripped of their tunes to become straight dramatic plays are very rare.

It may be true that some works of art should not be tampered with. It is hard to imagine a song and dance version of *Death of a Salesman* or *The Glass Menagerie*, for example. Yet even serious works can benefit from a musical score as background, to establish atmosphere. This is especially evident in some television productions, where music is not only expected by audiences, but, if tastefully selected, is a great enhancement. In some quarters, however, there is a perception that serious drama and musical drama are mutually exclusive.

In the current era this is certainly not the case, and it may be argued that it never was. Although much musical theatre is certainly lightweight and even superficial, there are notable exceptions dating back many decades, such as *Show Boat* (1927) and *Porgy and Bess* (1935), both of which were groundbreaking and controversial experiments in their own time.

Musical drama then, if inherently fantastic, is believable fantasy. Like escapist fiction or an adventure movie, it can be seen purely as entertainment, but often its content is anything but trivial. As with the two examples cited directly above, recent trends in musical theatre deal with significant social issues. Such plays are entertainment, but also much more than that. And equally important, they are now disseminated much more widely. Thanks to film and electronic media, audiences are no longer limited by ease of access to the larger cities. Some of the best of Broadway can be enjoyed in our own homes.

The technological revolution of the twentieth century changed forever the definitions of musical theatre, not only due to the advent of motion pictures, but to the availability of stage productions through the media of film and television, and most recently via home entertainment devices (VHS tape and DVD). To be fair, Hollywood produced some very credible film versions of musical stage plays as early as the 1930s. Perhaps the best early example is the 1936 version of *Show Boat*.[9] Similarly faithful were at least two Rodgers and Hammerstein films, *Oklahoma!* and *The King and I*, and both *West Side Story* and *The Music Man* also came very close to capturing the essence of the stage versions.

Nevertheless, mediocre adaptations and outright failures were more numerous than triumphs. The movie industry was much more successful when working with original material. The so-called "Hollywood" musicals, especially those from the studios of MGM, established a successful form of entertainment that is quite distinct from the Broadway style.

The ever-increasing expansion of television networks created a further opportunity for a new approach, as well as greater exposure to a larger audience. As early as 1954, the small screen presentation of *Peter Pan* had the definite appearance and flavour of the stage production, including the same principal actor, Mary Martin, in the lead role. As an added bonus, a high-quality film of that TV show preserved for future audiences the opportunity to witness an original Broadway cast performing in a close approximation of the stage setting.[10]

Subsequently some well-established composers and lyricists tried their hands at television[11] and the movies,[12] which with the advent of wide-screen technology gave musical vehicles much more scope and presence. There were also attempts to film some productions directly on stage, although without much success until the last quarter of the twentieth century. These early efforts lacked the ambiance and immediacy of being in the theatre. They tended to be static and somewhat remote, especially to audiences accustomed to the close-ups and scene changes of conventional motion pictures.

This situation changed with the filming of several Stephen Sondheim musicals, resulting in the most faithful mass-produced versions of stage musicals to date: *Sunday In the Park with George*, *Sweeney Todd*, and especially *Into the Woods*. These productions were filmed directly on stage, with no effort made to disguise that fact, and they provide an extra dividend.

Through skilful direction, close-ups and camera angles, these motion pictures focus the audience's attention on the elements of importance inherent in every scene.

These versions preserve the distinctive elements of stagecraft that theatre audiences have come to expect. The clever sets of *Sweeney Todd* and *Into the Woods*, for example, are typical of theatrical trickery: revolving sets, trap doors and flyaway scenery. However, the close-ups, panned shots and other decisions by the directors give the plays the intimacy of a movie, characteristics that could not be achieved simply by filming a play with a stationary camera or two. At the same time, these efforts come very close to achieving the illusion of being in the theatre.

More recently, Andrew Lloyd Webber's phenomenally (and in the opinion of some, unaccountably) successful *Cats* has been filmed directly on stage for VHS and DVD release. The essentially static style of that show lends itself well to this approach, but much of what made it so popular on stage is lost when viewed on a television screen. *Cats* is packed with clever lyrics and lovely melodies, but almost totally lacking in linear story, and the splendour of the setting and the costumes is muted when removed from the expanse of a theatrical stage. When separated from the ambiance of Broadway and the confines of a darkened theatre, the play loses some of its ability to command sustained attention.

A more recent and successful approach to certain types of musicals is the concert presentation, the most famous of which to date is the filmed performance of *Les Miserables*. With minimal sets and very little overt action, this format carries the story line primarily through the power of the music. Although interspersed with a few brief projected visuals from the stage play to reinforce certain climactic moments, the performance is mounted with limited dramatic interaction between the characters, confined as they are behind their microphones.

Nevertheless the format is decidedly appropriate to this type of production, due in part to very strong casting, which includes the original Jean Valjean in the English language edition (Colm Wilkinson). But the most important factor of its effectiveness lies in the fact that the core of *Les Miserables* is the music. In a conventional musical, the songs are interspersed throughout a spoken dramatic presentation. Like a traditional opera, however, *Les Miserables* is entirely sung, with recitatives, arias and choruses replacing what would be spoken dialog in a more conventional musical.[13]

This element of continuous music becomes even more significant when the concert presentation is compared to the three Stephen Sondheim works cited above. In *Sunday In the Park with George*, *Sweeney Todd*,[14] and *Into the Woods*, the balance between spoken dialog and lyrics is much more heavily weighted toward the latter. In this respect, Sondheim was one of the early pioneers in the movement toward the development of the operatic musical.

Sweeney Todd has also been filmed in a recent concert version. Although there is a small amount of spoken dialog, the story line depends far more upon the lyrics, and the minimal staging is entirely sufficient to engage the attention.[15] Other shows would lend themselves to this format, most notably *Miss Saigon*.[16] Although the presence of a helicopter on stage tended initially to dominate the publicity surrounding this show, its physical presence is not an essential element in the story, and the music is more than powerful enough to make a concert presentation successful.

The last decade of the twentieth century saw a resurgence of the Broadway-style musical in its many forms, traditional, operatic and experimental, and the new century finds it in good health. In North America, its history is said to begin with an obscure play entitled *The Black Crook* in 1866, but this is an oversimplification. Musical theatre is much, much older, and the form we commonly call the "Broadway" musical is not that different from some of its predecessors, either in subject matter or in structure. How this came to be is a fascinating story.

ONE
Pink Tights

475 performances![17] In 1866, this was an astonishing record for a dramatic presentation in North America.

Little more than a year after the close of the American Civil War, the reconstruction of the southern states had barely begun. Economic conditions throughout the United States were gradually improving, but transportation was primitive and very slow. The vast distances across the North American continent differed greatly from the compact geography of Europe, and the major population centres of the United States were relatively isolated by comparison.

A network of roads linking major cities such as Boston, New York and Philadelphia was in place, but they were unpaved in the modern sense. A journey of any significant distance normally required a horse-drawn coach. This mode of transportation was not particularly comfortable over such rough surfaces, given the primitive suspension systems and cramped interiors of the vehicles. In any case, the majority of people rarely saw the necessity to travel more than a few miles from their homes.

Major changes had begun during the previous decade with the almost explosive development of the first true mass transportation system, the railroad. In 1850, just 9,000 miles of track was in service, mostly in the northeastern states, but by 1860 this figure had tripled, and rail lines reached the Great Lakes in the north and the Mississippi delta in the south.[18] However, travel by rail was arduous and sometimes even dangerous, and for the average person, long-distance travel was a rarity, to be undertaken only under the pressure of necessity.

Today we enjoy almost unlimited access to the cultural centres of the world. Nowhere is more than a day away by air. But in 1866, especially in North America, almost no one would consider a journey to a far distant city just to see a play or to hear a concert. This severely limited the potential audience for such cultural events to the numbers who were within reasonable traveling distance.

Theatrical productions were popular in the large cities of 19th century America, but in more isolated and rural locations, traveling companies of players were the only source of such entertainment. The actors went to the people, rather than vice versa, and gave only one or at most a few performances in any given community. Only in large urban areas such as New York could one expect to find productions that were repeated over the course of several weeks.

Furthermore, the inclusion of music in the theatres of the United States was generally the exception rather than the rule. Unlike Europe, with its concentrations of urban populations, North America could boast few permanent orchestras and even fewer opera companies. Cultural entertainment of this magnitude was most often imported, and while visits from European ensembles were increasing, they were still far from common. In order to make a reasonable profit, such groups had to perform where a large potential audience was within close proximity, such as Boston or New York.

The first permanent theatre in North America is generally considered to have been established in 1753, the New Theatre on Nassau Street in New York,[19] but it was not intended primarily for musical productions. Occasional European imports with music were performed there, such as John Gay's *The Beggar's Opera*, and over the next century, home-grown musical plays appeared occasionally. But the expense of such plays and the lack of available musicians limited their production mostly to major centres. While the inclusion of songs in a play was not unheard of, they were seen as embellishments.[20] Original indigenous productions to which the music was central were uncommon.

"The early years of the 19th century were barren indeed for the American Musical Theatre."[21] Only in cities such as New York or Philadelphia could companies afford to keep singers, dancers and musicians on the payroll,[22] and they were employed mainly to provide entertainment between the acts of strictly dramatic works.[23] The major staple of the 19th century playhouse continued to be conventional drama.

One such play, a Faustian effort of questionable quality, was scheduled to open at Niblo's Garden in New York City in the autumn of 1866. Essentially a melodrama, and a mediocre one at that, *The Black Crook* was not expected to be a hit. At best the promoters hoped to break even, and except for a fortuitous accident, the play would almost certainly have had a very short run.

Earlier that year, impresarios Henry C. Jarrett and Harry Palmer had booked a French ballet troupe to perform at the Academy of Music on 14th

Street.[24]   Productions of this sort were very expensive in the 19th century, necessitating ocean travel and accommodation for the more than one hundred dancers, in addition to their stipends.   Therefore it was a major blow to the promoters when the Academy burned to the ground, and they were forced to seek an alternate site for the ballet to which they were irrevocably committed.

Apparently an auditorium large enough to accommodate the needs of the dance troupe was almost impossible to find.   Among the limited number of options the promoters considered was Niblo's Garden, but that theatre was obliged to honour its contract for *The Black Crook*.   Jarrett and Palmer found themselves saddled with a stranded ballet troupe and no venue, and therefore no means by which to pay their expenses.   The manager of Niblo's Garden, William Wheatley, was similarly encumbered with a second-rate play that held little promise of economic success.   That these three men conspired to join forces is one of the luckiest accidents in the history of theatre, and one that made them financially secure for life.[25]

With the addition of the ballet troupe to the production, *The Black Crook* was transformed into an extravaganza of epic proportions, each performance lasting more than five hours.   It touched a sensitive nerve in those repressed Victorian times, one that begged to be exploited.   Then as now, the audience for cultural events such as opera or ballet was a selective one, and did not for the most part include the average inhabitant of New York City.   At the same time, theatre in general was severely constrained by the moral climate of the times.   And so, when *The Black Crook* opened on September 12, 1866, two worlds came together with astonishing results.

Wheatley, Jarrett and Palmer embellished the play with music, song and dance, and a lavish assortment of special effects, even including a simulated hurricane.   To make the best use of the dancers, the plot was expanded by the addition of alluring spirits and water sprites.[26]   Most significantly, "whenever the melodrama began to drag, the girls rushed on and danced."[27]   The ballet troupe retained the basic elements of their traditional costumes, in which their shapely limbs, encased in pink tights, were constantly on display.   However, the manner of their dancing was modified from the artistically stylized movements typical of *Swan Lake* or *The Nutcracker*, becoming more suggestive and close to erotic.

If it may be assumed that the ballet troupe was classically trained and its members devoted to their art, they must have found themselves in severe financial straits to have been willing to change their approach so dramatically.   To the average Victorian gentleman, this revelation of the female form, in the comparatively respectable surroundings of the theatre, must have been an irresistible attraction. As a result, the mostly male audiences came in record numbers, night after night.

In a tradition begun by *The Beggar's Opera*, much of the music was borrowed from existing compositions that were already well known to the audience, to which new lyrics were added. This guaranteed instant familiarity for the audience, a technique that the 20th century Broadway stage has used extensively to promote success.[28] In addition to the dances, songs were added which had little to do with the plot, and which were blatantly suggestive in nature. One such tune, "You Naughty, Naughty Men," attained great popularity, and marked the inception of the musical comedy-inspired hit song.[29]

Although remarkably tame by modern standards, *The Black Crook* achieved almost instant notoriety. Denounced from pulpits and attacked in published reviews, it blossomed under all the attention,[30] and lasted a full sixteen months in New York. There followed a series of successful tours and many imitative shows. Whereas a classical ballet would have excited little prurient interest, despite the similar display of the dancers' bodies, the combination of apparent nudity[31] and risqué lyrics signalled the inception of a new era in entertainment.[32]

Even though attendance at the legitimate theatre was, if not always highly regarded, at least considered decent, the unsavoury reputation of *The Black Crook* led some customers to go there in disguise.[33] Rumours of the play's supposed eroticism kept the box office busy, and the attempts of censors to vilify the production had the opposite effect. Rather than discouraging attendance, the self-righteous sermons and explicit reviews titillated prospective audiences, and everyone associated with the production prospered.

One often-overlooked element in the success of *The Black Crook* was the clever combination of two tantalizing ingredients. In addition to implied sex, the muddled plot also portrayed the Devil himself, and the threat of sin and corruption to one's immortal soul. The use of sex to sell tickets is probably as old as theatre itself, and by pairing it with such pseudo-religious overtones, the producers transformed it into the main attraction. It became a banquet of forbidden fruit that radically changed the direction of theatre in North America.

The play was a triumph of style over substance. While the plot was dismissed as "rubbish" and "trashy" in the press,[34] it was nevertheless praised for the quality of its staging and its scenic effects. In an attempt to attract repeat business, the promoters invested heavily to keep the production fresh, periodically adding new scenes and dances. Proving that money makes money, these infusions of cash kept the play on stage for an astonishing 475 performances. The concept of the musical spectacular was born.

The Black Crook ushered in an entirely new style of North American theatre, and was quickly imitated. Within a short time, similar productions could be seen in fourteen New York City playhouses.[35] In a variety of guises, popular musical theatre became the dominant form of live entertainment in North America, unrivalled until the advent of radio, motion pictures and television.

TWO
Of Satire And Slavery

The various categories of musical theatre and the names by which they are called are not always clearly defined, and are inclined to overlap. Prior to the phenomenon of *The Black Crook*, most musical productions, whether serious or comic, tended to be described by the catch-all term "opera." In theory and general practice, an opera[36] is a drama in which all of the dialog is sung and the music is continuous, or almost so.

Today we usually associate opera with large-scale productions, most specifically those from the 18th century forward, that are associated with well-known composers of serious music. But in the 18th century, especially in England, the term was often applied to any production that featured both songs and dialog in various combinations.[37]

Modern opera may be said to begin with the reform movement of the middle 1700s,[38] when the fantastic plots and excessive ornamentation of the Baroque era gave way to an emphasis upon simpler, more beautiful melodies and plot lines that dealt with real people and real issues. Whether serious or comic, an opera was first and foremost intended to be entertainment. Those that have survived and have been elevated to the status of great art owe that position largely to the skill of their composers, although some were originally considered to be little more than transient entertainment.[39]

The Marriage of Figaro, for example, is primarily associated with the name of Mozart, as *Fidelio* is with Beethoven. We speak of Wagnerian opera, and of the grand operas of Verdi and Puccini and Strauss. This emphasis upon the creators of the music tends to de-emphasize the many elements that must come together for a successful production, not the least of which is the story line.

To cite one example, the music Wolfgang Mozart wrote for *The Marriage of Figaro* makes it perhaps the best known 18th century opera, and deservedly so. However, in the context of the times, the commercial success of an opera depended in equal measure upon its dramatic or comic content. In that regard, *Figaro* is a prototype musical comedy.

At times satire,[40] at times almost farce, and frequently with a subtext of sexual innuendo, the story line reflects the social climate of the times. Great humour is derived from contrasting the cleverness of the common person with the supposed stupidity of members of the ruling class. The librettist, Lorenzo da Ponte, fashioned the original tale (by Beaumarchais) into an intricate and amusing comedy that poked merciless fun at the nobility.

Today, for reasons of social change and the problem of language, *Figaro* is known more for the beauty of its music than for the wit and wisdom of its plot, but this was not the case when it was written. The political overtones of the story accounted for much of its original commercial success. Theatre was seen as a viable instrument (and weapon) of social change, and while the genius of Mozart has preserved his opera beyond its immediate social value, the most successful popular entertainment in the 18th century was often topical.

That the ruling classes of the 18th century were corrupt and removed from the people is an undeniable fact. Those in power, then as now, were too often concerned with amassing their own personal fortunes. However, a growing literacy among the general population meant a greater awareness of these excesses, and social commentary in literature and theatre gained in popularity.

The most famous theatrical attack upon the aristocracy was undoubtedly *The Beggar's Opera*, written by John Gay and first presented in 1728. Despite the inclusion of the word "opera" in its title, its form was totally unlike the Baroque art of the day. Gay's lyrics were set to tunes already well known to audiences, and the emphasis was upon their satire and wit, rather than upon the music. Among the targets of the satire, the members of the ruling class, enthusiasm was understandably lacking, but the general audiences responded with delight.

In fact, Gay had inadvertently created a new form, today usually referred to as the ballad opera. Unlike the art opera, which was almost invariably in Italian, the ballad opera was written in the language of the people (in this case English), and was therefore instantly accessible to the audience. All of its elements, the humour, the familiar music and the satire, combined to make it the most successful English theatrical production of the century. At a time when successful plays were presented only once, or at most four or five times consecutively, *The Beggar's Opera* lasted sixty-two performances, a record unequalled for nearly a century thereafter.[41]

John Gay's success depended in great part upon the growing level of education among the public.[42] Whereas in the previous century opera was entertainment created primarily for the enjoyment of the nobility, his cynical ballad opera recognized the ever-increasing sophistication of the common people, as well as their ability to grasp and react to the politics of the times. It was the beginning of a form of social commentary that would exert profound influence upon the revolutionary spirit of the latter 18th century.

The development of musical theatre, or more specifically "musical comedy" in the modern sense, owes much to John Gay. He was the first librettist and lyricist to integrate song and story by having the musical numbers relate to and grow out of the plot.[43] In this respect, *The Beggar's Opera* also satirized the prevailing form of Baroque opera, in which the vocal talents of the singers were emphasized at the expense of the story line. This was an important factor in the reform movement that eventually led to such successes as Mozart's *Figaro*.

In many respects there is a direct kinship between *The Beggar's Opera* and *The Black Crook*. Both are essentially ballad operas, with music drawn from the popular repertoire and not specifically composed for the occasion. Both reflected the times in which they were written, although it may be argued that John Gay's work had a somewhat higher purpose.[44] And both exerted a profound influence upon those who came after.

Another similarity is sometimes overlooked. Like *Crook*, *The Beggar's Opera* was also attacked by some elements of society for its moral degeneracy. The whores and criminals who were the principal characters in John Gay's plot served to draw parallels with the corrupt activities of the ruling class. Those who failed to recognize the implied social commentary were affronted instead by the portrayal on stage of such symbols of immorality. And as with *The Black Crook*, the controversy contributed greatly to the play's popularity and success.

The forms of popular theatrical musical entertainment during the century prior to *The Black Crook* were somewhat restricted, most falling roughly into the categories of art opera or ballad opera. One divergent type that appeared, however, was uniquely American. The black-face minstrel show, which dates from the early 1840s, grew out of the social climate in the United States in the middle of the 19th century.

Some background to the phenomenon of minstrelry is in order. Slavery was arguably the most divisive social issue to afflict the young American nation. While the northern states had moved toward industrialization and manufacturing as mainstays of the economy, the agricultural south required cheap labour to sustain its plantations. The enslavement of black (Negro) Africans to work the fields ensured maximum profits, but it was a practice so devoid of human rights that it led ultimately to the Civil War (1861-1865, also known as the War Between the States).

The concept of slavery would seem to be anathema to the very principles upon which the United States was founded. Its Constitution and Declaration of Independence were crafted in accordance with the belief in the equality of all men, and their right to the freedom to seek their own destiny. This attitude came largely as a reaction to the social divisions between commoners and aristocracy that existed in Europe. But the very wording of these noble principles is significant. The laws of the new country were based upon the concept that all *men* were created equal. And while not so specifically stated, the word "men" referred almost exclusively to white protestant male citizens. Women and members of other races and non-Christian religions were simply neither considered nor included.

It is a great temptation to interpret the actions of previous generations in terms of our contemporary standards, and therefore to condemn the white male-dominated society of 19th century America. This simplistic approach fails to recognize that social conditions are products of many interwoven factors, the most significant of which is usually economic. The domestic dependence of women in pioneer America, for example, may have had some of its roots in religious tradition, but it was also seen as essential to simple survival.

In a time when infant mortality, disease and the dangers of frontier living exacted a huge toll, the preservation of the family was of primary importance. To produce and raise many children was seen as desirable, if not absolutely essential. Any tour through a colonial cemetery will encounter the graves of huge numbers of children who did not survive infancy. A woman's primary responsibility was seen as the bearing and nurturing of as many offspring as possible, in the hope that at least some would survive to adulthood. To do so safely, she required economic support and physical protection. This accounted in large part for each gender's social position and responsibilities.

It has long been believed that the American nation was founded upon acceptance of religious diversity. While this is to some extent true, in that religious freedom was granted by law to various denominations, it was widely interpreted to apply only to branches of Christianity. Toleration for diversity did not extend to those considered to be pagan, or to those whose racial origins were widely believed to be inferior.

Whereas the framers of the United States system of government championed equality of opportunity, many of them were also owners of African slaves, and apparently did not choose to recognize the contradiction between such ownership and the principles they espoused. In simple terms, the African slaves were not defined as "men" by the standards of the time. Instead they were *property*, with neither rights of citizenship nor control over their own destiny.

In fairness, this attitude was not universal. In the south, slavery was promoted as absolutely essential to the survival of the agrarian economy. The laws of the more industrialized northern states did not permit slavery, although the social and economic position of the relatively small African population in the north was definitely inferior, and in many cases precarious. Sadly, it is safe to say that the prevailing majority attitude, north and south, was one of discrimination against, and a feeling of superiority toward, any race other than white.

As the debate over slavery increased, it became fashionable to derive humour from the imitation of Negro life and character. This brand of comedic exploitation quickly found its way into the theatre, as presented by white actors in blackface makeup. Through songs, dances and comic repartee, the minstrel show presented idealized characterizations that bore little resemblance to the truth, and "fashioned a romantic and sentimental recreation of a plantation experience that never existed."[45]

The minstrel show exerted several different types of influence upon musical theatre. First, it inspired the creation of new music specifically for the stage, the most famous of which were the melodies written by a northern white composer named Stephen Foster. Although he lived most of his life far removed from the cotton plantations, such songs as "Old Folks At Home" and "My Old Kentucky Home" evoked the romantic but fictional image of a genteel southern life in which benevolent masters provided for the contented Negroes who worked their lands.[46]

The minstrel shows also featured dance sequences that were included for their own sake, rather than as part of an overall plot. This type of entertainment would later become a staple of burlesque and especially of the *revue*, that peculiarly American form of stage entertainment that would culminate years later in such shows as the Ziegfeld Follies and George White's Scandals. In fact, the related forms of burlesque and revue, and the more sanitized vaudeville, all adopted much of the basic format of the minstrel show.

Although blackface entertainment survived well into the 20th century,[47] a variety of competing formats arose after the Civil War, and especially after the success of *The Black Crook*. Significantly, Negro entertainers, as opposed to white performers in blackface makeup, took the first steps toward acceptance in their own right, although it would be many years before their talents would be properly recognized.

In the intervening years, and in fact well into the years following World War Two, mainstream entertainment remained primarily a white domain. The influences of 18th century ballad opera, the minstrel show and the infant concept of musical comedy as represented by *The Black Crook* came together to create a dominant format known as burlesque, and its slightly less disreputable cousins, vaudeville and the revue.

THREE
The Naughty Shows

Whatever its ancillary contributions to music and drama may have been, the primary revolution of *The Black Crook*, in terms of popular culture, was to put the female body on display in a theatrical setting. Although the play spawned many imitators, eager to cash in on the same sort of success, its greater influence was the development of entirely new formats, one of which came to borrow from the parody and satire of the traditional English burlesque, and from the format of the American minstrel show.

A burlesque is by definition a form of theatrical entertainment based upon spoof and ridicule. In that sense, it also owes its origins in part to *The Beggar's Opera*. The elements of burlesque are comic imitation, exaggeration and caricature. As adapted for American audiences in the latter 19th century, it borrowed the structure of the minstrels, becoming a series of skits, songs and dances that would today be called a variety show. And from the very beginning, sex was a central theme.

In 1868, hard on the heels of the success of *The Black Crook*, New York's Niblo's Garden imported a risqué troupe of comediennes from Great Britain, billed as *Lydia Thompson and her English Blonds*. It was an era when female performers were often considered to be of low repute, even those who confined their participation to the more respectable forms of drama. Lydia Thompson not only appeared to fit this unsavoury stereotype, she flaunted it.

Her act consisted of parodies of classic plays and mythological themes, a type of satire calculated to appeal to the working class public who viewed such art forms as highbrow and therefore fair game for ridicule. Although actual nudity was never an issue in her troupe's performances, their skin-tight costumes revealed more than they concealed, and the juxtaposition of ample female flesh and supposedly artistic drama was the source of much humour for the exclusively male audiences. It was forbidden entertainment, and therefore all the more desirable.

Thompson also knew how to work the media. Using reverse psychology, she stoutly[48] defended the dignity and professionalism of all women in the theatre. She conveniently ignored the differences between those whose talent lay in dramatic portrayal, and her own company of satirists whose most obvious attraction was their sex appeal. It is said that "one of her girls once horse-whipped a *Chicago Times* writer who impugned their morals."[49] In show business there is no such thing as bad publicity, since any kind of notoriety usually results in increased box office traffic.

A typical 19th century burlesque show made fun of traditional culture, as did *The Beggar's Opera* in its sendup of Baroque operatic excesses and societal corruption a century and a half earlier. In crude comic skits, figures of importance such as judges and policemen were mercilessly lampooned. Another favourite target was the legitimate theatre, wherein excerpts from well-known legitimate plays were presented in comic imitations, replete with innuendo, double entendres and overt sexual humour. The comedy was obvious and often lewd, and depended greatly upon outrageous puns of a sexual nature.

As the genre developed, competition for the working man's dollar became intense, and promoters constantly sought new and ever more risqué acts to feature. An important step forward (or backward, depending upon one's point of view) occurred at the 1893 World's Fair, with the importation of that middle eastern staple, the harem or belly dance. Displaying her naked midriff in gyrations of undeniable erotic intent, an exotic performer named Little Egypt ushered in a new level of suggestive entertainment, one that would eventually grow into the strip tease three decades later. This style came to be known as the "cooch" or "hootchy-kootchy" dance. At about the same time the forbidden French can-can crossed the Atlantic, also to be met by fierce hostility from the self-appointed censors of the day. And as with most forms of censorship, opposition of a moral nature translated into increased popularity and revenues.

In addition to its sexual content, burlesque comedy tended toward the physical, or "slapstick" variety. The term slapstick is derived from a basic tool in the comedian's repertoire, a two-piece hinged board that echoed with a resounding crack when struck against a hapless victim's posterior. Burlesque comedians developed gymnastic-like pratfalls in response to such assaults, always for comic effect.

With the wave of immigration into the United States in the early years of the 20th century, ethnic humour invaded the burlesque house. It focused on stereotypes such as the drunken Irishman or the avaricious Jew to an extent that would be considered offensive today. A favourite comic ploy was the use of dialect, such as a Yiddish or Russian accent, a brand of humour that, however demeaning, has never gone completely out of style.

Interestingly, the most appreciative audience for ethnic humour was often found among the immigrant populations themselves. They could relate to the linguistic accents that resembled their own, and to the portrayal of characters, however exaggerated, that were much like their friends and neighbours. It somehow made them feel a part of their new adopted country.[50] Rather than being insulted, they felt accepted through the portrayal of their images in mainstream forms of entertainment.

Burlesque was a principal form of "adult" entertainment until the 1920s, when it began to face competition from the newly popular nightclubs that thrived during the era of liquor prohibition. In an effort to hold onto audiences, an enterprising team of promoters, the Minsky Brothers, transformed the cooch dance into the best-known symbol of burlesque, the strip tease. This more blatant display of sexuality became the defining element of the burlesque show, and undoubtedly extended its life span in the face of other competing formats.

The attraction of burlesque was undeniable, appealing as it did to male audiences with its aura of forbidden excess. It was also very cheap. In an era when a ticket to the legitimate theatre might cost several dollars, burlesque admission could be as low as twenty-five cents. The genre thrived until other forms of entertainment adopted its most attractive features. As sexual mores changed rapidly during the Roaring Twenties and the subsequent Depression years, theatrical sexual expression found an outlet in ways that were somewhat more respectable.

Not all theatrical amusement in the variety show format was sexually based. A concurrent style of entertainment called vaudeville borrowed some of the elements of burlesque but aspired to be accessible to families. It had its roots in fifteenth century France with the balladeers of the village of Val de Vire, but first became an American stage attraction in 1865 with the opening of Tony Pastor's theatre in Paterson, New Jersey.[51]

Pastor's policies forbade both drinking and smoking on the premises, and the acts he booked were scrupulously censored to eliminate vulgar humour. Whereas burlesque catered to the male members of the population and women and children were unwelcome in the audience, vaudeville encouraged their attendance. With entertainment that included dramatic monologues, animal acts, magicians and circus performers, as well as operatic singers, musicians and dancers, vaudeville offered something for almost everyone.

Vaudeville survived well into the 20th century, but finally fell victim to the economic collapse of the Great Depression and competition from other forms of entertainment, notably radio[52] and motion pictures. First, however, it helped to spawn one important variation that drew upon three other sources: the minstrel show/variety show concept, the idea of spectacle as developed in *The Black Crook*, and the focus upon sex as presented in burlesque, but in a more refined and polished form. This new form became known as the revue.

The revue aspired to a higher level than the typical burlesque, and came closer to the concept of musical comedy in that some of the shows contained a story line, however insubstantial.[53] The emphasis upon sex, topical comedy and satire was pure burlesque, but with the added elements of elaborate costumes and extravagant staging, the promoters hoped to give it an element of class and refinement, and thus acceptability to a wider segment of the population.

The sexual component remained central to the revue, sometimes even to the extent of female nudity (at least from the waist up), but the emphasis was different. Whereas in burlesque the performers gyrated in their tights and harem costumes, the revue girls more often sat in languid display amid lavish settings, or paraded in stately, dignified processions. They were often simply displayed upon pedestals, in the manner of fine art. The story line of a typical revue was secondary to the spectacle, and the central focus of the performance was to showcase the beauty, and only secondarily the talent, of young American women.

The revue achieved its highest level and its greatest popularity in the twenty-three productions staged from 1907 through 1931 by impresario Florenz Ziegfeld. To elevate his shows above the level of burlesque, he sought to imbue sex with glamour, "the glorification of the most beautiful American girls in settings of incomparable style and splendor."[54] The *Ziegfeld Follies* developed the concept of spectacular entertainment far beyond the special effects of *The Black Crook* and its imitators.

While still firmly rooted in the mould of the variety show, the *Follies* capitalized upon the finest talent available from all branches of show business. Ziegfeld commissioned music from composers of operettas, including Victor Herbert and Jerome Kern, and hired celebrities who were already familiar to audiences. He employed the finest set designers, choreographers and technicians available to create production numbers of remarkable beauty and extravagance.

A typical Ziegfeld show might feature as many as seventy-five elaborately costumed women, as well as high-priced featured performers such as Fanny Brice[55] and W. C. Fields. The expense was enormous, often as much as five times the cost of a traditional musical.[56] But the revenues more than compensated, at least until the Depression and the relatively cheap entertainment provided by the movies brought an end to this popular form of entertainment.

Not all revues were as fabulous as the Ziegfeld productions. A more sophisticated variety appeared in the 1920s, in which the emphasis shifted to quality scripts and witty lyrics. Such composers as Richard Rodgers[57] and Arthur Schwartz began their careers writing for these more intimate, urbane shows. While not musical comedies in the true sense, and still closer to the variety show format, they tended to have more coherent, linear structures, and were meant to appeal to a more refined audience than the Ziegfeld spectaculars.

Burlesque, vaudeville and revue all existed side by side with more legitimate forms of musical theatre, such as the operettas that were either imported from, or imitative of, the musical theatre of Europe. All of these forms would eventually come together in the creation of the true American musical.

FOUR
From Across The Sea

Whereas an opera is generally defined as a music drama in which all of the roles are sung throughout, an *operetta* is almost exclusively comic or romantic in nature, and may intermix song and dance with traditional spoken dialog. In many respects, Wolfgang Amadeus Mozart was an originator of the form with such productions as *The Marriage of Figaro* and *The Magic Flute*, but whereas all of the roles in these productions are sung throughout, they are usually classified as "comic operas" instead of operettas. Nevertheless, in style, content and intent, they bear a close relationship to the European style of operetta that enjoyed great popularity in the United States from the close of the Civil War until the 1930s.[58]

At a time when the burlesque and vaudeville houses were flourishing in such major cities as New York, the quintessential English operetta, Gilbert and Sullivan's *H.M.S. Pinafore*, enjoyed a full one hundred different American productions within the span of one year (1879).[59] Unlike the variety show forms of entertainment, operettas featured linear plot lines and original scores, as well as humour designed to appeal to a more sophisticated and educated audience. Even works presented in languages foreign to most Americans, such as the French operettas of Offenbach, were successful in New York.

A defining difference between these imported productions and home-grown efforts such as *The Black Crook* and its imitators was the level of artistry inherent in both plot and music. Despite their light comic and romantic nature, these operettas were written by composers and librettists of international stature.[60] The highly professional approach to dialogue, lyrics and music, when combined with the talents of accomplished European actors and vocalists, gave the shows an undeniable artistic cachet.

Operettas are most often escapist theatre. With subject matter far removed from everyday life, they frequently portray romance in exotic locales, characters of royal heritage, and adventurous exploits that skirt the borders of fantasy, but stay within the bounds of imagination. In the hands of composers such as Johann Strauss and Franz Lehar, they sweep an audience into a world perhaps fictitious, but somehow attainable, if only in dreams. The tradition is one in which "impossibly perfect heroes and heroines lived happily ever after against scrumptious backgrounds, fairy stories for grown-ups."[61]

As works of art, the English and Viennese operettas have enjoyed the greatest longevity of all of the European imports. Gilbert and Sullivan societies flourish, and such works as *The Merry Widow* have been given Broadway revivals and countless regional theatre productions. By contrast, indigenous American musicals from the late 19th century have virtually disappeared from the repertoire, and it is not surprising that the first original American operettas to achieve success were cast in the European mould. Furthermore, many of the composers of supposedly American shows were either foreign born or trained overseas.

Usually acclaimed as the first great American theatre composer, Victor Herbert was born in Ireland and educated in Germany.[62] His works shifted the major emphasis of operetta from the story to the music, and his songs are the earliest examples of so-called "standards" to emerge from North American musical theatre. Such works as *Babes In Toyland* have attained enduring popularity, far beyond the length of their initial presentations.

Arguably the first major success of an original American operetta, *Babes In Toyland* played 192 performances beginning in 1903, a respectable run for those times. Essentially a children's fantasy, the music survives to this day, and at least three film versions have been made.[63] Two songs, "Toyland" and "March of the Toys," are permanent fixtures in musical theatre repertoire.

And yet in style and format, the Herbert operettas owe much more to their European roots than to the new world country in which they were created. The same is true of the scores by Rudolf Friml, a Czechoslovakian composer who immigrated into the United States in 1906 at age 26. Counting among his teachers the symphonist Antonin Dvorak, Friml's prodigious skills at the keyboard and his compositional heritage were firmly rooted in the romantic nature of the classical European school. At a time when truly American music was moving toward syncopation, ragtime and rhythmic exaggeration, his melodies recall instead the lush Viennese tradition.

Although changing tastes have left Friml's story lines behind, some of his music survives. More important to the development of the genre, his operettas were among the first to stress the integration of the songs into the story line. Whereas Victor Herbert emphasized the music at the expense of the plot, Friml kept them in symbiotic balance. In the 1924 production *Rose-Marie*, only five of the many musical numbers were identified by name in the program notes, "because the authors felt that most of the score was interwoven into the story."[64]

If the music is European, the plot line of *Rose-Marie* is all North American, blending Indians, Canadian Mounted Police and the Rocky Mountains in an elegant romantic melodrama. Its commercial success was not surpassed on Broadway until *Oklahoma!* in 1943.[65] The only really well-known melody to survive from that production is "Indian Love Call," somewhat regrettably because of comic parodies of the filmed version, in which the tune was sung by Jeanette MacDonald and Nelson Eddy (1936).

A contemporary of Rudolf Friml, the Hungarian composer Sigmund Romberg studied in Vienna and in London before moving to New York. A prolific musician, his fifty-five scores span the years from 1914 to 1954. His last work, a tribute to *The Black Crook* entitled *The Girl in Pink Tights*, was completed after his death by Don Walker, and lasted 115 performances on Broadway.[66]

Romberg's greatest successes were *Maytime* (1917), *Blossom Time* (1921), *The Student Prince* (1924) and *The Desert Song* (1926). As with Herbert and Friml, his music is strongly European, but unlike his Czechoslovakian counterpart, he often avoided American themes and settings.[67] *Blossom Time* is based loosely upon the life of the Viennese composer Franz Schubert, for example, and *The Student Prince*, his most popular achievement, was set in Heidelberg, Germany. Most exotic of all, the locale for *The Desert Song* was the Sahara in Africa.[68]

Romberg's music has proven to be even more durable than Friml's, thanks in part to film versions of *The Desert Song* (1929, 1944 and 1953) and *The Student Prince* (1954).[69] Perhaps his best-known melody is "The Drinking Song" from the latter production. In many respects, *The Student Prince* is the best example of all European-influenced American operettas. The enduringly popular plot (that of a person of royal blood in love with a commoner)[70] and the lushly romantic melodies sum up the entire genre.

The established form of operetta and the newly emerging style of purely American musical comedy vied for attention and audience popularity throughout the 1920s, and an amalgamation of the two styles was inevitable.[71] Given the associations between Oscar Hammerstein II and both Rudolf Friml and Sigmund Romberg, it was perhaps to be expected that the lyricist's innovative 1927 collaboration with Jerome Kern on *Show Boat* would defy easy classification (see Chapter Eight).

Prior to about 1915, the American musical was a still somewhat crude and immature form that had yet to find its own voice and personality.

Nevertheless, the jazzy and impertinent style was distinct from everything else on Broadway at the time. Neither operetta nor revue, and a substantial cut above vaudeville and burlesque, the American musical struggled for attention, and served as the proving ground for composers and lyricists who would later make their mark. And the major arena for its development was the unassuming stage of the tiny Princess Theatre in New York.

FIVE
The Book

In terms of format, popular musical theatre in America took two different paths after *The Black Crook* in 1866. One concept, and for a time the most commercially successful, was the variety show model, which included the minstrel show, burlesque, vaudeville and eventually the revue. In the other direction lay two types of dramatic presentations with a musical component, the operetta, and the form that would come to dominate as the 20th century progressed, the book musical.

The term "book" does not refer to the literary source of a music drama. For example, the Jerome Kern-Oscar Hammerstein musical *Show Boat* was adapted from the book (novel) of the same name by Edna Ferber, but the "book" for that musical was written by Oscar Hammerstein II. In this context, the book is defined as the overall package of plot, dialog and characterization, and the way in which these elements are combined and interrelated. The music and lyrics are treated as separate elements. The actual dialog and lyrics are combined into the working script, called the libretto.

By this definition, the American version of the operetta could qualify as a book musical. However, the thematic material and especially the style of operetta are much more limited in scope, given that genre's European roots (musically and contextually) and the overriding atmosphere of old world romance and fantasy that pervades most examples of them.

The decline of the operetta in the 1930s was due to a number of factors. Paramount among them was the emergence of the most powerful musical form to originate in America, jazz in its many and diverse forms. The upbeat, syncopated rhythms that characterized ragtime were adopted by mainstream popular music throughout the 1920s, and stood in stark contrast to the prevailing lush romanticism of the operetta. European-trained composers could not or would not adapt to these changes, but a whole new breed of native sons did so enthusiastically.

The mood of the times also had some effect. The Great Depression,[72] with its prevailing harsh economic and social realities, negated the positive, fanciful world of the operetta, making that genre seem somehow shallow and superficial. In an atmosphere of prohibition, gangsterism and poverty, images of old world royalty and fantasy no longer appealed to the masses as they once had.

By the latter 1920s, musical theatre was poised to go in a new direction, and its roots had already sunk deep into the soil of society. In an era when Broadway was dominated by lavish operettas and the grand spectacles of vaudeville, burlesque and the emerging revue, a small playhouse in New York City, the Princess Theatre, became the artistic centre for a group of talented collaborators with refreshing new ideas.

In the late nineteenth century there was a deliberate movement among professions such as art and architecture to eliminate the influences of European models. In similar fashion, composers of stage and concert music who were born or trained in North America considered it essential that their music reflect a style that was distinctly American. "The honor of being one of the first truly American writers of theatre music went to Jerome Kern."[73]

The three most influential personalities involved in this transformation were composer Jerome Kern, lyricist P. G. Wodehouse[74] and author Guy Bolton. This brief but significant partnership crafted an entirely new species of musical theatre: "the intimate, simple, adult, intelligent, economical, small-cast musical show."[75]

Compared to huge auditoriums like Niblo's Garden, the Princess Theatre was tiny and intimate. With a modest stage and only a few hundred seats, it could not accommodate even the least pretentious revue or operetta. Nor could the revenue generated by the box office support a large payroll, imposing severe limits upon the size of cast and crew.

The Princess did not have an auspicious beginning. Located somewhat apart from the main theatre district, it opened in 1912 with a series of trivial one-act plays that failed to find a consistent audience. In an effort to attract new business, the owners turned their attention to the musical, but in a style more suited to the drawing room atmosphere of the little playhouse than the extravagant productions then in vogue elsewhere. With such a restricted budget, the theatre owner, F. Ray Comstock, could not afford to hire an already established team of writers. For his first effort, he asked English playwright Paul Reubens to adapt his play *Mr. Popple of Ippleton* as a musical. The results of the playwright's work were unsatisfactory.

Hoping to salvage the show, Comstock turned to a young composer who had contributed a few songs to a 1907 show entitled *Fascinating Flora*. Although only one Kern melody survived into the final version of that show, its quality was such that Comstock felt confident of Kern's ability, and contracted with him to rewrite Reuben's play under a new title: *Nobody Home* (1915).[76]

Jerome Kern had already established a modest reputation on Broadway. A native New Yorker, he began writing songs at an early age and refined his talent with studies at the New York College of Music and later in London.[77] After returning to New York, he found work as a rehearsal pianist on Broadway, and as a result soon met influential people who were willing to listen to his original songs, and eventually to buy them for inclusion in major productions.[78]

The typical musical of the very early 20th century tended to be an amalgam of many different people's work, which is not surprising considering the roots of the genre. From minstrel show to revue, most Broadway productions were the result of collaboration between many different personalities, and the infant book musical was no exception. By the time Ray Comstock approached him, Kern was already chafing at the restrictions imposed by writing to order for someone else's shows. Although he had never written the score for a complete musical himself, he had acquired substantial experience in all aspects of theatre craft, and was ready to experiment with his own ideas.

Given the limited resources of the Princess Theatre (a full house could yield a gross of only about $3500 for a full week of performances), the management could not afford the luxury of having a large creative staff. The budget restrictions also precluded having more than thirty in the entire cast, including the chorus,[79] a number far below the sometimes hundreds who appeared on stage in traditional productions. Rather than being an obstacle, these limitations proved to be fortuitous in setting the tone and style of these more intimate musical plays.

Jerome Kern's first writing partner was an immigrant from Great Britain, St. George Guy Reginald Bolton. Their early efforts for another producer were not especially successful, but when entrusted with running their own show, they revelled in the lack of restrictions and completely revised the existing loose structure of the book musical. With playwright Reubens no longer involved, Bolton set about rewriting *Nobody Home* with an almost clean slate.

Whereas the limited amount available for salaries mandated a low-paid and therefore virtually unknown cast, Kern and Bolton could not depend upon having an established star to bring in paying customers. They needed a new approach to attract attention. In its initial incarnation, the play had failed to find favour with audiences, and the producers gave the writers free rein for a complete revision, featuring all new songs. This enabled them to experiment with an idea of Kern's that would set their work apart from the existing tradition.

Kern proposed creating a fully integrated book and score, wherein the songs and plot were woven inescapably into a coherent whole, to an even greater extent than in the European-style operetta. Contrary to the traditional practice of writing songs as adjuncts to the dramatic situation, Kern envisioned his music as integral to the plot, and especially to the individual personalities of the characters, believing that such a unified approach would produce the most satisfying results. "Jerome Kern became America's first great theatre composer because he attempted to so immerse his musical talent in the characters of the book as to write songs for them alone. He believed the composer's mission must be to reveal character, thought, or feeling to the audience in suggestive musical images."[80]

This approach proved to be essential to the success of the small-scale musical. Without the trappings of spectacle and glamour inherent in big-budget productions, a quality script was fundamental to capturing and maintaining an audience's interest. In Kern's hands, the songs assumed the added responsibility of conveying both the dramatic action and the essential emotion of any given situation. The combination of a quality book and quality songs, mutually supportive of each other and specific to the plot, resulted in substantial success for *Nobody Home*. After an initial run at the Princess, the producers moved it to a larger theatre to increase the gross, and later added three touring companies.[81]

Kern's next effort for the Princess Theatre, *Very Good Eddie* (1915), employed a substantially larger creative team. Guy Bolton collaborated with Philip Bartholomae on the book, and Schuyler Greene, Kern and several others contributed lyrics. *Very Good Eddie* created a new pattern for American musical theatre by giving the characters depth and realistic human characteristics. It avoided clichés and made the songs a part of and relevant to the comedic plot. It created a format that would influence the style of musical theatre for more than half a century.[82]

Like *Nobody Home*, *Very Good Eddie* was a substantial success, but to achieve the total integration and coherence that Kern envisioned for his third play, the composer once again abandoned the committee approach. He formed instead a more limited three-way partnership, charging the author and wit P. G. Wodehouse to supply all of the lyrics, working in concert with Guy Bolton on the book. Their first collaboration was the highly successful *Oh, Boy!* in 1917.[83]

Such was the quality of this play that the theatre management invested a generous $29,000 to launch it, and raised ticket prices to $3.50 per seat,[84] a huge increase over the $1.50 they had charged for *Nobody Home*. Driven by an intense publicity campaign and a successful tryout tour on the road, it recorded 463 performances,[85] not a record but nevertheless a substantial hit for a small theatre. The modern interpretation of the book musical had arrived.

Later Kern-Bolton-Wodehouse efforts met with varied audience approval, although the best of them, *Leave It To Jane*[86] (1917) and *Oh, Lady! Lady!!* (1918) had respectable runs. Kern and Bolton wrote the very successful *Sally* (1920) with lyricists Clifford Gray and others, but by that time they had moved from the restrictive Princess Theatre to the more spacious New Amsterdam. Wodehouse began work on this project, but he withdrew after a disagreement with Kern, and the two never collaborated again.[87] The lasting influence of their partnership, however, proved to be greatly disproportionate to its brevity, as their style helped shape the work of many who came after them.

The Kern musicals for the Princess Theatre altered the way other composers and authors approached the book musical. Although Broadway continued to be dominated by operettas and lavish revues (*Ziegfeld Follies, George White's Scandals* and the *Music Box Revue*, for example), there were signs of change on the horizon. Amid *Rose-Marie* and *The Student Prince* in 1924, George and Ira Gershwin produced the first of their fourteen distinctively American musicals, *Lady Be Good!* And a year later, the team of Richard Rodgers and Lorenz Hart turned from writing for revues to create their first true book musical, *Dearest Enemy*.

Despite the quality inherent in many of them, with almost no exceptions the book musicals from the years before 1927[88] are not revived today. To modern audiences, most of the plots are lightweight and somewhat inconsequential, and the once topical scripts are now dated. Nevertheless, the music from this period is significantly durable. Still played today are such standards as Kern's "They Didn't Believe Me" (which preceded the Princess years) and "Look For the Silver Lining," the Gershwins' "Fascinating Rhythm," and Irving Berlin's "A Pretty Girl Is Like a Melody."[89]

The Princess musicals established a new pattern, and while the rest of Broadway slowly came to take notice, it was left to Jerome Kern to take the next major step forward, this time in partnership with two of the foremost talents in the business, producer Florenz Ziegfeld and author and lyricist Oscar Hammerstein II. In 1927, they gave us *Show Boat*.

SIX
Enter Oscar

Oscar Hammerstein II was born in New York City on the twelfth of July in 1895, into a world of contrast and conflict between many diverse and strongly opposing forces. Slavery had been legally abolished in the southern United States little more than three decades before, and its effects still dominated the pattern of life for those members of the population of African origin. In the states that had formed the breakaway Confederacy, many former slaves remained as unpaid labour on the plantations by necessity, as they were denied any other means of earning a living. In the supposedly more enlightened north, educational and employment opportunities were severely limited for "persons of colour."

Economic disparity and inequality plagued much of the United States. Corrupt financiers and politicians conspired to cheat the public of land and resources. The most blatant of these robber barons ran the railroads,[90] and while they fully deserve credit for opening the western continent to settlement, they extracted an exorbitant price through their land grabs.

The entire North American continent had begun the slow but inexorable shift from a rural agrarian economy to an urban one. This process spanned many decades and altered and distorted social patterns to a great degree. Unionism, laws governing child labour, minimum wage provisions, universal public education and economic reform would gradually transform the sweatshop mentality of the early industrial revolution into a more socially conscious twentieth century civilization. But these reforms were slow to materialize.

As the standard of living gradually rose for the middle class, it was accompanied by increased awareness of and emphasis upon intellectual and artistic pursuits, encouraged by seemingly wondrous technological advances. Hammerstein's birth coincided almost exactly with the advent of the recording industry, the first commercial motion pictures, and that most personal form of communication, the telephone. While transportation still consisted primarily of animal power (horse and buggy) or public conveyance, in the form of railroads and trolleys, the personal automobile was just over the horizon. Perhaps most important, reliable electric lighting had begun to replace candles and gas lamps, not only in homes but also in public theatres, and it would soon become nearly universal.

Hammerstein was born into an affluent family, one with strong ties to the theatre. His grandfather Oscar, for whom he was named, became quite wealthy through his real estate transactions and his ownership of a number of profitable apartment buildings and vaudeville houses. Among the latter was New York's lucrative Victoria Theatre. He used the proceeds from these investments to sponsor the building of opera houses in Manhattan and Philadelphia,[91] and organized a major opera company. Although this was a money-losing venture, it nevertheless satisfied his innate artistic ambitions.

William and Arthur, sons of the elder Hammerstein, were both actively involved in the theatre,[92] the former as a somewhat reluctant manager of his father's Victoria Theatre. In that capacity William also produced vaudeville shows, but exhibited little affinity for the artistic side of show business. In spite of his personal involvement, he attempted to keep his family insulated from the theatre, and before his premature death at age 40, he extracted from his son, Oscar II, a promise to seek a career in law. Uncle Arthur, by contrast, was dedicated to the stage, and became a successful dramatic and operatic producer.[93]

Honouring his father's wishes, Oscar II attended Columbia University to prepare for the legal profession. While an undergraduate, he wrote both book and lyrics for, and appeared on stage in, a 1917 Columbia University student production entitled *Home, James*. Concurrently he secured an apprentice position with a law firm,[94] but was neither happy nor especially successful in this pursuit. After only a year, despite the promise made to his father before the older man's death, he left both the university and the law firm and approached his uncle Arthur for help in becoming established in show business.[95]

His father's insistence on a law career for his son was understandable. William Hammerstein had become relatively prosperous as manager of the Victoria Theatre, but this was due more to his efficient and conservative management skills than to a natural affinity for the stage. Furthermore, as a Jew he must have encountered to some degree the anti-Semitism that infected much of North American society at the turn of the century. To William Hammerstein, economic success would have been seen as an antidote to such attitudes, and a career in something so insecure as the theatre promised little hope of stability, security and social acceptance.

The arts have often been cited as being more liberal than society as a whole, and although prejudice certainly existed in the theatre as elsewhere, anti-Semitism was less apparent there than in the general population. With the eventual rise of the Nazi party in Germany, the world's attention was especially drawn to this pernicious variety of racism in the years preceding World War Two, but this was by no means its first appearance. In the middle of the 19th century, for example, the artistic world was severely contaminated by anti-Semitism, fomented in part by the composers Franz Liszt and Richard Wagner.[96]

Nevertheless, the arts seem to have been more hospitable to racial minorities than mainstream society, including both those identified by skin colour,[97] and the less apparent factor of religious affiliation. In the latter category, the success of Jewish entertainers, producers and directors, especially throughout the first few decades of the Twentieth Century, is notable.

Careers connected to the stage have never been associated with secure and regular income. For every adherent who attains stardom, there are countless others who labour in the chorus lines for mere subsistence wages, and for every successful songwriter, there are dozens of hacks. William Hammerstein wanted more for his son than this, and was somewhat dismayed at young Oscar's attraction to the theatre.

Under his Uncle Arthur's guidance, Oscar Hammerstein II learned virtually every facet of the theatrical trade, including management, production and writing. His early efforts were not commercially successful, but with each new script that he turned out, he became more skilled in the techniques of drama. Significantly, he came to recognize that among all of the elements that go to make up a successful theatrical presentation, the most important is, first and foremost, a quality plot. That approach would shape his work for the rest of his life.

American musical comedy was an immature art form in the nineteen-teens and early twenties, having developed side by side and in competition with the more risqué forms, burlesque and revue, that followed the success of *The Black Crook* in 1866 (see Chapters One and Two). Like the other two, the true musical comedy depended to some extent upon sex to sell tickets. It was, however, presented less crudely.

Musical comedy differed from the sex shows mainly by offering true drama, as opposed to melodrama, with a developing story line from start to finish. However, the scripts tended toward stereotypical boy-meets-girl scenarios and stock comic situations. The appeal of these shows stemmed more from the songs and the talents of the performers than from the simplistic story lines.[98]

The more artistic side of popular musical theatre remained the province of the European-style operetta, with its class-conscious emphasis upon royalty and fairy-tale endings (see Chapter Four). The competing American-style shows, the musical comedies, "depended upon the girls, the jokes, the dancing, and the sets,"[99] and usually in that order. While not as blatant as burlesque, they were closer to outright girly shows than to operetta.

This is not to say that there were not many fine efforts in the musical comedy genre in the early years of the 20th century. At first, however, serious-minded writers such as Oscar Hammerstein II were best known for their work in collaboration with European-trained composers such as Rudolf Friml and Sigmund Romberg. These operettas are remembered today, however, more for the quality of their songs than for their plots. It was the strength of Hammerstein's lyrics, as much as the beauty of the music and more than the quality of the drama, that led to the popularity of *The Desert Song* and *Rose-Marie*, his two significant early successes.[100]

Hammerstein's collaborator on the book and lyrics for a handful of productions, including both *Rose-Marie* and *The Desert Song*, was Otto Harbach, who was born in Utah of Danish immigrant parents. Harbach's academic aspirations (he taught English at a college in Washington state) led him to seek further study in New York, but failing eyesight ended his teaching career,[101] and he gravitated toward the theatre. In partnership with Bohemian composer Karl Hoschna he wrote six operetta-like musicals, only one of which, *Madame Sherry*, was reasonably successful at 231 performances, in 1910. He also worked with Rudolf Friml (*The Firefly*, 1912) before teaming up with Hammerstein for *Rose-Marie*.

Hammerstein and Harbach's first major effort with a native American composer, Jerome Kern, broke with tradition.[102] *Sunny* (1925) cannot be described as an operetta, although there are some similarities in the approach to the romantic plot. However, the music bears little resemblance to the European pattern. Kern's melodic style, grounded as it was in the popular music of the New World, tended toward the short and snappy,[103] as opposed to the flowery romanticism of Friml and Romberg.

The plot of *Sunny* spans two continents, beginning in England and ending in New York, and elements of the story include a "circus, an ocean liner, a ladies' gymnasium, and a fox hunt,"[104] hardly the stuff of operetta, excepting perhaps only the last. The script is almost zany and somewhat contrived, but attractive nonetheless. Most important, it gave the composer enough pegs upon which to hang an excellent and very original score. Helped by the casting of the very popular Marilyn Miller in the lead role, the play was a substantial success, but it is the promise of the score that made audiences remember the name of Jerome Kern.

Apart from Broadway, the period of the mid 1920s was a significant watershed in American music. The concert stage was dominated by Europeans, and the most artistic of the stage musicals were still in the old world style of operetta. In popular music, however, a slow but steady cultural infusion was beginning to take hold. The concept of ragtime, with its heavy emphasis upon syncopation, was most closely associated with Negro composers such as Scott Joplin, but more mainstream composers had begun to adapt its style and even its nomenclature. For example, Irving Berlin's first major success, *Alexander's Ragtime Band* (1911), employed not only the syncopated rhythms, but also the name of the rhythmically energetic genre.[105]

In addition, white musicians had begun to adapt the instrumental style of their black colleagues during this period. The nascent category of jazz, crafted almost exclusively by black musicians in the beginning, was generally considered to be lowbrow, and in fact was not well known to the general public. With very little access to the recording industry, black musicians did not have a wide following outside their own culture.

Among white musicians, however, the style was soon eagerly embraced. The appellation "Dixieland" is often mistakenly attached to music played by black performers, but it originally referred only to those all-white ensembles that imitated the Negro style.[106] White musicians more easily obtained recording contracts, and it was through their efforts that the black style of jazz became more widely disseminated.[107]

Rhapsody In Blue (1924) was the first serious attempt to infuse jazz elements into an extended orchestral work, and the composer, George Gershwin, followed it up a year later with his three-movement *Concerto In F* for piano and orchestra, in a similar style. Both works are now considered part of the standard repertoire. Gershwin's bread and butter at that time, however, was the stage musical, and he produced three scores in 1925, with lyrics by his brother, Ira: *Tell Me More*, *Tip-Toes* and *Song of the Flame*. (In an interesting footnote to stage history, the original title of *Tell Me More* was *My Fair Lady*, which was determined to have too little commercial appeal, and was subsequently dropped.[108]) Although not as popular nor of as high quality as their effort the previous year (*Lady, Be Good!*), these works by the Gershwin brothers firmly established a jazzy, self-consciously American style on Broadway.

Somewhat earlier in the century, the concept of operetta began to succumb to gradual Americanization. Although the genre was dominated by European-trained immigrants such as Sigmund Romberg, Franz Lehar and Rudolf Friml, native American composers began to invade the field. In the first two decades of the 20th century, the outstanding operettas were imports such as *The Merry Widow* (1907) and *The Chocolate Soldier* (1909). However, they were increasingly forced to share Broadway with home-grown material.

Naughty Marietta (1910) was set, not in Europe, but in late 18th century New Orleans. Although the composer, Victor Herbert, was old-world trained, American lyricist Rida Johnson Young gave the story a distinctly down-home atmosphere. And the producer, Oscar Hammerstein (grandfather of Oscar II) imbued it with production values that rivalled his Manhattan Opera. There can be little doubt that operettas such as this were a powerful influence not only upon the younger Hammerstein, but also upon other aspiring composers and lyricists.

By the 1920s, the distinctions between the diverse genres of musical theatre in North America were becoming less well defined. The principal change of emphasis was in the relative importance of the plot. Unlike the more elaborately scripted European-style operetta, the American format emphasized singing and dancing at the expense of the story. The scripts tended toward simplistic, lightweight narrative that relied heavily upon boy-meets-girl situations, romantic misunderstandings, clearly drawn good-versus-evil characters, and a wide variety of comedic devices.

Despite their lack of literary importance, these embryonic musical comedies benefited from the talents of very creative writers and performers, many of whom, like the Gershwin brothers, expanded their careers into more significant avenues in later years. But these early stage shows, from which many excellent songs were derived, are rarely revived today.

In 1924, the first true hit among the Gershwin musicals, *Lady Be Good*, opened at the Liberty Theatre in New York on December 1st, and ran a respectable and profitable 330 performances.[109] With lyrics written by George's brother Ira, the score included three tunes that rapidly became standards in the emerging Jazz Age: "Oh, Lady Be Good," "The Man I Love" (inexplicably dropped from the show in pre-Broadway trials) and the immensely popular "Fascinating Rhythm." The cast featured a young brother and sister song-and-dance team out of the vaudeville tradition, Fred and Adele Astaire, the first of whom would go on to redefine the concept of stage and film dancing over the next three decades.

Without the memorable songs and exceptional talents of the Astaires, however, the show would probably have become a mere footnote to theatrical history. The elements of the plot were improbable and somewhat simple minded at best: a poor but talented vaudeville couple, unable to get that "big break" to succeed in show business; a failed attempt by the female lead to steal an inheritance by posing as a Spanish heiress; a nick-of-time escape by the male lead from a disastrous marriage.[110]

In addition to their skill in the faster tempos, the Gershwins were masters of the ballad style, as exemplified by the best-known song from *Tip-Toes*, "Looking For a Boy." While lacking the rhythmic elements characteristic of jazz, this lovely melody exploits the "blue" note,[111] the bending of pitch that was characteristic of much black music, and distinguished it strongly from the European style.

Productions such as *Lady Be Good* captured the imagination of the public, partly for the relief they offered from the heavy-handed operettas that had previously dominated the more serious side of the musical stage. And they offered at least some semblance of a story, as compared with the ubiquitous revue, which was an amalgamation of songs, dances and short sketches (mostly comic) amounting to little more than an elaborate variety show. The revue was an important proving ground for composers and lyricists, however.

1925 marks a significant effort by another well-known songwriting duo, Richard Rodgers and Lorenz Hart. Their first fully successful score, *The Garrick Gaieties*, was in strict revue format,[112] and is remembered chiefly for the attractive tunes, especially their first true standard, "Manhattan." A second version of the show the following year showcased one of their most durable melodies, "Mountain Greenery." However, it wasn't until Rodgers and Hart turned their attention to the book musical that the full extent of their talents became apparent.

Hart's work on the *Gaieties* exerted lasting influence on lyricists who followed him. At the time, lyrics were generally considered secondary to the music, dances and staging of a revue. The words of a song were often heavily influenced by the romantic sentiment of German operetta, and frequently shoehorned into pre-existing melodies that did not really complement their mood or meaning.

Hart believed that the words of a song should do more than simply entertain. His creative and imaginative use of language transformed the typical trite and clichéd verses of the day into witty and meaningful poetry, equal in quality and importance to the music and staging. In his able hands, the lyrics moved from mere adjuncts to the action into the realm of true dramatic expression.[113] This was a concept that would later come to full fruition in Oscar Hammerstein's lyrics for *Show Boat*.

At that time, the most famous of the revues were staged by impresario Florenz Ziegfeld under the title *Ziegfeld Follies* (see Chapter Three). Because these shows emphasized glamour rather than the more blatant sexual displays of burlesque, they achieved a certain level of legitimacy on Broadway. Similar productions such as the *George White Scandals*, *The Garrick Gaieties* and the *Music Box Revue* offered similar entertainment. The best of these nearly plot-less extravaganzas showcased the music of promising composers, and while Gershwin cut his teeth writing for *Scandals*, Irving Berlin gained attention for his work on the *Ziegfeld Follies* and the *Music Box Revue*. But except for the tunes, these shows exerted little influence on the development of Broadway as a whole.

In spite of the writing and compositional talents that emerged from these various productions, Broadway continued to be dominated by the "girly show" as the 1920s progressed. Sixty years after *The Black Crook*, the musical comedy,[114] as a truly original American form, was still rarely more than a song-and-dance extravaganza. It would have been hard to predict that it would come to exceed the popularity of all other types, except for the singular influence exerted by the "Princess Musicals" (see Chapter Five).

Most of the Princess Theatre productions had similar and relatively inconsequential story lines: romantic entanglements, family conflicts and the triumph of love over adversity. The plots were less important than the way in which the music supported and embellished the dramatic possibilities. This integration of score and story was the most significant contribution of these plays. They established a format that was more tightly knit than the variety-show amalgam of the revue, and more approachable than the opulent, artificial old-world ambience of the operetta.

Almost of equal importance, they created among American audiences an appetite for home-grown, relevant theatre, and were the training ground for the most influential composer of the 1920s, Jerome Kern, who, in partnership with Oscar Hammerstein II, would take the genre to the next logical level.

In the two decades leading up to December of 1927 (a monumental month at the end of a monumental year in Broadway theatre history), the most successful New York productions could therefore be divided roughly into three categories: operettas, revues (along with their less savoury cousin, burlesque), and those that could more properly be called true musical comedies. All, of course, fell into the broad category of musical theatre, but the dividing lines between them remained at that time relatively clear.

In 1927, the American musical finally grew up. And the landmark production of that year, *Show Boat*, sounded the first death knell of European domination of the more artistic side of the Broadway musical stage.

SEVEN
That Wonderful Year

The relatively affluent year of 1927 was an active one on Broadway. Thanks to a buoyant economy and the lack of strict government controls to limit abuses, business and industry were expanding at a rapid rate, and disposable income among the general population was at an all-time high. Reflecting this prosperity, Florenz Ziegfeld[115] opened what was arguably the continent's finest, most opulent theatre for the production of musicals,[116] the Ziegfeld Theatre, on February 2nd.

The floor plan was unusual and innovative, elliptical in shape instead of the more familiar fan-shaped design, with a high domed ceiling and extravagant appointments, including even a gold-trimmed mural. The seats were arranged so that all members of the audience had an unobstructed view of the stage.[117] It quickly became the first choice for large-scale productions that could be expected to earn enough to justify such luxury.

The show that inaugurated the house was *Rio Rita*,[118] a lavish book musical that in both story and melodic style had many overtones of operetta. Although cast in a conventional mould and with a relatively unmemorable score, the play benefited from the opulent surroundings of the new theatre and a visually spectacular production in the Ziegfeld tradition. It lasted well into 1928.[119]

It is notable that the first success of 1927, and the last, represented opposite poles of the musical theatre spectrum, and that both were showcased in the magnificent Ziegfeld Theatre. With its somewhat exotic flavour (a sort of Mexican variation on *The Desert Song*) and romantically melodic score, and despite the up-to-date writing style of Guy Bolton, *Rio Rita* owed more to operetta than to the pattern set by Bolton's Princess musicals. Less than eleven months later, the first of a whole new breed, *Show Boat*, replaced it on the same stage.

Following *Rio Rita*, new productions by well-known creative talents met with audience resistance. Neither a foreign setting (Japan) nor the melodic talents of Sigmund Romberg could lure many patrons to *Cherry Blossoms* in March. The same month, Jerome Kern's *Lucky* lasted only 71 performances,[120] despite an expensive set and elaborate costumes and the considerable talents of such well known performers as a teen-aged Ruby Keeler[121] and the entire Paul Whiteman[122] Orchestra. The only new revue of the late winter, *The New Yorkers*, also failed to capture public approval, as did several lesser efforts. Examining the situation in hindsight, it is apparent that public tastes, if not already changing, were anticipating change, and audiences were increasingly unwilling to accept stale, overly familiar formats.

It was not until April that the next major success came (literally) aboard. With music by Vincent Youmans, *Hit the Deck!* was based on a 1922 play entitled *Shore Leave*, and its clever seagoing story line equalled its fine score in quality. Two of the songs, "Hallelujah" and "Sometimes I'm Happy," are among the most enduring of American standards.[123] (Youmans' latter melody was originally burdened with the title "Come On and Pet Me."[124] It's tempting to speculate on its place in musical theatre history, had they not changed the lyrics.)

Hit the Deck! was strongly American in theme and realization. The boy-meets-girl plot was far from original, but the Navy setting gave the show a flavour of novelty in costuming and set decoration. The plot and book (by Herbert Fields) may have lacked depth, but the rapid pacing provided a strong showcase for the very contemporary score. The dances were derived from the popular Black Bottom and Charleston, with the aggressive syncopation in such tunes as "Hallelujah" being typical of the Roaring Twenties.

At 352 performances and with very low overhead (no star performers and a very small chorus, similar in size to those of the Princess musicals[125]), *Hit the Deck!* returned a substantial profit. With a relatively lightweight story line, however, it broke no new ground. As pure entertainment, it stood out from a lacklustre season, and was later filmed three times. But it was the new season that began halfway through the calendar year that was to produce a string of successes of unprecedented quality.

Summer offerings were uniformly slight, and there were no notable productions until September, but on the 6th of that month, *Good News* opened at the 42nd Street Theatre. This lively and topical show epitomized the entire era with its jazz-oriented score, memorable melodies and carefully crafted comedy. Set on a college campus, all aspects of the production echoed the theme. Ushers and members of George Olsen's band were costumed to match the young actors on stage, and the musicians "shouted college cheers as they ran down the aisle and into the orchestra pit."[126]

Again, the boy-meets-girl plot is hardly the stuff of good literature, but that is not the major appeal of the show. It is the context into which the story is woven that makes it work so well. Singing and dancing fit right in with the college atmosphere, and provide a logical reason for production numbers featuring the latest dance crazes. Audience familiarity with stylistic elements can be a strong attraction, and in the case of *Good News*, it contributed substantially to the run of 551 performances.

It was the right show for the times, handsomely staged and with a wonderful score that produced some enduring hits: "The Varsity Drag," "Lucky In Love" and "The Best Things In Life Are Free" among them. Ray Henderson provided the music, the first in his series of successful book musicals. With lyricists B. G. De Sylva and Lew Brown, Henderson was a veteran of the *George White's Scandals* revues.

Good News is the first major American book musical to achieve repertoire status. The popular 1947 film version featured some new material by Betty Comden and Adolph Green, and the most recent Broadway revival was staged in 1974.[127] It is a perennial favourite for high school and college productions.[128] And while perhaps less well known than his contemporaries, Ray Henderson was in good company on Broadway in the fall of 1927.

Within the space of just two months, the three most influential songwriting teams of the 1920s and 1930s launched significant new book musicals. Two of these shows were polished confections with excellent scores that spawned enduring standards and presaged their creators' more mature works to come. By contrast, however, the third production was revolutionary.

After *The Garrick Gaieties* revue, Richard Rodgers and Lorenz Hart enjoyed modest success with two slight book musicals, *Dearest Enemy* (1925) and *Peggy-Ann* (1926). The first was a novel spoof on the American Revolution, while the second was a surreal comedy. In spite of their commercial success,[129] the music from these two shows is largely forgotten today. Rodgers and Hart were extremely prolific in those years, with five productions on Broadway in 1926 alone, but these formative efforts, while promising, were somewhat routine and uninspired in terms of plot and structure. Four of the five were not as enthusiastically received as *Peggy-Ann*, although *The Girl Friend* (in March) yielded the very beautiful standard, "The Blue Room."

Their next big hit opened on November 3rd in 1927. Based on the story by Mark Twain, *A Connecticut Yankee (In King Arthur's Court)* was a milestone for several reasons. The score contains two of the team's most memorable melodies, "Thou Swell" and the deeply emotional ballad "My Heart Stood Still." The plot, a dream fantasy interwoven into the Arthurian legend, was cleverly constructed to be more than the usual boy-meets-girl scenario, thanks to its quality literary source and to the polished reworking by Herbert Fields.

The story derives much of its humour from anachronisms. In a decade entranced by the novelty of electricity, radio and the telephone, the insertion of such devices into medieval England was received as both witty and very modern. The producers also expended considerable expense and effort to create their Camelot set in a riot of colours,[130] and the dancing, staged by a young Busby Berkeley, was athletic and exciting. At 418 performances, *A Connecticut Yankee* was Rodgers and Hart's most successful production to date.

It came amid a crowd of winners that month, a total of six profitable musicals. All are generally forgotten today with just one exception, *Funny Face*, by George and Ira Gershwin.[131] As was the case with *Yankee*, this show's appeal was due to a variety of factors. The score is exceptional, with "He Loves and She Loves," "My One and Only" and the title song capturing substantial popularity, but the standout tune was "'S Wonderful."

The premier marked the opening of the new and elegant Alvin Theatre, and in the lead roles were the team of Fred and Adele Astaire, a major box office draw. The plot was a "lighter-than-air concoction"[132] riddled with outrageous puns, but it did serve to establish Astaire's trade mark tuxedo image in the production number "High Hat." But even with the allure of a brand new theatre and established stars in the cast, it was primarily the Gershwin brothers' music and lyrics that guaranteed success.

The proof of the superiority of the music over the story can be seen in two subsequent events. The very attractive film by the same name, with Astaire again in the lead role and opposite a young Audrey Hepburn, kept four of the songs but none of the plot.[133] And in 1983, six songs from the show were combined with other Gershwin classics (including "Strike Up the Band") for the modestly successful musical, *My One and Only*, also with an entirely new story line.[134] As with virtually every American-format musical prior to *Show Boat*, the life span of the music from *Funny Face* far exceeded the play itself.

With one major exception, the remainder of 1927 was relatively lacklustre. *Take the Air* was a modest success at 106 performances, and a revue by Harry Delmar played for fourteen weeks. Oscar Hammerstein II co-wrote *Golden Dawn*,[135] which ran a disappointing and only marginally profitable 184 performances. A throwback to the operetta format, *Dawn* was notable as the first production in the newly opened Hammerstein Theatre.

There was no lack of new dramatic material in December, as fully eleven new shows premiered on the day after Christmas, but the only musical among them, *The White Eagle*, was a failure. However, the next day at the Ziegfeld Theatre, *Show Boat* opened to become "the outstanding commercial success and artistic triumph of the 1927-28 season, and it has survived as one of the masterpieces of our lyric stage."[136]

EIGHT
Coming Of Age

Virtually everything about the hit musicals of the early to mid 1920s would be unfamiliar to most modern audiences, were it not for the enduring quality of the music. The shows' titles are either obscure (*Poppy; Sunny; Tip-Toes*) or quaintly old-fashioned (*Rose-Marie; No, No Nanette*). However, the songs that gave life to the overly romanticized or simplistic plots have endured as pop standards and jazz classics, and rank among the finest efforts of significant American popular music composers.

Jerome Kern's *Sally* gave us "Look For the Silver Lining," and from *Rose-Marie* came "Indian Love Call" (sung infamously by Nelson Eddy and Jeanette MacDonald in the 1936 movie version). *No, No Nanette* provided "Tea for Two" and "I Want to Be Happy." Among other songs from 1920s musicals that are still recorded today are "Birth of the Blues," "Someone To Watch Over Me," "St. Louis Blues" and "I Can't Give You Anything But Love."

Most of these adolescent musicals are rarely or never staged today. The one notable exception from among those produced prior to December of 1927 is *Good News* (see Chapter Seven), an evocation of Roaring Twenties collegiate life that still finds great favour as a college or high school vehicle. The score by B. G. DeSylva and Lew Brown is infectious: "Varsity Drag" (a Charleston clone), "Lucky In Love," and a truly enduring standard that would later become a message of hope during the Great Depression, "The Best Things In Life Are Free."

When *Good News* opened on Broadway on September 6th, 1927, it seemed to be the culmination of all that the American musical strove to be, a slick and stylish blend of boy-meets-girl dramatic comedy and modern, dance-based music. The collegiate setting captured the prosperous, upbeat feeling of the times, as did its imaginative staging. *Good News* continues to strike a resonant chord with audiences generation after generation, as evidenced by the successful 1947 motion picture version and the 1974 Broadway revival, an unusual event for what is essentially a period piece.

Part of the credit for its appeal lies in the plot resolution: "…how the girl who has never had anything hits it off with a Universal Dream Man."[137]

But it remains a product of its times, a logical climax to the trend begun by the Princess musicals, rather than an innovative new form. The appeal of *Good News* was evolutionary. The revolution was just around the corner.

By 1927, Oscar Hammerstein II was a familiar but only moderately successful fixture on the Broadway theatre scene. After several promising but failed attempts, he scored his first big triumph in operetta style, in collaboration with composers Rudolf Friml and Herbert Stothart in *Rose-Marie* (1924), for which he and Otto Harbach were credited jointly for the book and lyrics. The production was staged by the lyricist's uncle, Arthur Hammerstein. The following year, Hammerstein again teamed with Harbach to write *Sunny* (see Chapter Six), significantly with music composed by Jerome Kern, who had not had a major success on Broadway since the 1920 production of *Sally*. Essentially an updated Cinderella story, *Sunny* proved to be immensely popular, with 517 first-run performances.

For the 1926 season, Harbach and Hammerstein wrote the lyrics for Sigmund Romberg's operetta *The Desert Song*, assisted on the book by Frank Mandel. The production was something of a departure for the authors, an old-fashioned vehicle in the European tradition that nevertheless found favour with audiences for a substantial 471 performances. It was filmed in three different versions (1929, 1943 and 1953) and was revived on Broadway in 1973, although for a very short run.

Despite the success of *The Desert Song*, Hammerstein abandoned the operetta concept, never to return to it.[138] Seeking new territory instead, he again sought out his first major American collaborator, Jerome Kern. Both Kern and Hammerstein had felt for some time that the Broadway musical theatre was suffering from too much sameness and tameness. After reading Edna Ferber's sprawling novel of life on the Mississippi, they became convinced that it was the story best suited to help them make the kinds of changes they felt were needed.[139]

That novel was *Show Boat*. Hammerstein saw in it the opportunity to lift traditional musical theatre above and beyond the time-honoured and somewhat moribund pattern of stage entertainment then in vogue, and to elevate it to the level of serious drama and social commentary. But rather than return to the established format of operetta, he infused the book with a modern and essentially American plot treatment that rivalled the best in straight dramatic theatre. And by writing both the book and the lyrics without a collaborator, he was able to attain the fullest possible integration of the songs and the story.

As a stage play, *Show Boat* succeeded on every important level. Following in the tradition of the Princess musicals, it was a fully unified production, in which the songs were a fundamental and essential element in the plot development. This was unlike the majority of earlier musicals, wherein the interpolation of songs and dances signalled a break in the action rather than a continuation and development of it.

Show Boat carried the concept of plot/music fusion to a new level. Each of its musical numbers flows naturally out of the preceding dialog and action. Not only do they convey and drive the tale, they provide the audience with insight into the characters' lives and thoughts. (This was a technique that Oscar Hammerstein would later employ to great advantage during his collaboration with Richard Rodgers.[140]) Following the pattern established by Lorenz Hart, Hammerstein gave the lyrics equal importance to the music. Capable of standing alone as poetry, they are also absolutely essential to the development of the story.

While the average Broadway musical of the times might contain one or possibly two memorable songs, an unprecedented six from *Show Boat* became almost instantaneous hits. The emotional content of these songs was also unmatched among contemporaneous musicals, from the intense pain and suffering in the lyrics of "Old Man River" to the tender longing in "Bill" and "Can't Help Lovin' That Man." *Show Boat* also contains the first of Hammerstein's trademark "what if" songs: "Make Believe" (see also Chapter Twenty).

Most theatre music fits into specific categories: patter songs, dance tunes, inspirational songs, and several other types, the most common of which is the love song, in all of its various guises. Almost every successful stage musical has featured the element of romantic love, and in many it is the central theme. There are only just so many ways to say "I Love You," but songwriters have been amazingly creative throughout the years in finding new ways to approach this universal sentiment.

Beginning with his lyrics for *Show Boat*, Hammerstein developed a formula that would become almost a signature for him, although he did not overuse it. In the early encounter between Magnolia Hawks and the gambler Gaylord Ravenal, he sought to portray at one and the same time the growing attraction between the couple and their concomitant reluctance to express their emotions to each other. Hammerstein's solution was the earliest example of his "what if" songs, in which the characters skirt the issue of their increasing affection by imagining what a relationship between them might be like.[141] Through this device, Hammerstein manages to convey a wide range of emotions in a dramatic and curiously affecting way.

Kern's melodic line emphasizes the essential message of the song by a simple but effective mechanism. The opening words, "Only make believe," are in the low register, while the next words "I love you" skip a full octave upward, allowing the sentiment to soar.

The lyrics of "Make Believe" reveal and describe the complex emotions of two people experiencing, and possibly somewhat frightened by, the powerful attraction they feel for each other. In a beautiful and transparent paradox, they tell each other of their love while seeming to deny it. Occurring as it does early in the play, "Make Believe" sets up the emotional framework for the tragic relationship between the two characters in a manner far more subtle than the passionate declarations of love often found in classic operettas.

The musical adaptation of Ferber's novel necessarily took many liberties with the original story. Although forced by constraints of time to focus only upon portions of that expansive work, Hanmmerstein captured and commented upon social issues of the day that had hitherto gone almost unnoticed in popular musical theatre.

The play spans the period between the 1880s and the "present day" (1927), those pivotal years following the abolition of slavery in the United States that saw little improvement in the material well-being of the Negro[142] population. Hammerstein was no stranger to racial prejudice. His surname, of which he was justifiably proud, given the accomplishments of his forebears, branded him a member of a large and distinctive minority. The Jewish population had long been the target of racial hatred in Europe and elsewhere. As a group, they were readily identifiable by their religious practices and even by their clothing, which set them apart from the predominately Christian population.

Furthermore, the considerable talents of some members of the Jewish race, especially in the economic sector, had often helped them to amass both wealth and political power, inciting some jealousy. Anti-Semitic sentiment was, however, less overt than the racial prejudice practiced against Negroes in many areas of the United States. Although recognizable by surname or religious practice, Jews were much less discernible in appearance from the rest of the primarily Caucasian population. Negroes, by contrast, were instantly distinguishable by the colour of their skin.

There is little doubt that Hammerstein identified with the suffering of the Negro people. Racism in various forms was a topic to which he would return many times in the future. The plot device of mixed-blood children in *South Pacific* (1949) and the doomed romance between one of that musical's Caucasian characters and a Polynesian girl, made a powerful statement in the years immediately following World War Two. And although not primarily concerned with racism as such, *The King And I* (1951) deals with cultural differences in much the same way. The issue of slavery also forms a significant subplot, wherein the subjugation of the young girl Tuptim is compared graphically to the anti-slavery book by Harriet Beecher Stowe, *Uncle Tom's Cabin*.

The topic of cultural difference arises once again in *Flower Drum Song* (1958). In each of these examples, it is the Oriental races whose position in society is exposed to close scrutiny, and in Oscar Hammerstein's hands, always sympathetically. Finally, it was in his last collaboration with Richard Rodgers, *The Sound Of Music*, that the lyricist focused directly on the issue of anti-Semitism as it existed in Europe during the years preceding World War Two.

While *Show Boat* depicts compellingly and compassionately the plight of Negroes working on the docks along the Mississippi, Hammerstein was not content to leave it at that. In what was to be regarded as the most controversial plot element of the musical play, he tackled the issue of miscegenation, specifically the laws then in force that prohibited marriage between members of different races. These laws were directed primarily against members of the Negro population, and were punishable by imprisonment.

Although rarely discussed openly in those days, sexual exploitation of slaves by white plantation owners was a common occurrence, and resulted in the birth of many thousands of mixed-race children. Even such highly respected founders of the United States as Thomas Jefferson[143] were known to have fathered children with the Negro women in their "service." And while this situation was tacitly accepted, legitimizing any such union through the institution of marriage was strictly proscribed by law, and punishable by harsh penalties, both legal and societal.

Hammerstein deftly portrayed the consequences that accrued to those who would defy these laws, and thus drew attention to the innate racism that lay at their core. By first invoking affection for the interracial couple, he invited outrage among the audience members for the way in which they were later treated by local law enforcement officials. The ultimate decline and tragedy of the mulatto woman, Julie La Verne, was fashioned by Hammerstein into a powerful and effective statement against prejudice in America.

It was many years before any significant segment of American society began to accept the portrayal of interracial unions on stage, and such acceptance is still not universal. As late as 1962, in Richard Rodgers' first effort after Hammerstein's death, *No Strings*,[144] the central characters are a black woman and a Caucasian man (played by Diahann Carroll and Richard Kiley). Their romantic involvement on stage, which included kissing, resulted in some members of the audience walking out in protest during initial tryouts in Detroit, and Rodgers received a considerable amount of hate mail. However, there was no such reaction in a subsequent run in Toronto or at the New York opening.[145]

The treatment of the primary plot in *Show Boat*, the romance between Magnolia Hawks and the riverboat gambler who abandoned her and their young daughter, established another theme that would resurface in much of Hammerstein's later work. A heroine worthy of respect in those pre-feminist times, Magnolia is portrayed as independently capable of providing for herself and her child. Rather than accept the financial support of others, she, and her daughter after her, survive by their talents and their determination to make their own way in the world.

Show Boat was a revelation in its time, a radical departure from the accepted forms of musical theatre in almost every way. The universality of its themes prompted three film versions and numerous revivals, including two subsequent Broadway productions. The first of these stage revivals was in 1946; the second was a lavish stage production that opened in Toronto amid considerable controversy in 1994. The producers of that revival chose to remain faithful to Hammerstein's original portrayal of Negroes, prompting charges of racism among modern black activists and misguided white liberals.[146]

As Hammerstein first penned the lyrics to "Old Man River", the song begins "Niggers all work on the Mississippi." Taken in the context of the play, the use of the word "nigger," sung by a black man, is not framed in the form of an insult. Rather, it serves to point up the plight of the race, and zeros in on the injustice of pejorative labels that ignore and deny the essential humanity of all people.

This offensive word was completely expunged from most subsequent stage productions and all of the movie versions.[147] The phrase "coloured folks" was substituted for the 1928 London production and in the 1946 Broadway revival. Sometimes the generic term "people" was used instead, completely negating the message that the author intended.

For the 1994 stage revival, the producers apparently concluded that to whitewash the script would be to rewrite theatre history, and would also be a disservice to the intent of the lyricist. It is a tribute to the quality of Hammerstein's original concept and libretto that modern audiences ultimately recognized in the script not racism, but a strong statement against racial hatred taken within the context of 1920s America.

The 1994 *Show Boat* revival was moved from Toronto to a successful run on Broadway: 947 performances at the Gershwin Theatre. The play had previously been filmed three times, with varying results. The first version was released in 1929, within two years of the advent of sound motion pictures. Like the first sound film, *The Jazz Singer* of 1927, it mixed sound-augmented musical scenes with silent dramatic portions. The story line is said to have been changed substantially from the stage play, and no prints are known to exist.[148]

In 1951, the third version was lavishly captured in full Technicolor with the considerable vocal talents of Howard Keel, Kathryn Grayson and William Warfield. The original Kern-Hammerstein score was beautifully presented, and the budget for scenic effects, especially the magnificent riverboat, was immense. However, the story line was distorted to such an extent that the power and drama of the book all but vanished. The end result is a visually stunning but dramatically confusing movie that does great injustice to the original.

It is the second film version, expertly filmed in 1936 in black and white, that captured the essence of the musical. The screenplay was essentially faithful to the stage version, and retained most of the plot elements and social commentary. The producers assembled an extraordinary cast, including the exceptional actress who originated the role of Julie La Verne on stage, Helen Morgan. Ms. Morgan's portrayal of this tragic figure ranks high among the great performances in film history.

The controversial baritone Paul Robeson was featured in a dramatically filmed version of "Old Man River."[149] Acclaimed actors Irene Dunne, Charles Winninger,[150] Hattie McDaniel and Alan Jones (father of pop singer Tom Jones) succeeded in bringing each of the characters to life. The portly Winninger's surprising athleticism was a high point of the play-within-a-play sequence, and McDaniel managed to infuse great humanity into the stereotypical role of a Negro "mammy."

While perhaps no film version of any musical can be said to equal the power of a well-produced stage presentation, the 1936 *Show Boat* comes very close, especially in a medium (sound motion pictures) that was still in its infancy. More than six decades later, it remains remarkably fresh and entertaining.

Show Boat "was the beginning of the serious musical, the point at which the all-encompassing term 'musical theatre' would replace 'musical comedy,' marked by the supreme achievement of the integration of book, music and lyrics."[151] Strangely, it failed to engender equally compelling stage musicals during the next decade and a half. With the significant exception of Gershwin's *Porgy and Bess* in 1935, most stage musicals of the 1930s and early 1940s steered clear of truly controversial topics. (*Porgy and Bess* is an anomaly among 1930s musicals, and is more often classified as a folk opera; see Chapter Ten).

This is not to say that they were all trivial, but the musicals of this time period are, like those written during the years leading up to *Show Boat*, memorable much more for their music than for their plots, and few are ever revived today. This was in part due to the world-wide economic reversal caused by the Great Depression, beginning in 1929 and not eased until World War Two. Theatre productions faced serious competition from sound films, as audiences seemed to prefer lighter, less sombre plots to help them forget the deteriorating economic conditions.[152]

Having achieved monumental freshness and originality with *Show Boat*, Kern and Hammerstein were unable to repeat their success. Audiences inevitably compared their next productions to that ground-breaking effort, and found them somewhat less compelling. For example, *Sweet Adeline* was an attempt to capitalize on Helen Morgan's success in *Show Boat*, as well as nostalgia for the late 19th century.[153] Although profitable at 234 performances, it lacked the immediacy and social importance of the previous show. Nor was the score of comparable quality. Only one song attained the status of a standard: "Why Was I Born?"

In 1929, Hammerstein returned to the operetta format in collaboration with Sigmund Romberg. *The New Moon* was well received but not innovative, although the lovely score included the popular "Stouthearted Men" and "Lover, Come Back To Me."[154] Later Kern-Hammerstein efforts were also relatively conventional. *Music In The Air* (1932) fared somewhat better than *Sweet Adeline* at 342 performances, enough to turn a substantial profit, but was not memorable as to plot. The score is excellent, however, and two songs from that production, "I've Told Ev'ry Little Star" and "The Song Is You," achieved widespread popularity.

Because of the onset of the Great Depression, just two book musicals were introduced in New York in 1934,[155] and some composers and lyricists, Rodgers and Hart among them, gravitated toward Hollywood. Throughout the rest of the decade, Hammerstein and Kern worked on other projects, together and with other collaborators, but without achieving their previous artistic success. And in commercial terms, following 1932's *Music In The Air*, Hammerstein would not have another hit musical for a full eleven years.

NINE
Before Porgy

The fact that Kern and Hammerstein were unable to create another musical to equal *Show Boat* over the next decade emphasizes the substance and importance of that ground-breaking show.[156]   Nor could any other creative individual or team equal that artistic triumph, at least not until Gershwin's *Porgy and Bess* in 1935. And the true transformation of musical theatre that was begun in 1927 would not come full circle until the advent of *Oklahoma!* in 1943.

Despite three more attempts at collaboration,[157] Kern and Hammerstein achieved greater success when working with others. The lyricist's association with Sigmund Romberg on *The New Moon* (1928) was his only major success for over a decade, and even Kern's work with Otto Harbach, *The Cat and the Fiddle* (1931) and *Roberta* (1933), seemed somehow out of step with the new direction being taken by the Gershwin brothers, Rodgers and Hart, and especially Cole Porter.

The enduring nature of *Show Boat* derives from the total package: fine music, sensitive lyrics and a significant story line by a skilful author, crafted by Hammerstein with equal proficiency into a powerful libretto. It was a synthesis of great ideas and masterful execution, and it is the very rarity of this combination that made the production great. Excepting perhaps only *Porgy*, the musical plays of the 1930s and very early 1940s lacked one essential element of *Show Boat*. While their music, lyrics and staging were admirable, they failed to deliver a compelling portrait of society that could capture the public's attention.

Kern's music certainly continued to be of very high quality. With Harbach he produced two lovely ballads, "Smoke Gets in Your Eyes"[158] and "The Night Was Made for Love."[159] The very haunting "Why Was I Born?",[160] the optimistic "I've Told Ev'ry Little Star," and the powerful ballad "The Song Is You,"[161] all with lyrics by Hammerstein, are equal to the best songs from *Show Boat*. And Hammerstein himself created two of his most enduring standards, "Stouthearted Men" and "Lover, Come Back to Me," in partnership with Sigmund Romberg for *The New Moon*.

But times were changing, and public taste shifted in response to technology, politics and especially economic deprivation. The emphasis turned away from period pieces toward a more urbane, contemporary approach in which wit, satire and a more blasé view of the world captured the imagination of the theatre-going public. And no one epitomized this change more than Cole Porter.

Porter's first success of the 1930s, although a minor one (168 performances), was indicative and predictive of the new trend. Gone were the opulent sets and dashing princes of operetta, the heroic women of *Show Boat*, and especially the underlying decency of humanity that these earlier shows so often reflected. *The New Yorkers* (1930) dealt with murdering gangsters, bootleggers, whores and other amoral characters in a seedy nightclub setting.[162] The music suited the context. The best-known number from the show, "Love For Sale," was consistently banned from performance on the radio because of its association with prostitution.

The survival of Broadway faced a very significant threat in the new decade, the advent of the movie musical. Talking pictures were now firmly established, and the rapidly declining economy eroded purchasing power and severely limited discretionary spending, especially for recreation and amusement. The low cost of a movie admission, just a fraction of that of a Broadway ticket, created a massive shift in how one's entertainment budget was spent. Except for those who lived near major cities, first-run musicals were generally out of reach. Hollywood quickly discovered that by usurping the theatre's most lively genre, the musical, it could bring the essence of Broadway to every corner of the nation, and handsome profits to the studios.

Despite the relatively small size of movie screens in those days, and the comparative blandness of the black and white images, the combination of low admission cost and broad accessibility gave motion pictures a substantial competitive advantage.[163] To meet the challenge, the entire complexion of Broadway changed. The number of extravagant revues and lavish operettas declined rapidly, and except for revivals of past successes, with their inherent lower cost, the newer musicals were smaller and more subdued and introspective.[164]

Stage personalities sought the wider recognition that films offered. Fred Astaire's last significant Broadway appearance (and without his sister, Adele) was in Porter's *Gay Divorce* (1932),[165] after which he began an extensive career in movie musicals for the MGM studio. Vaudeville performers took a similar route, finding in the cinema a more dependable source of income than on the stage.[166] Songwriters too, most notably

Rodgers and Hart, turned to the more financially secure venue of Hollywood.

An even less expensive form of show business made further inroads into the theatre audience with the rapid development of local and later network radio broadcasting. The one-time purchase of a home receiver brought a wide variety of entertainment directly into people's homes. During the 1930s and 1940s, many diverse styles of music, comedy, drama and variety became available to almost everyone at the twist of a dial.[167]

In the face of such competition, theatrical musicals moved upward to a level of sophistication unmatched in the other media. Cole Porter hit his stride in 1934 with *Anything Goes*, the most exemplary musical comedy of the decade,[168] for which he wrote both music and lyrics. The book was fine entertainment, with contemporary characters, refined humour and fast-paced action, and the cast carried it off well, especially trumpet-voiced Ethel Merman in a role that suited her strident stage presence.[169]

Whatever the quality of the script and the cast, however, it was the music that made the show. In a coup not seen since *Show Boat*, most of the score achieved the status of standards, including "Blow, Gabriel, Blow," "I Get a Kick Out of You," "The Gypsy in Me," "You're the Top" and the title song. Porter's lyrics were aimed at an educated and cultured audience. He frequently employed topical references[170] and shamelessly dropped the names of celebrities into his songs. Above all, his clever poetry appealed to a more intellectual and erudite clientele.

The intricate construction of the title song illustrates Porter's imaginative placement of rhyming words in places other than at the ends of symmetrical verses. He also employed multiple rhymes within a single line, and sometimes rhymed the first words of a pair of two-word groups, as in "better words/four-letter words."[171]

He also had a great penchant for internal rhymes, and never hesitated to alter or combine words in order to achieve lines that scanned well. In "I Get a Kick Out of You" he follows the words "if" and "sniff" with "terrific'ly," allowing the rhythm of the melody to emphasize the "if-sniff-terrif" rhyme.[172] This series fits perfectly with the sequences of rising notes in the melody to draw attention to the rhymes. And Porter loved the incongruity of diverse rhyming pairs, such as the lines in the song "You're the Top" that juxtapose the name of the composer Strauss with Mickey Mouse.[173]

The early 1930s also witnessed quality work from George and Ira Gershwin, and like most musicals of the period, their shows were polished, topical, and often satirical. *Strike Up the Band* (1930), for example, cast a jaundiced eye on the increasingly warlike developments in Europe, and at the posturing of politicians at home and abroad. *Of Thee I Sing* (1931) took shots at political campaigns, beauty pageants, marriage, the Supreme Court, the Vice Presidency, and even that most sacred of all institutions, motherhood.[174]

These shows produced a string of Gershwin brothers' standards, including "I've Got a Crush on You" and "Love Is Sweeping the Country." But it was their 1930 production of *Girl Crazy* that generated a score to rival those of Kern and Porter. In terms of plot, the show reverted to a more innocent, romantic style reminiscent of the previous decade, and lacked the biting satire and contemporary political commentary that was inherent in the other two works. Given a romantic theme, they produced memorable music to match: "But Not for Me"; "Bidin' My Time"; "Embraceable You"; and that tune beloved of jazz performers for generations, "I Got Rhythm."[175]

Also in a satirical mood, Irving Berlin wrote the music and lyrics for Moss Hart's book treatment entitled *Face the Music*. This time the targets were New York politicians and policemen, the reduced circumstances of society's elite during the Depression, and even the theatre itself.[176] Berlin and Hart followed it up with a revue-style show in 1933, *As Thousands Cheer*, cleverly structured to resemble a newspaper and so topical as to be mostly inaccessible to audiences today. The music, however, is wonderful, especially Berlin's second most enduring hit after "White Christmas," "Easter Parade."

During this period, the team of Richard Rodgers and Lorenz Hart was not prominent on Broadway. Their production of *America's Sweetheart* (1931) was generally pleasant but not memorable, and although it ran for seventeen weeks, the music is forgotten today. Because of their intervening sojourn in Hollywood, they did not create another stage success until *Jumbo* in 1935.

Often overlooked among better-known composers of the period is the team of Arthur Schwartz and Howard Dietz, perhaps because their shows were in revue style, rather than musical comedies or dramas. Their third effort, *The Band Wagon*, "may well have been the most sophisticated, imaginative, and musically distinguished revue ever mounted on Broadway."[177] The standout tune from the show was "Dancing in the Dark."

In general, the period from *Show Boat* to *Porgy and Bess* was one of transition, marked by tremendous political, economic and technological upheaval. The dramatic voice of *Show Boat* failed to spawn credible imitators, and was replaced instead by a more world-weary cynicism and a concentration upon comedy in musical theatre. The most enduring product of those years is the music itself, as the first truly American composers and lyricists reached their maturity.

TEN
The Anomaly Of
Porgy And Bess

Although there were quality productions on Broadway in the years between *Show Boat* and *Porgy and Bess*, the number of productions with a similar devotion to serious topics and an integrated book and score was minimal.[178]   However, this was not due to lack of creative talent. The productions of that period contain a wealth of fine music, and given the economic restrictions of the time and the competition from other forms of entertainment, they were reasonably well funded. The problem was more likely a matter of intent. Broadway composers and lyricists, concerned with making a living, had to cater to the demands of the public, and the market was for urbane comedy, topicality and satire, rather than serious drama.

Almost unique among stage composers of the time, George Gershwin aspired to create more serious works, first for orchestra and ultimately for the operatic stage. His *Rhapsody in Blue, Concerto in F* and *An American in Paris* had attracted considerable (if controversial) attention in the 1920s and thereafter, sparking debate over the appropriate inclusion of pop and jazz music conventions into classical forms. Billed as an "Experiment in Modern Music," the groundbreaking *Rhapsody* is not jazz in the improvisatory sense, but it was the first successful introduction of that style and language to the symphonic repertoire.[179]

Gershwin's background included a thorough grounding in the classical tradition, first from the composer and pianist Charles Hambitzer,[180] and later with Edward Kilenyi.[181]   His early works benefited from the assistance of established musicians, notably the American composer Ferde Grofe,[182] who orchestrated *Rhapsody in Blue*. His interest in more serious vocal forms (and in Negro culture) was first revealed in a one-act opera about blacks in Harlem entitled *Blue Monday*. It was presented as a part of the revue *George White's Scandals of 1922*, but was deleted after the opening night performance.[183]

Although American composers were beginning to attract attention, the vast majority of concerts and operatic productions were dominated by composers of European origin.[184] To their credit, however, promoters were actively searching for home-grown material. Just two years after *Show Boat*, Gershwin had explored the possibility of writing for the Metropolitan Opera, but the project did not materialize.[185]

Still hoping for the opportunity to create an opera on a purely American theme, Gershwin undertook certain preparations. He was apparently very much aware of his technical deficiencies,[186] and in an effort to acquire more exposure to 20th century compositional methods, he studied with the acclaimed theorist Joseph Shillinger between 1932 and 1936.[187] And most important, he went in search of a vehicle, a story worthy of his ambitions.

The subject he found was a best-selling 1925 novel by DuBose Heyward on an unlikely theme, and with an even more unlikely cast of characters. Although a white southerner himself, Heyward captured the unique flavour of the Gullah culture of South Carolina in his story of the crippled Negro Porgy.[188] He wrote sympathetically of that unique society, and imbued the story with an emotional authenticity that gave the characters both depth and universal appeal.

In an era when the average white citizen knew little or nothing about the lives of the black population, other than the pervasive stereotypes, Heyward's insights were atypical, and the way in which he treated the material was highly original. He professed great admiration for a way of life far different from his own, and sought mainly to give it sympathetic exposure through a valid artistic treatment.[189]

The author and his wife Dorothy turned the novel into a stage play, but the project languished throughout the 1920s and early 1930s. Several treatments were considered, including a proposed stage version to star Al Jolson in blackface, with music by Jerome Kern and Oscar Hammerstein II.[190] Given the success of that team's *Show Boat*, the intent, however misguided, must have been taken seriously at the time,[191] but it was finally shelved.

George Gershwin first encountered the novel in 1926, and approached the author with a proposal to collaborate on an opera, but they could not come to an agreement at the time. Dorothy Heyward's straight dramatic version took precedence in the author's list of priorities, besides which the Gershwin brothers were heavily involved in their series of lighter weight Broadway productions.[192] It was not until late 1932, with Heyward becoming thoroughly frustrated at the repeated unsuccessful attempts to bring his novel to the stage, that the author and the composer finally reached an agreement to join forces.

Heyward began developing a new libretto in 1933,[193] and Gershwin started work on the music late in the same year.[194] The composer approached the task as seriously as he had his musical studies, by going to the cultural source of the material. In 1934 he spent part of the summer, alone and in the company of the author, in the islands off Charleston, South Carolina. There he met with, observed and got to know well the people on whom Heyward had based his story. Equally important, the author and the composer formed a bond between them that allowed them to work on the opera with a common purpose and direction.

According to Heyward's own recollections of Gershwin's reaction to the Negro culture, what he found most interesting was the composer's empathy for a culture that must have seemed exceedingly alien to him. However, Gershwin's affinity for the jazz conventions that originated with the black population seemed to give him an instinctive understanding of this peasant society. Heyward described Gershwin's first exposure to a musical exercise believed to be of African origin that the Gullahs called "shouting," a complex rhythmic accompaniment to spirituals involving the participants' hands and feet. Heyward wrote: "I shall never forget the night when... George started 'shouting' with them. And eventually to their huge delight stole the show from their champion 'shouter.' I think that he is probably the only white man in America who could have done it."[195]

The book for *Porgy and Bess* is usually credited only to Heyward, although the contributions of his wife Dorothy should not be overlooked. Ira Gershwin received top billing for the lyrics, but with his intimate knowledge of the Gullah dialect, Heyward himself wrote at least the initial versions of many of them. Ira made the necessary changes so they would better fit the patterns of George's melodies, and also contributed some original material, but the essence of many of the songs came initially from Heyward. The three-way collaboration was apparently an easy one,[196] each of the men respecting the other's unique talents.

When *Porgy and Bess* opened in 1935, it was understandably controversial, but at first the main point of the discussion centred around the form or classification of the work, rather than its dramatic content. One *New York Times* reviewer, Olin Downes, wrote that Gershwin had "not completely formed his style as an opera composer" and that "the style is at one moment of opera and another of operetta or sheer Broadway entertainment."[197] Although the show opened in the mainstream Alvin

Theatre, as opposed to a venue such as the Metropolitan, it was billed not as a musical, but as "An American Folk Opera."[198]

Porgy originally owed much to the European operatic format, with recitatives substituting for spoken dialog.[199] However some critics, notably Virgil Thompson, vilified the composer's efforts, calling his recitatives "vocally uneasy and dramatically cumbersome."[200] This opinion prevailed at the time, and when the work was revived in 1941, spoken dialog was substituted instead.

With so much attention given to what was essentially an academic debate, questions of the quality of the show were relegated to second place. In addition, the grim, oppressive atmosphere of the play kept audiences away, and it closed after only 124 performances. Apparently in those Depression years, theatregoers were more inclined to seek out the escapism of less serious musical comedies than an artfully constructed portrayal of the woes of a minority race.[201] Another problem was the cost of the production. With an operatic-style orchestra, twice the size of those typically used on Broadway, only a full house could return even the barest profit.[202]

History has accorded the work its rightful place as a masterpiece, with four major revivals (1941, 1953, 1976 and 1983), some with the recitatives restored, and inclusion in the permanent repertoire of the Metropolitan Opera[203] and other companies. Unaccountably, the well-done 1959 film version has been withdrawn from distribution, depriving film and video audiences of a reasonably faithful interpretation. In the final analysis, all of the debate over format and category is meaningless. "*Porgy and Bess* is a one of a kind work of art that cannot be judged against anything else in the history of the American stage."[204]

The durability of its score is undeniable, and includes the hauntingly beautiful "Summertime" and "I Got Plenty 'o Nuttin'." Like the score from *Show Boat*, the individual songs have crossed racial barriers[205] and become standards in their own right. Regrettably, it marked the Gershwin brothers' last appearance on Broadway.[206] They turned their attention to writing for films before George's premature death from a brain tumour in 1938. Those movie years produced some of their most memorable tunes, including "Nice Work if You Can Get It."

Porgy and Bess stands out as the single most important Broadway production in the years between *Show Boat* (1927) and *Oklahoma!* (1943). In particular, it was a worthy successor to the Kern-Hammerstein effort in its intent to do more than merely entertain. With a score derived from fundamental black American genres (ragtime, jazz, blues and spirituals), it took the American musical in a new and significant direction.[207] While its initial reception was minimal, its lasting influence proved to be monumental.

ELEVEN
More Of The Same

In a pattern reminiscent of the years following *Show Boat*, Broadway returned to established formats after the anomalous production of *Porgy and Bess*. Given its initial commercial failure and the conflicting and controversial reviews that helped to sink it, it is understandable that its quality and innovation were not recognized at the time. Broadway was, after all, about making money, and escapist drama and comedy laced with sex were the big ticket draws in the middle of the Depression.

With the departure of the Gershwins, Cole Porter and the team of Rodgers and Hart were in the ascendancy, and with just a few exceptions, the quality of their music far outshines the shows from which they originated. For example, Cole Porter's *Jubilee* (1935) lasted a profitable but hardly exciting 169 performances, offering nothing but lighthearted, escapist fun in the story line,[208] but at the same time a rich and lasting score that included "Begin the Beguine" and "Just One of Those Things."

After some success in writing for films, Rodgers and Hart returned to Broadway in November of 1935 with *Jumbo*, a circus-theme musical that produced three fine standards, including an early example ("The Most Beautiful Girl in the World") of Rodgers' most significant form, the waltz.[209] They followed it up the next year with *On Your Toes*, a mostly conventional book musical with one significant innovation, one which Rodgers would use to good advantage in his work with Oscar Hammerstein during the next decade. The innovative ballet (*Slaughter on Tenth Avenue*) predated the extraordinary dream sequence that attracted so much attention in *Oklahoma!* seven years later.

Cole Porter's 1936 entry of note was *Red, Hot and Blue*, a political satire with a mostly mediocre score (at least by Porter's standards) from which only "It's De-Lovely" achieved the proportions of a hit. The able cast, however, which included Bob Hope, Ethel Merman and Jimmy Durante, kept it on the boards for 183 performances.

Rodgers and Hart had two more successful shows in 1937, *Babes in Arms* and *I'd Rather Be Right*. The first of these yielded the best tunes:

"My Funny Valentine," "Johnny One Note," "I Wish I Were in Love Again" and "The Lady Is a Tramp." The 1939 movie adaptation was the first of the Judy Garland-Mickey Rooney "let's put on a show" movie musicals, but only two of the Rodgers and Hart songs were retained.[210]

I'd Rather Be Right was a political satire, with George M. Cohan appearing as President Franklin Delano Roosevelt, but the script paled in comparison with the previous satire, *Of Thee I Sing*. Both of these shows made money, given a fairly low overhead for the simple sets, and in 1938 the team turned their talents to fantasy with very profitable results. *I Married An Angel* played 338 times, with a score highlighted by arguably the loveliest Rodgers and Hart ballad since "Valentine," entitled "Spring Is Here."

Somewhat out of the mainstream for Broadway musicals, German-born Kurt Weill mounted two significant musicals in the 1930s, the first of which was *The Threepenny Opera* (1933). A victim of the Nazi movement, Weill emigrated to Paris and eventually to New York, where he teamed with Bertold Brecht to update John Gay's *The Beggar's Opera*. Although unsuccessful at the time (it ran less than two weeks), it has since been frequently revived, and one number from the score, "Mack the Knife," has appeared in a wide variety of recorded interpretations ever since.[211]

Weill's second effort, however, the influential *Knickerbocker Holiday* of 1938 (book and lyrics by Maxwell Anderson) established him as a songwriter of uncommon depth and emotion. Although the politically-charged plot was far less coherent than his later *Lost in the Stars* (1949),[212] the eternal reminder that we all must grow old in "September Song" helped carry the show to 168 performances. (Walter Houston's performance on stage, as well as his recording of that tune, proved that a trained singing voice is not always essential to the effective delivery of an emotional song.)

Another 1938 production, Cole Porter's *Leave It To Me!*, is a comic political satire that is best known for one song and the actress who performed it. In her Broadway debut, Mary Martin sang "My Heart Belongs To Daddy," while performing an innocent and relatively modest striptease. This song is a classic double entendre number, and the naïve Miss Martin apparently had little idea of exactly what she was singing. Ironically, that very ingenuousness contributed greatly to the sexual heat of her performance.[213]

Porter was astonishingly prolific during this period, turning out major hits in each of 1939, 1940 and 1941.[214] Irving Berlin was similarly successful with *Louisiana Purchase* (1940, 444 performances) and the wonderfully melodic *This Is the Army* (1942), a revue-style show that was very much in tune with the times and spawned a successful film version in 1943.[215] And Kurt Weill's third Broadway effort, *Lady in the Dark* (1941) was a substantial hit at 467 performances, followed by a film version in 1944.

However, the two most significant musicals of the period, *The Boys From Syracuse* (1938) and *Pal Joey* (1940), came from the pens of Rodgers and Hart, although neither enjoyed the longevity of the Porter and Weill efforts. Nor were they as influential in the development of musical theatre as either *Show Boat* or *Porgy and Bess*, but the uniformly high quality of the books, lyrics and music set them apart. This songwriting team had four substantial hits between 1938 and 1942. The scores for two of them[216] are inconsequential in terms of continuing influence, but *The Boys From Syracuse* and *Pal Joey* generated five durable standards and helped to create new pathways for others to follow.

It is ironic that the lyrics of Lorenz Hart are among the most valid expressions of romantic love to come from the Broadway stage in those years, while their creator never enjoyed a stable personal relationship himself. In an era when intolerance toward homosexuality was almost universal, even in the normally liberal atmosphere of the theatre, Hart struggled with his own sexual identity[217] and with life-long alcoholism.

In his work with Richard Rodgers, Hart was fluent and imaginative, and until near the end, he was also prolific. Together they wrote twenty-seven stage musicals, eight musical films and reportedly as many as a thousand songs,[218] although this number is usually considered to be erroneous, and to have stemmed from an overly-enthusiastic article in *Time* magazine.[219] In many ways charming and affable, Hart was barely over five feet tall and rotund, and in the manner of Kern and Hammerstein, and of Rodgers himself, he was dedicated to the development of integrated musical theatre.

Rodgers found Hart's intellectual approach to writing lyrics to be refreshing and stimulating. They explored such intricacies as interior rhymes and feminine endings,[220] and also found themselves in fundamental agreement about the importance of the work of Bolton, Wodehouse and Kern in the Princess Theatre musicals. Both men shared a belief that musical theatre "was capable of achieving a far greater degree of artistic merit in every area than was apparent at the time."[221] But Rodgers was to experience both frustration and irritation in trying to work with a partner so essentially different from himself.

That irritation began almost from the onset of their professional relationship in 1919. A heavy drinker from an early age, Hart was frequently unreliable, and was his own worst enemy. One thing that never seemed to vary was the quality of his work, provided he was both sober and focused, but toward the end of the 1930s, his personal dissolution had reached almost unmanageable proportions. When working on *Too Many Girls*, for example, "Rodgers had to start writing lyrics himself because Hart would disappear for longer and longer periods. By the end of *Pal Joey*, …Hart was unable to write at all."[222]

After years of considerable productivity, there were no new Rodgers and Hart productions for 1941, mainly due to Hart's unreliability. His drinking had escalated out of control, and he would often be absent for long periods without warning. He could never be relied upon to keep appointments or to meet deadlines, and seemed to have lost interest in almost everything.[223]

In spite of his disintegration, Hart produced some of his most affecting lyrics near the end of his life. To another of Rodgers' flowing waltz melodies he wrote "Falling in Love with Love" for *The Boys from Syracuse*. The same show yielded "This Can't Be Love" and "Sing for Your Supper." And in the few lucid respites from his alcoholic fog he wrote "I Could Write a Book" and "Bewitched, Bothered and Bewildered" for *Pal Joey*, both among the very finest examples of American popular music from that period. But it was becoming apparent that the partnership was nearly over.

During the early stages of writing *By Jupiter* (1942), Hart was hospitalized for acute alcoholism. Rodgers resorted to a sort of forced confinement to get his partner to focus upon lyrics for the show. He arranged to have a room with a piano reserved in the hospital, and with the cooperation of Hart's doctor, the lyricist was not released until the work was finished.[224]

On the surface, it would appear that Richard Rodgers was taking advantage of the situation for his own benefit, but it is certain that he not only held his collaborator in high regard, but also felt concern for his well being. By keeping Hart confined to the hospital, he was insuring at least a short period in which the ailing lyricist was free of alcohol, and with his health problems attended to. While Rodgers did not profess personal responsibility for his partner, beyond the needs of their working relationship, his affection for the man motivated him to try to help. "We had worked together, struggled together and succeeded together, and I simply could not look the other way while this man destroyed himself."[225]

Despite the efforts of Rodgers and others who cared for Hart, his self-destructive behaviour resulted in his premature death in 1942. Richard Rodgers had already begun the search for a new writing partner, which culminated in his historic association with Oscar Hammerstein II, but the two late products of the Rodgers and Hart partnership, *The Boys from Syracuse* and *Pal Joey*, would prove to have lasting influence on the theatre, beyond the quality of the music.

The idea of adapting the works of Shakespeare and other classic plays to musical theatre was not a new one, but the skill with which Rodgers and Hart accomplished it deserves attention. Based on *Comedy of Errors*,[226] the book for *The Boys from Syracuse* was authored by George Abbott, in a witty and erudite manner that recognized the sophistication of the potential audience. Above all, it proved that highbrow drama could be translated into stylish musical comedy, and laid the groundwork for Cole Porter's *Kiss Me, Kate* a decade later and *West Side Story*[227] in 1957, among others.

But it was *Pal Joey* that would become the supreme monument to the Rodgers and Hart partnership. Although the book was ascribed to John O'Hara, at the time like Hart an unreliable alcoholic, it owes much to the additional uncredited work of George Abbott.[228] It was "a major breakthrough in bringing about a more adult form of musical theatre."[229] The lead role depicts "a cheap, handsome night-club hoofer,"[230] but the intense three-dimensional portrayal of his character, blended with the decadent atmosphere of the after-hours world he inhabits, led Rodgers to write (in the *New York Times*), "Nobody like Joey had ever been on the musical comedy stage before."[231]

The role of Joey Evans was played by dancer Gene Kelly, in his only major Broadway appearance before establishing his film career.[232] His performance, and the subject of the play as a whole, engendered considerable controversy. In a major departure from even the most risqué of its predecessors, *Pal Joey* dealt realistically with blackmail, adultery and sexual exploitation, and painted an unflattering portrait of the underside of Chicago society. The *Times* theatre critic, Brooks Atkinson, called it "entertaining" but "odius."[233]

This show was revived successfully in 1952, and a sanitized movie version, with Frank Sinatra in the lead role, was made in 1957. It is an interesting commentary on the times that even as late as 1957, the filmmakers found it necessary to expunge some of the more disturbing elements of the original stage play. While the language, morals and situations of *Pal Joey* would hardly turn a hair today, in 1940 they were explosively contentious, and far ahead of their time. Not much had changed by 1957.

Two unusual musical productions from the immediate pre-World War Two period predicted coming changes in theatre. Plays with all black casts and directed toward black audiences were comparatively rare in those years. Given the limited box office potential, such projects did not attract the attention of established authors and composers.

Nevertheless, perhaps influenced by the success of *The Boys from Syracuse*, Jimmy Van Heusen created a score for an ambitious retelling of Shakespeare's *A Midsummer Night's Dream*, entitled *Swingin' the Dream*. It was set in 1890 Louisiana with an all black cast that included jazz trumpeter Louis Armstrong and the very talented Butterfly McQueen. Despite the formidable talents of the Benny Goodman Sextet in the pit and a score that included the standard "Darn That Dream," the uneven book and some silly staging doomed it to thirteen performances. Nevertheless, it was a noble effort for 1939.

More successful in 1940 was *Cabin in the Sky*, with music by Vernon Duke, lyrics by John Latouche and book by Lynn Root. Cast in the form of a fantasy, it featured the wonderful voice of Ethel Waters in a comedic but emotional good-versus-evil struggle between the forces of the Lord and of Satan, all in a sympathetic parody of southern Negro life.[234] Audience appeal crossed racial lines, and it proved profitable at 156 performances.

A reasonably faithful movie version was made in 1943. In the film, Miss Waters repeated her stage role, and her rendition of the one standard from the show, "Taking a Chance on Love," is one of the few filmed records of her talent. The principal male lead was played by Eddie Anderson ("Rochester" on the Jack Benny radio program), and Butterfly McQueen's performance in a secondary role is a comic delight.

Despite the somewhat radical subject matter of *Pal Joey* and the tentative emergence of mainstream black theatre in *Cabin in the Sky*, the period between 1935 and the spring of 1943 produced no significant new directions in musical theatre along the lines of *Show Boat* or *Porgy and Bess*. But as was the case with those two milestones, another revolution was just over the horizon. Unlike *Show Boat*, however, *Oklahoma!* was to exert an immediate and powerful influence.

TWELVE
"No Gags, No Gals, No Chance"

Success often results from the courage to take chances. Never in the history of American musical theatre was this more apparent than in the first collaboration between Richard Rodgers and Oscar Hammerstein II in 1943.

Hammerstein's career had been somewhat moribund, with no truly outstanding productions since his 1927 partnership with Jerome Kern for *Show Boat*, and the subsequent *The New Moon* (1928), which he wrote with Sigmund Romberg. Several productions were modestly successful, including *Sweet Adeline* (1929) and *Music in the Air* in 1932, but seven other shows between 1928 and 1939 were total failures.[235]

By contrast, Rodgers had enjoyed a recent string of critically acclaimed and profitable shows in association with lyricist Lorenz Hart. But with Hart's decline into alcoholism, Rodgers began in 1941 to seek out someone with whom he could continue to find success. In his autobiography, he admits to feeling guilty over having to abandon the working relationship with Hart. Given their long association, they were almost inseparable in the eyes of the public.[236]

Richard Rodgers was a precocious musical talent who learned to play piano by ear from early childhood.[237] This very fact sometimes interfered with his education, as he was resistant to learning how to read music when he could so quickly reproduce on the keyboard any melody he heard.[238]

As a teenager growing up in New York, he attended productions at the Princess Theatre and developed a life-long respect for the music of Jerome Kern.[239] His exposure to such shows as *Very Good Eddie* and *Oh, Boy!* led him to appreciate the emerging style of small-scale musical theatre represented by the works of Kern, Guy Bolton and P. G. Wodehouse. He found them modern and relevant in their treatment of ordinary people, far removed from the imported operettas and their old-world preoccupations. "I was watching and listening to the beginning of a new form of musical theatre in this country. Somehow I knew it and wanted desperately to be a part of it.[240]

Rodgers was just sixteen when he first met Lorenz Hart. Less than two years later their first effort, *Fly With Me*, was chosen as the 1920 Varsity Show at Columbia University.[241] Over the next few years they contributed songs to several productions, and finally mounted the first of their completely original musicals in 1925, *Dearest Enemy*. Comparing it to a concurrent Vincent Youmans/Otto Harbach hit show, Gerald Bordman cites "the subtlety, inventiveness and sophistication (that) stood in direct contrast to the slap-on-the-back obviousness of *No, No, Nanette*."[242]

Little more than a decade later, the phenomenally successful Rodgers and Hart partnership had begun to collapse, even before the lyricist's death in 1942. The composer was, if not actively seeking a new partner, at least open to the idea. Richard Rodgers and Oscar Hammerstein II had worked together previously, and they were well acquainted, even good friends. They co-wrote two songs for an amateur production in 1919, and another during the following year. Hammerstein was a member of the selection committee that chose *Fly With Me* at Columbia in 1920. He also co-directed a Rodgers and Hart variety show in 1921, but the two men drifted apart as Hart's influence on the composer increased.[243]

During the preparation of *By Jupiter* in 1942, Rodgers had confided in Hammerstein his fears for Lorenz Hart's future as a songwriting partner.[244] Hammerstein even offered to assist the composer in the event that Hart became too incapacitated to work. However, while each respected the other's talent, Rogers had reservations about their compatibility of style, should they attempt to work together on a more permanent basis.[245]

There was also the nagging problem of Hammerstein's recent record of mediocre shows and outright failures. "By the early forties the once super-successful Hammerstein had inspired the odd line 'He can't write his hat' in Hollywood's ever-cynical community."[246] Nevertheless, as the two men skirted warily around each other, it became apparent to them that they shared very similar views on how a musical play should be constructed.

One fundamental area of agreement between them was a certainty that the music should be an integral part of any musical theatrical performance. Neither accepted the idea that a song could be inserted into a play unless it had a specific purpose other than entertainment. Except for a few such productions as *Show Boat*, it was uncommon for the music to be central to all aspects of a play. *Oklahoma!* would change that.[247]

In Richard Rodgers, Hammerstein sensed the same devotion to an integrated approach that had made his association with Jerome Kern so productive. In 1942 they chose as their first experiment a modestly successful stage play entitled *Green Grow the Lilacs*, by Lynn Riggs, and began to map out how the project would proceed. Rodgers had previously planned to write the musical with Hart as the lyricist, but other than recognizing that it would be a complete departure from any of his former shows, he had not planned a specific approach.[248]

There are many similarities, albeit perhaps superficial ones, between the Edna Ferber novel that spawned the musical *Show Boat* and the unassuming Riggs effort. Both had turn-of-the-century settings, and both were essentially rural. Both concerned societal and cultural conflict, although of a very different kind. While *Show Boat* had a strong component of racial conflict, the context for the opposing factions in *Green Grow the Lilacs* was economic and societal: ranchers and farmers, each with a different and competing approach to the proper use and development of the land.

Additionally, the characters in both stories were seen to be believable, probably more like the average citizen than the types of roles portrayed in the average 1930s musical. Whereas Broadway had moved almost exclusively toward the contemporary, gritty slice-of-life context exemplified in *Pal Joey*, the time seemed ripe for a return to the kind of values that are thought to represent rural America.

Rodgers and Hammerstein chose deliberately to eschew most of the conventions that had developed ever since *The Black Crook*. *Oklahoma!* would have no chorus of leggy beauties, no contrived and intricate comedy of misunderstandings or mistaken identities. Instead it would trace the lives of ordinary people, and would tell the story in a straightforward narrative manner. But it would seek to do so in an artistic, intelligent manner that respected both the literary source and the receptivity of a sensitive audience.

For close to a century, the typical Broadway production had opened with a brilliant overture and a splashy entrance, as if trying to capture attention purely by sound and fury. The pretty girls were introduced early, singing and dancing and generally entertaining the audience instead of telling the story. Had *Oklahoma!* followed this familiar pattern, it might have begun with a rodeo or a barn dance, or something equally exciting to quicken the pulse. But Oscar Hammerstein had other ideas: "We agreed to start our story in the real and natural way in which it seemed to want to be told!"[249]

One example of his unconventional approach was to delay the appearance of a woman's chorus until relatively late in the first act,[250] a break with typical musical comedy tradition. For this and other reasons, the word "comedy" seemed no longer appropriate,[251] despite its pervasive use on Broadway in those years. *Oklahoma!* was different, not just in structure but in its approach to narrative, formerly the province mainly of straight dramatic productions.

The beginning of *Oklahoma!* must have seemed magical to an audience accustomed to splashy openings: a woman stands alone; offstage the voice of a cowboy begins to sing of the beauty of the day. Rodgers writes, "we were, in effect, warning the audience, 'Watch out! This is a different kind of musical.' Everything in the production was made to conform to the simple open-air spirit of the story… certainly a rarity in the musical theatre."[252]

In and of itself, the clever and unexpected introductory scene cannot be considered sufficient to account for this play's place in theatre history. In fact, the entire show was a deviation from the expected norm. The depth of characterization as developed simultaneously by Hammerstein's book and lyrics quickly drew the audience into the story and made them care about the people involved. It is unlikely that this could have been achieved with the traditional formula of dialog and action interspersed with loosely related songs and dances. The music of *Oklahoma!* grows directly out of the story, the setting, and especially the personalities of the singers, and infuses the action with an uncommon intimacy.

For example, in a clever twist on his "what if" song ("Make Believe," from *Show Boat*, Chapter Eight), Hammerstein devised yet another original way to say "I Love You." In the time-honoured tradition of such tales, the centrepiece of the play is still boy-meets-girl: "Cowboy Curley woos and wins farm girl Laurey. How could audiences get excited about something as ordinary as that?"[253]

How, indeed! Using reverse psychology, Laurey and Curley caution each other against revealing their growing affection for one another in the song "People Will Say We're In Love."[254] This emotional dichotomy is familiar to any young person who, in the first throes of love, is desperately afraid of becoming the object of teasing by his or her friends. In this one simple but emotionally charged song, Hammerstein quickly adds depth and familiarity to the principal characters. Laurey and Curley become real people, very human individuals with whom the audience can identify.

Hammerstein's approach to songs was the direct opposite of the intricate, technically complex rhyme schemes and wry, satiric subject matter favoured by Lorenz Hart. By contrast, the libretto of *Oklahoma!* is lyrical and poetic,[255] never cunning for its own sake, and always supportive of the mood. The craft of the lyricist is never allowed to detract from the story, nor to get between it and the audience.

This element probably explains Hammerstein's relative lack of success during the 1930s. Whereas his almost operetta-like romanticism was exactly right for *Show Boat*, it was out of step with the prevailing atmosphere of the subsequent Depression years. By 1943, and especially in the midst of the growing pride of nationhood that wartime often engenders, it was time for a return to the style with which Oscar Hammerstein felt most comfortable.

To match this new direction, "Rodgers' music marked a change from the suave, brash musical lines he had turned out when working with Hart."[256] His ballad melodies came more closely to resemble those of Jerome Kern, although with a freshness and vitality that set them apart from anything on Broadway at the time. And the hoofbeat rhythm of "The Surrey With the Fringe On Top," like the naïve exuberance of "The Farmer and the Cowboy," owed nothing to the brittle intensity of the score to *Pal Joey*. In just one production, the composer expanded his palette to include a wide variety of new colours. His melodies imprint themselves almost immediately in memory, thus confirming the most important ingredient of success, "to send (the audience) out humming and whistling."[257]

In fashioning the character of Jud Fry, Hammerstein gave us one of musical theatre's first examples of that late 20th century phenomenon, the stalker. Attracted to Laurey himself, Jud becomes at first threatening and then violent as he recognizes her growing love for Curley. This plot element gave rise to Rodgers' most innovative conception, an artistic device that would seem to be completely foreign to a play about rural America: a ballet.[258]

Rodgers had experimented with this idea once before, in the 1936 production of *On Your Toes*.[259] But in that show, the ballet itself was a plot device appropriate to the story of a prima ballerina in a dance company. Its inclusion was a natural and realistic part of the story. In *Oklahoma!*, the ballet is an imaginative fantasy, an expressive tool employed to convey the emotional climate of the story and the innermost feelings of the principal female character.

Occuring almost at the mid-point, the ballet is the centrepiece of the entire show, in which Laurey falls into a drug-induced sleep. She dreams of her upcoming marriage to Curley, only to be menaced by the threatening Jud. In the context of a dream, the element of classical dance becomes not only acceptable, but somehow exactly appropriate, allowing the expression of emotion through movement in a manner much more effective than either dialog or song.

Had Laurey simply said or sung "I'm afraid," no matter how elaborately, the effect would have had far less impact. As choreographed by Agnes de Mille, Laurey's "Dream Ballet" elevated the concept of musical comedy dance from basic entertainment to an essential and compelling component of the plot, and of the overall production.

To dissect the diverse ingredients that went to make up *Oklahoma!* is to do a disservice to the play itself and to its creators. The play is so much more than the sum of its parts, and had a lasting effect upon the style of musicals until well into the 1960s. "It rejected the topical and even the contemporary and instead embraced a sentimental look at bygone Americana. For the most part it also rejected wit and patently polished sophistication for a certain earnestness and directness."[260]

Whereas *Show Boat*, for all of its innovation, was a culmination of the styles that came before it, *Oklahoma!* was a reversal of current trends, simultaneously resurrecting the past and also heading off in an entirely new direction. It was therefore much more influential than the earlier show. Almost immediately, composers and lyricists began adapting the Rodgers and Hammerstein innovations into their own productions. Such works as Irving Berlin's *Annie Get Your Gun* (1946) and Lane and Harburg's *Finian's Rainbow* (1947) owe much more to the style of *Oklahoma!* than to the slick, contemporary ambience of shows like *Pal Joey*. Even the normally glib and sometimes acerbic Cole Porter revealed a mellower side in *Mexican Hayride* (1944). And of course the subsequent Rodgers and Hammerstein vehicles exploited the new style to great effect.

To their credit, almost every critic immediately recognized the quality of *Oklahoma!* There were exceptions, however. The superficial dismissal "No gags, no gals, no chance," variously credited to producer Mike Todd or journalist Walter Winchell,[261] completely missed the point, and was a demeaning insult to the intelligence of the theatre-going public. More thoughtful reviewers praised it unequivocally, resulting in an astounding first run of 2,212[262] performances in New York, followed by extended tours on the road. For the first time, a stage musical achieved national exposure approaching that which previously had been the exclusive territory of the movies. "Some of its records were later surpassed, but *Oklahoma's* importance in opening a new era in American Musical Theatre will never be challenged."[263]

THIRTEEN
Some Insights

One of the most affecting songs from *South Pacific* (1949) was "A Cockeyed Optimist," written by Oscar Hammerstein II to illuminate the character of nurse Nellie Forbush, but it might as well have been written about Hammerstein himself. He was essentially a positive man who believed in the power of the happy ending, and sought to infuse his work with a spirit of hopefulness.

It may be said, and with some justification, that the sincerity inherent in many of his scripts and lyrics was not necessarily genuine, for in his private life, Hammerstein was not always the benevolent, cheerful man his songs suggested. As befits a man whose profession was language, his wit could be caustic and cruel.

Despite the sympathetic and often idealistic portrayal of young people in his librettos and songs, Hammerstein's own children were often the targets of his unkind humour. He was demanding of them and frequently critical. His protégé Stephen Sondheim has said, however, that it was the man's deep love for his children that impelled his behaviour. He set high standards for them, ones which he drove them to achieve. One might disapprove of his methods, but not of his intent. And in fact, Sondheim was himself the beneficiary of an almost parental affection from his mentor, for whom he felt deep respect.[264]

Nevertheless, it was apparent that Hammerstein did not know how to relate to his own offspring on a personal level when they were still fairly young, perhaps reflecting his strained relationship with a father who opposed his son's theatrical ambitions. His humour was often cruel, although apparently not from a conscious intention to inflict emotional harm. However much he may have loved them, he simply did not seem to know how to treat his offspring with affection.[265]

Hammerstein's own youth must have shaped his attitudes toward child-rearing, as toward life itself. It was his own father who steered him away from the theatre, with a firm and forceful insistence, and toward a career in law (see Chapter Six). But it was also his father's death (Oscar was nineteen at the time) that freed him to follow his passion for writing.

By the time he was twenty, and lacking direct parental influence to guide his life choices at a time when he felt compelled to make a change, he sought out other models.

It was understandable that he looked for a role model in his uncle Arthur,[266] who considered a career associated with the stage to be a reasonable ambition for his nephew. Thus conflicted by these opposing influences, it may be that in later years Hammerstein was somewhat unsure of his own role and fitness as a father. But it is undeniable that he held great hopes for his children, and for the young Stephen Sondheim, whom he saw as an extension of his own family.

Children feature prominently in a number of his stage works. *The King and I* (1951) and *The Sound Of Music* (1959) are the two most notable examples, although *Flower Drum Song* (1958) contains similar elements, and it is a teenager around whom much of the plot of the latter half of *Carousel* (1945) revolves. It is interesting to note that in the first two plays mentioned above, the children are initially pictured as strictly controlled, restrained, and even possibly unloved, at least in the conventional sense.

The Baron Von Trapp (*The Sound Of Music*) is an authoritarian figure, in many ways not unlike the King of Siam in *The King and I*. Left to raise his seven children alone after the death of his wife, the Baron runs his household with military precision, and the children are portrayed as having no playtime, being forced to study daily even in the summer, and apparently without conventional parental affection. In *The King And I*, the children are similarly regimented. Like the Baron, the King is depicted as being distant and severe, and having little contact with them, emotional or otherwise.[267]

It is tempting to draw parallels between these plots and Hammerstein's own youth, which was characterized by the pressure of a domineering father and, during his middle and late teen years, the absence of a mother who might have mediated on his behalf. To be fair, it must be remembered that while he wrote both the book and lyrics for *The King And I*, Hammerstein supplied only the lyrics for *The Sound Of Music*. Whatever his influence may have been upon the character of the Baron, Howard Lindsay and Russel Crouse wrote the book for that production.[268] Nevertheless, the plot of *The Sound Of Music* resounds in so many ways with the elements of Hammerstein's previous works that it is impossible to believe he had no input into the book. In fact, the lyrics of the songs seem almost to drive the plot, rather than vice versa.

The ultimate resolution of the relationship between parent and children is a major element in *The Sound Of Music*. The Baron Von Trapp is transformed from a cold and dictatorial figure into a loving and attentive father. The scenario is idealized and overly simplistic, but it strikes a sympathetic chord that is one of the contributing reasons for the success of that musical. Is Hammerstein's personal orientation a factor in the direction the story takes here? It is highly likely. It reflects many of the essential attitudes that permeate most of his stage plays, most especially those productions that he created with Richard Rodgers.[269]

The plots, books and scripts that Hammerstein chose to adapt for the theatre all contain elements of his essentially optimistic outlook on life. Although he steadfastly (but not always successfully) resisted the impulse toward melodrama, his lyrics and librettos almost invariably contain elements of triumph over adversity. Nowhere is this more apparent than in the plot resolution of *Show Boat*: the success of Magnolia Ravenal and her daughter Kim by their own efforts, against substantial odds.

Tragic figures abound in his stories, however: the mulatto Julie La Verne in *Show Boat*; the criminal Billy Bigelow in *Carousel*; the slave girl Tuptim in *The King And I*; and the Polynesian girl Liat (*South Pacific*), who suffers ultimate rejection by her soldier lover, a basically good man who cannot reconcile himself to a mixed-race marriage. And in *The Sound Of Music*, the ultimate tragedy of World War Two serves as the backdrop for the entire play. Nevertheless, the plots of most Hammerstein musicals, especially those written in collaboration with Richard Rodgers, have at their core a fundamental and positive belief in the goodness of humanity, and almost invariably end in triumph, as reflected in the titles and lyrics of many of his compositions:

Climb Ev'ry Mountain
Happy Talk
A Hundred Million Miracles
I Have Dreamed
Oh, What A Beautiful Mornin'
Something Wonderful
You'll Never Walk Alone

Consider for example the title of the hymn-like song of courage from *Carousel* (1945), "You'll Never Walk Alone." It is tempting to read religious significance into this title, as if it were a reference to a specific deity's presence in one's life. However, Hammerstein's lyrics seem almost to skirt the issue. In his original script, he conceived of "Mr. and Mrs. God" in a heaven that was "a bare New England parlor,"[270] but dropped the idea in favour of a slightly more conventional view, a strangely stylized heaven that is far removed from the prevailing popular concept,[271] wherein the deity is perched on a ladder, polishing stars.[272]

Upon careful examination, however, the words of the song itself in fact contain no explicit reference to belief in a deity that governs human affairs, in spite of the pseudo-religious plot devices in the play. The mood is one of generalized hope for the future rather than faith in a higher power, especially in the final denouement, wherein Billy Bigelow, who dies before the birth of his daughter, is allowed to return to earth to help her through one of life's trials.[273]

Although Richard Rodgers was widely believed to have been an atheist, there is little direct evidence of Oscar Hamerstein's religious orientation. Apparently he was not a practicing Jew, but he nevertheless entertained a personal philosophy that provided him with an essentially optimistic view of humanity. Even in *Carousel*, in some ways his bleakest effort for the stage, he blunts the tragedy with a cautiously hopeful denouement.[274]

Perhaps the lyricist's strongest sentiments of confidence are expressed in "Climb Ev'ry Mountain" (*The Sound Of Music*, 1959), in which the Mother Superior urges the young nun Maria never to give up striving. The mood is one of hope and the inference is spiritual (after all, it's sung by a nun!), but the words of the song themselves are generic rather than explicitly religious, and the objective is the achievement of a "dream" rather than a heavenly reward.[275] Hammerstein wisely chose to shape his lyrics around universal human aspirations, as opposed to those specific to any particular faith.[276]

Hammerstein's love songs are similarly full of promise:

Hello Young Lovers
I Am Going To Like It Here
If I Loved You
People Will Say We're In Love
Some Enchanted Evening
We Kiss In A Shadow
A Wonderful Guy

The least well known on this list, "I Am Going To Like It Here," has an especially beautiful melody, one of Richard Rodgers' simplest and most affecting, built on the Oriental-sounding pentatonic scale. It is sung by a Chinese immigrant girl, newly arrived in San Francisco. In it she sings first of her fondness for her new country. Then Hammerstein takes the listener from the general affection she feels for her surroundings to the specific attraction she feels for a certain young man. This tender and indirect yearning for love, and the quiet confidence in its realization, is Hammerstein at his best.

Another affecting song convention is the "be brave" lyric that appears most prominently in *The King And I* and *The Sound Of Music*. In both of these plays, the character singing the song is thrust into a new and frightening situation. In the former play, Anna Leonowens arrives in Siam with her son, preparing to become a tutor for the King's children in a culture very foreign to her English upbringing. To reassure her son, she tells him in the song "I Whistle a Happy Tune" that, when faced with a fearful situation, she simply pretends that she isn't afraid at all.[277]

Similarly in *The Sound Of Music*, the naïve young nun Maria is pushed into alien surroundings as a governess to the Baron's children. She comforts them during a thunderstorm with the song "My Favorite Things," but it is apparent that her own insecurities are reflected in her brave words.

The major criticism levelled at *The Sound of Music* when it opened in 1959 concerned the romanticized and idealized nature of the plot, and the ways in which it was resolved. Much of it was, of course, fiction, based only very loosely on the experiences of the Trapp Family Singers,[278] but audiences don't go to the theatre for history lessons; they go to be entertained.

Whereas poor reviews most often spell the end of a musical, *The Sound of Music* was kept afloat by substantial advance ticket sales, long enough for public opinion to overcome the printed criticisms.[279] In what Meryle Secrest calls "a backhanded compliment to operetta,"[280] Rodgers and Hammerstein's last work found favour with the changing taste of the public, and was made into the most successful film of its time. Even though the music was originally said to be quite ordinary, time and the movie have made it as well known and loved as any of their other scores.

It is too simplistic to say that Hammerstein was merely reflecting the taste of his prospective audiences, or that he was shaping his plays according to what would guarantee success on the stage. Oscar Hammerstein II truly had a positive view of the world, and it permeates almost all of his work. In this respect he exerted great influence upon his contemporaries. *Oklahoma!*, the first of the Rodgers and Hammerstein collaborations (1943), set the pattern for other composers that would distinguish the majority of musicals throughout the 1940s and 1950s.

Brigadoon (Lerner and Loewe, 1947), *Finian's Rainbow* (Lane, Harburg and Saidy, 1947), *Paint Your Wagon* (Lerner and Loewe, 1951) and *The Music Man* (Meredith Willson, 1957) are just a few examples of shows that owe their formats to the pattern of plot and song integration that Rodgers and Hammerstein developed into their own signature during their eighteen-year association (see Chapter Sixteen). These and many other shows exhibit the same essential confidence and "happily-ever-after" plot resolutions that found so much favour with audiences during those years after the Second World War. They were an affirmation that everything was getting back to normal.[281]

The same elements infuse the early works of Hammerstein's most famous protégé, Stephen Sondheim, whose first major success came in association with Leonard Bernstein in 1957. Bernstein had initially intended to write both music and lyrics for *West Side Story*, and examples of the words he wrote for some of the songs still exist. Had he not consented to work with Sondheim, *West Side Story* might very possibly have become a mere footnote to music theatre history. While Bernstein's mastery as a composer is unquestioned, his poetry simply didn't work.[282]

It's hard to conceive of these sentiments being sung convincingly by two inner city New York teenagers. Compare them, for example, to the simplicity and honest emotion (not to mention the inherent beauty) that Sondheim brought to his lyrics for the songs "Tonight" and "Somewhere." Another illustration is the very quiet, very tender scene between Maria and Tony as they pledge their love to one another in "One Hand, One Heart." The gentle and straightforward sentiment behind the words is proof that when it comes to expressing emotion, less is often more. The mood of these songs is hope, an unshakable belief in the future, expressed in simple, straightforward terms.

Despite the fact that *West Side Story* is a tragedy, the Hammerstein influence of optimism pervades the lyrics that Sondheim used to illuminate the characters and their relationships. Listen to the dizzy anticipation that Tony feels as he sings "Something's Coming," and compare it with *Oklahoma!'s* serene confidence in the opening number, "Oh, What a Beautiful Mornin'."[283]

Following the success of *West Side Story*, Sondheim collaborated with composer Jule Styne and author Arthur Laurents[284] on *Gypsy*, an adaptation taken from the biography of exotic dancer[285] Gypsy Rose Lee. The centrepiece of the show was Ethel Merman's performance of "Everything's

Coming Up Roses," a quintessential Hammerstein-like statement of hope and triumph (although with overtones of the bittersweet cynicism that would later become a Sondheim staple). Following the show's success (702 first-run performances), the lyricist was ready to broaden his approach, and to employ his compositional talents as well.

A Funny Thing Happened On The Way To The Forum opened on Broadway May 8th, 1962, and lasted a substantial 964 performances. Sondheim wrote both music and lyrics, to a book by Burt Shevelove and Larry Gelbart. Sondheim himself, however, contributed substantially to the content of the book.

Forum is a farce, but a very literate one, owing its existence to the pattern set by the twenty-one plays of the ancient Roman author Plautus.[286] In it, Sondheim began to find his own voice, and the play is totally unlike any that Oscar Hammerstein (who had died two years earlier) could ever have conceived. Nevertheless, the opening number, "Comedy Tonight," expresses all of the confidence and buoyancy of the elder man's vehicles, and sets the tone for the entire production.

Following the success of *Forum*, Sondheim began to explore new territory, and his next independent effort initiated the distinctive and revolutionary style that would transform Broadway in the latter half of the twentieth century.[287] But it was at least partly the influence of Oscar Hammerstein II that impelled him in this new direction, a concentration upon the content of the material rather than the manner in which it is expressed. Above all, Hammerstein espoused the idea that the meaning must always be perfectly clear to the listener.[288]

Sondheim's works after *Forum* would turn by times darker and more cynical than those of his mentor, but the optimism frequently shines through, albeit often touched with irony.[289] In Sondheim, however, that "happily-ever-after" feeling is usually missing, although he once even tried unsuccessfully to fashion a musical from *Mary Poppins*.[290] His view of the world in the post-Hammerstein years is inherently more reflective of reality. Even in his most light-hearted efforts, the underlying message is most frequently dark. Sondheim entertains, and he challenges. But above all, he makes you think.

FOURTEEN
Whither Oscar

Concurrently with *Oklahoma!*, Oscar Hammerstein II was working on the book for what is surely the least typical musical play of the 1940s, one for which the source of the score was a composer who had been dead for many years. *Carmen Jones* was an adaptation of the 1875 libretto of the opera *Carmen*, by Meilhac and Halevy, with music by Georges Bizet.[291]

Updating the story to the then-present day (World War Two) gave it immediacy and popular appeal, and the operatic score lent an artistic cachet to the whole endeavour. In a departure from his usual upbeat style, Hammerstein retained the tragic ending of the original. But most significant is the choice of an all black cast, the first such show to achieve the status of a certified hit.[292] It enjoyed a substantial run of 502 performances, a tribute to its serious intent, a talented cast, and some very astute promotion by producer Billy Rose.[293]

In some respects, Hammerstein's lyrics for *Carmen Jones* suffer by comparison with the original operatic libretto, partly because of the popularity of Bizet's enduring work. In the face of the public's widespread familiarity with "The Toreador Song," for example, the new lyrics fall strangely on the ears. Nevertheless the story is powerfully told, and the best of the songs, especially "Beat Out That Rhythm of the Drum," are exciting and dramatic. The 1954 film version was very well received (see Appendix).

Carmen Jones was the only one of Hammerstein's major efforts without concurrent collaboration with a composer, and after 1943 he worked almost exclusively with Richard Rodgers. Given the impressive reception accorded to *Oklahoma!*, and the manner in which audiences embraced its innovations, it is understandable that the team was tempted (some would say driven) to try to repeat its success.

Oklahoma! was the right play, in the right style, at the right time.[294] The United States was still deeply embroiled in war, both in Europe and in the Pacific, and the certainty of victory was still illusory. Economically, the country was only just beginning to emerge from the financial chaos and deprivation of the Depression, and then only because of the industrial requirements of the war effort. But with so many young men fighting and dying overseas, the revitalized economy was viewed by many as an empty accomplishment. Audiences could be forgiven for looking to the theatre for escape, and for a picture of America that would be in stark contrast to the war years. *Oklahoma!* provided just such a portrait.

The many innovations of the play attracted wide attention among critics and theatre-goers alike, and exerted a powerful influence upon other composers and lyricists, but no less upon Rodgers and Hammerstein themselves in their subsequent works. [295] These innovations were not limited to the folksy, reflective script that painted a portrait of the pioneering spirit Americans have so often loved to embrace. The costumes were also a distinct departure from the norm. Gone were the long-legged chorus girls in skimpy outfits, gone were the flashy suits, the city urbanity, the sophistication. If theatregoers were expecting the traditional sex-laced extravaganza of the 1930s, they were to be sorely disappointed.

The plot was not particularly challenging; in fact, therein lies much of its charm. It is in essence a classic romantic triangle with overtones of violence, set against the confidence of a pioneering people in a new and promising land. The execution of the play, however, was far-reaching in its influence, as was the way in which the elements of the plot were organized, developed and revealed.

In a musical by Cole Porter, Irving Berlin or George Gershwin, dancing could be an integral part of the action, but not necessarily of the plot. In a nightclub scene, for example, dancing would be a logical activity for the participants, but not a reason for their conduct. And it was considered essential that any dance sequence show plenty of female leg. The context of *Oklahoma!* mitigated against any such display, and it would have been logical to assume that dancing would be minimized or even entirely absent. But instead, Rodgers and Hammerstein redefined the entire concept, at least as it applied to the popular Broadway stage. They created an almost classical ballet that forms a centrepiece for the entire production (see Chapter Twelve).

To stage the ballet, the authors turned to Agnes de Mille, and the excellence of her work in *Oklahoma!* served as a springboard for her later career. Her interpretation melded classic forms with characteristic western American motifs, in an arresting panorama that succeeded in taking the audience into the mind of the principal character, experiencing vicariously her hopes and fears.

In the 1930s, most musicals had one or two signature songs that attracted wider popularity beyond the stage. Cole Porter's *The New Yorkers* (1931), for example, included the enduring "Love For Sale," but the remaining tunes are obscure, such as "Where Have You Been?" and "Let's Fly Away."

By contrast, almost every tune in the score of *Oklahoma!* achieved immediate popularity, partly due to a new phenomenon: the original cast album. "The Surrey With The Fringe On Top," "People Will Say We're In Love" and the title song all became much-recorded hits by other artists, and even the lesser melodies quickly became well known to audiences who had never seen the play.

Oklahoma! launched an entirely new model for Broadway-style musical theatre, and its creators turned it into a formula that characterized their most successful subsequent productions. Their second effort, *Carousel* (1945), centred around the same elements that had made *Oklahoma!* so successful: an essentially American setting, period atmosphere, an evocative ballet sequence (again staged by Agnes de Mille), and a score replete with popular hits.[296]

The inclusion of ballet in *Oklahoma!* and *Carousel* demonstrated to other composers the viability of the concept, and they adopted it with great success in such musicals as *Brigadoon* (Lerner and Loewe) and *Finian's Rainbow* (Harburg, Lane and Saidy), both in 1947, and in *Guys And Dolls* (Frank Loesser and Abe Burrows, 1950). The latter features what is probably the most unlikely setting ever for ballet: a crap game in a New York subway, to the melody "Luck, Be A Lady Tonight." The idea of ballet in a musical reached its full flowering, however, in 1957 with *West Side Story*. Building upon the foundation laid by Agnes de Mille, choreographer Jerome Robbins transformed the posturing of opposing New York street gangs into an artistic statement of great power and intensity.

Equally compelling was *Carousel's* other major innovation, the soliloquy set to music. In its most famous incarnation in the Shakespearian play *Hamlet*, the soliloquy opens a window into the innermost thoughts and motivations of a character. Similarly, Hammerstein adapted the concept to explain the driving force behind Billy Bigelow's fateful decision to turn to crime.

The ne'er-do-well Billy, faced with the prospect of impending fatherhood, meditates on the wonders of having a son, and the jaunty flavour of the tune ("My Boy Bill") reveals his shallow character and immaturity. Then in a mixture of spoken dialogue, moving recitative and a gentle aria, he acknowledges that the child may be "My Little Girl," and the sudden insight shocks him into the reality of his responsibility. Billy's mental attitude undergoes a profound change, from carefree lack of concern for the future to intense anxiety over his inability to provide for a dependent child. In Hammerstein's able hands, the soliloquy provides not only a revelation of his character, but more importantly the impetus for the robbery that later costs Billy his life.

Other musicals have used this device, although rarely in so extended a fashion or with such emotional intensity. One significant example is a late scene in *My Fair Lady*, as Henry Higgins comes finally to acknowledge his love for Eliza during a solitary walk on the street. The song that follows ("I've Grown Accustomed To Her Face")[297] is part aria and part recitative, in which Professor Higgins vacillates between his infatuation with the young woman and a defence of his own masculine pride and independence. Through the device of the soliloquy, the audience achieves an otherwise unattainable insight into his character and motivation.

In a perhaps unconscious tip of the hat to Hammerstein, *My Fair Lady* creators Lerner and Loewe later wrote the most imitative example of a *Carousel*-like soliloquy, although not for a stage play. The film *Gigi* (1958), however, is so like a Broadway musical both in conception and execution, that its inclusion here is not unwarranted. As in the Rodgers and Hammerstein work, the soliloquy represents a change in direction for the character, expressing his inner thoughts and emotions through song.

The character Gaston, a successful but world-weary Parisian, comes to a surprising conclusion. The daughter of an acquaintance, whom he sees as an awkward teenager, has suddenly blossomed into a lovely young woman. At first he tries to convince himself that she is still nothing but a child, but in the course of the soliloquy, which culminates in the title song, he finally recognizes and accepts his own feelings of love for her.[298] Like the earlier example from *Carousel*, this soliloquy is a major turning point in the development of the plot.

Even if others such as Lerner and Loewe successfully copied the innovations of Rodgers and Hammerstein, that team was not content merely to repeat the formula that had produced their first two extraordinary successes. Their third collaboration was *Allegro*, in its own way as innovative and unusual as their first musical. In a departure from his previous practice, Hammerstein did not adapt an existing work, but instead created an original story line, dealing with a man beset by the pressures of life who cannot realize his goals.[299] This hardly seems to be exciting thematic material, but as with *Oklahoma!*, Hammerstein was exploring new and untested territory, including commentary by a chorus in the ancient Greek tradition.[300]

Allegro has been described as the first concept musical, in which the staging plan is a vehicle for telling the story. A more familiar example would be the entertainment in the Kit Kat Klub in *Cabaret* that serves to comment upon the story. Like *Oklahoma!* just a few years before, *Allegro* broke the rules and took musical theatre in a new direction,[301] although its effects were not to be realized fully for more than a decade.

It was this very unconventionality that doomed it to an unprofitably short run of only 315 performances.[302] It was too far ahead of its time. Audiences were accustomed to the pattern set by the first two Rodgers and Hammerstein masterpieces, and went to the theatre expecting it. *Allegro* was too different, too soon, although its format would later find success in the works of such composers as Stephen Sondheim. Nevertheless *Allegro* holds a place of great importance in music theatre history. Its pioneering conception and structure were bold and experimental, and in effect said to authors, composers and producers that risks were worth taking.[303]

The team returned to more familiar ground with conventional musicals (that is, conventional by their own unconventional standards) in *South Pacific* (1949) and *The King And I* (1951). A lightweight comedy entitled *Me And Juliet* (1953) met with little success,[304] and is considered obscure today. A television production in 1957, *Cinderella*, was hugely popular on the CBS network, however, and 1958's *Flower Drum Song* had a respectable run of 600 performances, due largely to an excellent score that included the exquisite "Love, Look Away" and the comic protest of the perennial bachelor, "Don't Marry Me." These efforts are basically in the format and style that had made *Oklahoma!* and *Carousel* so popular.

There is an interesting sidelight to some of the Rodgers and Hammerstein musicals after *Allegro*. Beginning with *South Pacific*, wherein the principal romance is between the middle-aged Emile De Becque and the much younger Nellie Forbush, there appears a pattern in the plays that may have resulted primarily from Rodgers' influence. He was well known for his frequent and inconsequential sexual liaisons with cast members, and like Frederick Loewe, his choice of bed partners tended toward very young women, especially as he himself grew older. The story lines seemed to reflect this preference.

As with *South Pacific*, the male-female relationship of most importance in the next Rodgers and Hammerstein success, *The King and I*, is again between an aging man, the King, and a younger woman, the teacher who joins his court to instruct his many children. The pattern is repeated in *The Sound of Music* less than a decade later, wherein a young woman is employed as the governess for a wealthy widower's children, and later becomes his wife.

After Hammerstein's death, Rodgers revisited the theme in *No Strings*, in which the main characters are a well-known author and a younger black model. Although this theme was uncommon in musicals at the time, it reflected a pattern already extant in American life, one that persists today. It is seen as appropriate that a man's social and economic position is his most important quality, while a woman's most significant advantage is her youth.[305] In this respect, as in so many others, the musicals of Rodgers and Hammerstein reflected the culture, anticipated it, and by their pervasive influence, encouraged it.

One outright failure experienced by Rodgers and Hammerstein was *Pipe Dream* (1955). With a mediocre score and a book that never achieved coherence,[306] it failed to repay its investors. But their last work together, *The Sound Of Music* in 1959, quickly became what is probably the best-loved and best-known of all Rodgers and Hammerstein creations. The nearly faithful film version has made their work familiar to audiences the world over.[307]

No other team created so many musicals, nor had so many substantial hits, in the two decades following World War Two. No other team influenced the theatre in so many fundamental ways. But the impact of Oscar Hammerstein II outlasted his death in 1960 in another important way, for Hammerstein's work was a profound stimulus to the creative force that would reshape the American Musical Theatre in the 1970s and beyond: Stephen Sondheim. First, however, there came Lerner and Loewe, Leonard Bernstein, and the mature works of older composers and lyricists who had earlier found success in the decade preceding World War Two.

FIFTEEN
Hammerstein To Sondheim

The mature association between Richard Rodgers and Oscar Hammerstein II lasted for a period of less than two decades,[308] from the preparations for 1943's *Oklahoma!* to the latter's death in 1960, early in the run of *The Sound Of Music*. Their partnership produced eight commercial successes and only three productions that were generally considered marginal or outright failures (indicated by asterisks; see Chapter Fourteen):

Oklahoma! (1943)
State Fair (1945)[309]
Carousel (1945)
*Allegro (1947)
South Pacific (1949)
The King And I (1951)
*Me And Juliet (1953)
*Pipe Dream (1955)
Cinderella (1957)[310]
Flower Drum Song (1958)
The Sound Of Music (1959)

Such a string of achievements was unprecedented in the postwar years, and represents an astounding output, better than one major musical every two years. Even more impressive is the fact that both men were concurrently involved in other projects. To cite just three examples: they jointly sponsored the production of composer Irving Berlin's *Annie Get Your Gun* (1946); working independently, Hammerstein reinterpreted Bizet's operatic masterpiece *Carmen* with an all-black cast in 1943 (see Chapter Fourteen);[311] and Rodgers wrote in excess of an astounding thirteen hours of original symphonic music for the twenty-six episodes of the acclaimed mid-1950s television series *Victory At Sea*.[312] (Rodgers undoubtedly spent less time on this project than his long-term associate,

Robert Russell Bennett. Rodgers wrote the themes, but it was Bennett who created the magnificent orchestrations, a much more time-consuming task.[313] Like most Broadway composers, Rodgers rarely worked on his orchestral scores himself.)

Of their eight major successes, only two have a context and setting roughly contemporary to their production dates: *South Pacific* and *Flower Drum Song*. These two focus upon elements of cultural exoticism and conflict. In three others,[314] the sense of period Americana dominates the mood. *The King And I* combines period atmosphere with an exotic foreign locale. And by the time *The Sound Of Music* opened, its historical placement (the years leading up to World War Two) had receded to the point where it also became a period piece. Finally, *Cinderella* is a fantasy.

Consider, by contrast, the three "failures," in which the period setting is relatively unimportant. Two are indeed period pieces, while *Me And Juliet* is essentially contemporary. *Allegro* takes place just after the turn of the century, and *Pipe Dream* is set in the 1930s, but in neither case is the atmosphere or mood essential to the play, as was the case in *Oklahoma!* and *Carousel*.

Another element of contrast between the successes and the failures is the source of the material. Only two of the story lines, both failures, were original with Hammerstein: *Allegro* and *Me And Juliet*. All of the remainder had as their basis some other literary, dramatic or historical source, and only one of those, *Pipe Dream* (based on a work by novelist John Steinbeck) failed to live up to expectations. Two inferences may be drawn from this: Rodgers and Hammerstein as a team were at their best when evoking exotic cultures, fantasy or period Americana rather than contemporary life; and Oscar Hammerstein II was a master interpreter of the works of others,[315] but somewhat less skilled as an original storyteller.

It is apparent from an examination of the successful musicals by other composers and lyricists of the postwar years that period pieces and fantasies satisfied audiences the most. They far outnumber plays with contemporary settings. Beginning with the *Oklahoma!* revolution, the list is impressive. All of the following enjoyed profitable Broadway runs:

Song Of Norway (1944; the life of composer Edvard Grieg)
Bloomer Girl (1944; turn-of-the-century, a la *Oklahoma!*)
Up In Central Park (1945; 1870s Americana)
Annie Get Your Gun (1946; the "old west")
Finian's Rainbow (1947; fantasy)
Brigadoon (1947; fantasy)

High Button Shoes (1947; New Jersey in 1913)
Where's Charley (1948; London in 1892)
Kiss Me, Kate (1948; contemporary but also Shakespearian)
Gentlemen Prefer Blondes (1949; set in the 1920s)
Guys And Dolls (1950; evoking the 1930s gangster era)
Paint Your Wagon (1951; the 1853 gold rush)
Can Can (1953; Paris in 1893)
Kismet (1953; exotic turn-of-the-century Arabia)
The Threepenny Opera (1954; an updated *Beggar's Opera*)
The Boy Friend (1954; set in the 1920s)[316]
My Fair Lady (1956; early 20th century England)
The Most Happy Fella (1956; California in the 1920s)
The Music Man (1957; the American Midwest in 1912)
Redhead (1959; turn-of-the-century London)
Destry Rides Again (1959; the "old west")
Once Upon A Mattress (1959; fairy tale fantasy)

There were some notable successes with contemporary and essentially realistic settings in the span of years from 1943 through 1959. *On The Town, Call Me Madam, The Pajama Game, West Side Story* and *Damn Yankees* come to mind, but they are far outnumbered by those that fit more closely into the format established by Rodgers and Hammerstein. Around 1960, however, the first signs of impending change occurred.

Bye Bye Birdie (1960) introduced rock and roll, albeit satirically, to the Broadway stage. *Irma La Douce* (1960) portrayed contemporary Paris. *How To Succeed In Business Without Really Trying* (1961) and *No Strings* (1962, with music and lyrics both by Richard Rodgers) continued the trend.

Fantasies were few and far between, and in general they failed to find favour. For example, despite a lovely score, *Greenwillow* (1960, music by Frank Loesser) lasted for only three months.[317] Two notable exceptions to this trend were an off-Broadway production, *The Fantasticks*, which posted a probably unbeatable run of more than forty years, and *Camelot*, both in 1960. And although period pieces continued to find success (such as *Oliver!* in 1963 and *Fiddler On The Roof* in 1964), it was apparent that public taste was beginning to change.

Stephen Sondheim found early success in collaboration with established Broadway figures, including Leonard Bernstein and Arthur Laurents in *West Side Story* (1957) and composer Jule Styne and Laurents again in *Gypsy* (1959). His first solo effort as composer and lyricist, *A Funny Thing Happened On The Way To The Forum* (1962), while clever and literate to a degree far beyond the typical musical, was a farcical comedy that owed much to the styles of the past.

However, *Forum* is most especially notable for the exceptional wit and fluidity of the composer's lyrics. In a manner reminiscent of the word play of Cole Porter, Sondheim manipulated the English language in many delightful ways, in what has been called "the cleanest dirty musical of the decade."[318] In the song "Everybody Ought To Have A Maid," he turned sexual innuendo into a fine art, replete with exquisite rhymes.[319]

However, it is with his next work, the sadly unsuccessful *Anyone Can Whistle* (1964, book by Arthur Laurents), that the true genius of Stephen Sondheim began to emerge (see Chapter Twenty-one). His characters began to take on a depth and emotionality unprecedented in an art form that far more often had relied on comedy or more extroverted sentiment for its power. The title song "provides the key to all Sondheim's subsequent emotional opacity. His characters cannot unashamedly belt out songs of unrestrained passion. They are filled with doubt and insecurity."[320]

Where did Sondheim find a pattern for this type of introspection? Surely the "Soliloquy" from *Carousel* must have been one of his models. In that startlingly innovative sequence, Oscar Hammerstein II reinterpreted the dramatic Shakespearian soliloquy in musical terms and took the audience completely inside the mind of Billy Bigelow, as he contemplates the enormous responsibility of his impending fatherhood (see Chapter Fourteen). But while he undoubtedly built upon the past, Sondheim took the portrayal of his characters' emotions to a new and ever more introspective level.

Despite its imperfections, *Anyone Can Whistle* marked a significant departure from the Broadway norm. It changed the public's view, and that of the critics, of what a musical drama was and could be. Its failure was in part its greatest success, for it awakened and alerted audiences to the kind of experimentation that would permeate the last quarter of the twentieth century.[321] It further allowed Sondheim to explore and develop new avenues of approach. Like *Anyone Can Whistle*, his next effort was almost startlingly original, although somewhat more approachable by the general public. In *Company* (1970, book by George Furth), Sondheim at last found his voice.

The almost nonexistent plot of *Company* was of much less importance than the depiction of the characters and their relationships.[322] The protagonist, a bachelor named Bobby, celebrates several birthdays in world-weary New York among materialistic and fundamentally dissatisfied friends. In a pattern begun by *Allegro*, *Company* was the most fully realized concept musical to date. The songs were used not just to advance the action, but as commentary upon the characters and situations themselves.[323]   No less important than the personalities is the milieu, a big, impersonal city that impacts upon people with an implacable force, as in the song, "Another Hundred People."   And the instability of marital life as characterized by 1960s America is deftly handled in the breakneck comic song, "(I'm Not) Getting Married Today."   The satire is also pungent and reminiscent of Cole Porter, especially in the comic masterpiece, "The Ladies Who Lunch."

Despite its unconventional and somewhat stark atmosphere, *Company* struck a sympathetic chord with audiences, and lasted a substantial 706 performances.[324]   It established Sondheim, and his collaborators George Furth (book) and Harold Prince (producer), as major forces in the reconstruction of what had become by that time a moribund and predictable art form, the Broadway musical.

But between Hammerstein and Sondheim, some other very important voices had their say.

SIXTEEN
A Tip Of The Hat

Imitation need not be conscious, but anyone working in musical theatre in the years following *Oklahoma!* would have found it difficult to avoid being influenced by the productions of Rodgers and Hammerstein. The following musicals, in chronological order, owe at least part of their style and substance to the pioneering work of these two men, and span the period of that team's productive years (1943 to 1959).

Bloomer Girl, 1944, by Harold Arlen (music), E. Y. Harburg (lyrics), Sid Herzig and Fred Saidy (book).

Built around the women's reform movement and the struggle for civil rights, this light-hearted play continued the Americana tradition of *Oklahoma!*,[325] and even recognized that heritage in its advertising campaign.[326] It also featured a ballet by Agnes de Mille.[327] The title derives from Amelia Bloomer, the 19th century abolitionist and promoter of more practical women's clothing, specifically the undergarments that came to bear her name. Neither the score nor the shallow story line promised it a place in the permanent repertoire, but it did enjoy a reasonable run of 654 performances.

St. Louis Woman, 1946, by Harold Arlen (music), Johnny Mercer (lyrics), Arna Bontemps and Countee Cullen (book).

Talented performers and a fine score failed to keep this all black-cast musical on the boards for more than a few months. Continuing the fashion for American period works, the era depicted was the late 19th century. The lightweight plot (based on Bontemps' novel *God Sends Sunday*[328]) attracted little attention.[329] The show's style owed much to *Porgy and Bess*, especially the staging by *Porgy's* director, Rouben Mamoulian,[330] but it was probably prompted more by the success of Hammerstein's *Carmen Jones* (see Chapter Fourteen).

Annie Get Your Gun, 1946, by Irving Berlin (music and lyrics), and Herbert and Dorothy Fields (book).

Although so fine and original a composer as Berlin cannot be said to be especially imitative, this popular musical (1,147 performances) is nevertheless derivative, and having Rodgers and Hammerstein on board as producers undoubtedly had an effect on both its style and content. In fact, it was Rodgers himself who spearheaded the project, based on an idea by Herbert and Dorothy Fields.[331] With its period setting (the west in the 1880s) and a bona fide American heroine, Annie Oakley, it was more properly defined as a comedy rather than a musical drama like *Oklahoma!*, but its artistic construction was superior to many more serious efforts of the era.

Ethel Merman's dynamic portrayal of Oakley established her status as a star, and much of the score has attracted recording artists ever since. The standout number was "There's No Business Like Show Business," belted out in Merman's rafter-rattling delivery, but the ballads and comedy numbers are equally compelling.[332] The most recent long-running Broadway revival opened with Bernadette Peters in the lead role, and the 1950 movie version, with Betty Hutton in the title role, captured the spirit of the production fairly well.

Finian's Rainbow, 1947, by Burton Lane (music), E. Y. Harburg (lyrics and book) and Fred Saidy (book).

This clever fantasy owes much to Hammerstein for several reasons. It tackles the topic of racial prejudice head on, although in a much more comic and satiric vein than in *Show Boat*. Like the first two Rodgers and Hammerstein musicals, the inclusion of dancing (choreographed by Michael Kidd),[333] in this case emphasizing Irish ethnicity (leprechauns and such), is central to the production. The songwriting team almost equalled Rodgers and Hammerstein in creating a uniform, hit-laden score,[334] and the authors developed strong, memorable characters who, although steeped in fantasy and magic, were as endearing and complex as any in *Oklahoma!* or *Carousel*. The 1968 film is excellent, especially the performance by an aging Fred Astaire.

Brigadoon, 1947, by Frederick Loewe (music) and Alan Jay Lerner (lyrics and book).

This is another fantasy, with a startling chase sequence in the form of a ballet, choreographed by *Oklahoma!* veteran Agnes de Mille,[335] and a cleverly woven plot that ranges from 18th century Scotland to contemporary New York. The show embodied many of the stylistic conventions introduced by Rodgers and Hammerstein,[336] and featured a lovely score that helped establish Lerner and Loewe commercially. It differed, however, in the whimsical and otherworldly plot.[337] Although not as enduring as their later work on *My Fair Lady*, many of the tunes enjoyed wide popularity and were frequently recorded. (See Chapter Seventeen for additional information.)

Kiss Me, Kate, 1948, by Cole Porter (music and lyrics) and Samuel and Bella Spewack (book).

Given the success of *The Boys From Syracuse*, which set the pattern for witty interpretations of classic plays, this updating of *The Taming of the Shrew* was probably no gamble. The libretto is excellent, as is Cole Porter's score, probably the most melodic and entertaining effort of his career. The action depends upon a play-within-a-play structure, in which the principal characters are actors in the Shakespearian comedy. Their battling off-stage relationship is a comic parallel to the Bard's two leads.

Almost half of the score achieved widespread popularity outside of the theatre, and even the less well known tunes are both witty and literate.[338] For example, the composer captured the essence of Shakespearian language and style without playing down to the audience in "Were Thine That Special Face," and in the comically clever "I've Come to Wive It Wealthily in Padua," surely the most inventive way ever devised to say, "I'm going to marry rich." In another comic masterpiece, he achieved outrageous rhymes for "Brush Up Your Shakespeare," and the song "Always True to You in My Fashion" is a wonderful take on the benefits (principally economic) to be derived from flirting and cheating.

Most important of all, this wonderful play is the ultimate realization of the integration of song and story in the Hammerstein tradition. The characters are convincing, and virtually all of the music relates directly to the plot and advances it.[339]

Miss Liberty, 1949, by Irving Berlin (music and lyrics) and Robert E. Sherwood (book).

This show was "very much in the Americana mold of *Oklahoma!* and *Bloomer Girl* that offered a comforting view of the past to make audiences confident about the future."[340] The story was slight, the dances were unmemorable (choreographed by Jerome Robbins, later to make history with *West Side Story*), and the score produced none of the more impressive and long-lasting Berlin standards. At 308 performances, it is perhaps that composer's least remembered effort.

A Tree Grows in Brooklyn, 1951, by Arthur Schwartz (music), Dorothy Fields (lyrics), George Abbott and Betty Smith (book).

With a turn-of-the-century setting and its portrayal of a strong female character, this slight musical, based on the best-selling book, was pleasant, but its unprofitable run of 270 performances would probably have been even shorter except for the presence of a young Shirley Booth in the lead role. It has been suggested that by this time, "the vogue for Americana may have been overplayed."[341]

Paint Your Wagon, 1951, by Frederick Loewe (music) and Alan Jay Lerner (lyrics and book).

This "western musical with a sound score but a slight book and a muddled structure"[342] was the only Lerner and Loewe production with an entirely American theme, centred around the 19th century California gold rush. "Of all those influenced by Rodgers and Hammerstein, Lerner and Loewe are virtually acolytes, for *Paint Your Wagon* (1951) could be seen as *Oklahoma!* by a different route."[343] Compared to *Brigadoon* and *My Fair Lady*, however, the score is essentially undistinguished, suggesting that the foreign-born Loewe did not have a feel for American style and conventions. Only "They Call the Wind Maria" caught on,[344] and at 289 performances, the show lost money.[345] (Also see Chapter Seventeen.)

Kismet, 1953, by Robert Wright and George Forrest (lyrics, with music adapted from Alexander Borodin), Charles Lederer and Luther Davis (book).

This lavish operetta is included here for two reasons: the exotic setting in the manner that Hammerstein created for *South Pacific* and *The King and I*, and the adaptation of music from another source, as with *Carmen Jones*. The score was lifted reasonably intact from the works of the late 19th century Russian romantic, Alexander Borodin (primarily his *Polovetzian Dances* and *Second String Quartet*). The well-crafted lyrics led to several substantial popular hits: "Baubles, Bangles and Beads," "And This Is My Beloved" and especially "Stranger in Paradise."

Peter Pan, 1954, by Mark Charlap, Jule Styne (music), Carolyn Leigh, Betty Comden, and Adolph Green (lyrics), based on the play by James M. Barrie.

With Mary Martin, the original Nellie Forbush of *South Pacific* in the lead role, this fantasy was stylishly directed and choreographed by Jerome Robbins. The influence of Rodgers and Hammerstein can be seen in the effective use of children in the cast, as well as in the overall staging and style of the production.

House of Flowers, 1954, by Harold Arlen (music and lyrics) and Truman Capote (lyrics and book).

In spite of a talented cast that included Pearl Bailey, Diahann Carroll, Juanita Hall and Ray Walston[346] (who later played the wonderfully Satanic Mr. Applegate in *Damn Yankees*; see Chapter Eighteen), this somewhat exotic and interracial musical by the acclaimed author of *In Cold Blood* owes some of its thematic orientation to *South Pacific*, but "deteriorated into simple monotony"[347] and collapsed after 165 performances.

Plain and Fancy, 1955, by Albert Hague (music), Arnold B. Horwitt (lyrics), Joseph Stein and Will Glickman (book).

This depiction of an atypical side to American rural life borrowed a leaf from *Brigadoon*, in that two urbane New Yorkers are plunged into an antique culture, that of the Amish in Pennsylvania.[348] The score produced one popular hit, "Young and Foolish."

My Fair Lady, 1956, by Frederick Loewe (music) and Alan Jay Lerner (lyrics and book).

This most successful musical of the 1950s[349] was based on the play *Pygmalion,* by George Bernard Shaw, which is notable for having been rejected as appropriate musical material by both Noel Coward and the Rodgers and Hammerstein team.[350] The plot is overwhelmingly British rather than American, but it revolves around class distinction, and reached new heights in characterization. See Chapter Seventeen for a more comprehensive analysis.

West Side Story, 1957, by Leonard Bernstein (music), Stephen Sondheim (lyrics) and Arthur Laurents (book).

As conceived by Jerome Robbins, this interpretation of *Romeo and Juliet* took the concept of integrated ballet,[351] as first introduced in *Oklahoma!*, to new heights. See Chapter Nineteen for a more detailed description.

The Music Man, 1957, by Meredith Willson (music, lyrics and book).

Equal to *Oklahoma!* and *Carousel* in its evocation of "the innocent charm of a bygone America,"[352] this is perhaps the most personal of all musicals, based as it was on the composer's own boyhood memories of

1912. Robert Preston's performance defined the slick-talking con man Harold Hill[353] in both the stage and movie versions. See the Appendix for an analysis of the 1962 film, which is possibly the most faithful recreation of a Broadway musical ever made (excepting only those filmed directly on stage), equal to or surpassing the movie version of *The King and I*.

Once Upon a Mattress, 1959, by Mary Rodgers (music), Marshall Barer (lyrics and book), Jay Thompson and Dean Fuller (book).
The influence here is probably more genetic and familial than situational. The composer is Richard Rodgers' daughter.

Gypsy, 1959, by Jule Styne (music), Stephen Sondheim (lyrics) and Arthur Laurents (book).
Employing the talents of Hammerstein's protégé, Stephen Sondheim, and the choreography and direction of Jerome Robbins, "*Gypsy* was one of the musical theatre's most distinguished achievements."[354] Hammerstein himself encouraged Sondheim to accept the assignment, at a time when the younger composer was already contemplating *A Funny Thing Happened on the Way to the Forum*, and was intent on writing his own music as well as lyrics.[355]
The show seems to have one foot planted in each of two worlds. Aside from the personalities involved in the creation, it gave Ethel Merman a role of considerable depth, especially compared to the old-style parts that had made her famous as a song belter (*Annie Get Your Gun* and *Call Me Madame*). In an interesting twist, it also harked back to the days of burlesque and revue in its portrayal of the career of ecdysiast Gypsy Rose Lee. But the main ingredient of the show, and the one that gave it its artistic and popular success, was the profound characterization of the principal role of Mama Rose, a trend-setting development that would strongly influence musical theatre in the decades to come. In later works by Sondheim and others, the element of character would come to supersede action, situation, and even plot.

SEVENTEEN
Fritz And Alan And The Lady

The most talked-about production of 1956 was Alan Jay Lerner and Frederick Loewe's interpretation of the George Bernard Shaw play, *Pygmalion*, by far the most coherent and finely crafted product of their sporadic partnership. Unlike Rodgers and Hammerstein, who worked together almost exclusively from *Oklahoma!* until that lyricist's death in 1960, Lerner and Loewe joined forces on a less regular basis.[356] Their collective output was therefore somewhat smaller.

Their four major stage works are period pieces, and the three most successful ones, *Brigadoon*, *My Fair Lady* and *Camelot*, are old world in nature, all set in the British Isles and reflecting the European orientation of the composer. Frederick (Fritz) Loewe was born in 1901 and educated in Germany, and appeared as piano soloist with the Berlin Philharmonic at the age of thirteen. He moved to the United States in 1924, but his style of composition remained forever immersed in the European tradition. "Fritz Loewe never became an American composer in the way (fellow German) Kurt Weill did. He was Viennese to the day he died."[357]

Younger by a little more than seventeen years, lyricist Alan Jay Lerner was a native New Yorker, educated at Harvard and well established in a career writing for radio when he first began working with Loewe in 1942.[358] Their initial collaborations were undistinguished. *Life of the Party* (1942) lasted just nine weeks on Broadway, and the subsequent *What's Up?* (1943) fared even worse. They tried again in 1945 with *The Day Before Spring*, which lasted a longer but still not lucrative 167 performances.[359] It was out of step with the times, owing more to the style of the 1920s than to the new trends begun by *Oklahoma!* Nevertheless, *Spring* was promising, with a more literate book and better music than their first two efforts.

The team finally succeeded in 1947 with *Brigadoon*, a fairy tale-like fantasy about a Scottish town that appears in the Highlands for just one day each hundred years.[360] Hoping to capitalize on some of the elements that made the first two Rodgers and Hammerstein vehicles so popular, they sought out Agnes de Mille to serve as choreographer, and also secured the impressive Ziegfeld Theatre as a venue. In a year that saw the opening of yet another fantasy, *Finian's Rainbow*, Broadway was receptive to the romantic story line and the excellent score. The beautiful set, colourful period costumes and de Mille's innovative chase ballet earned positive reviews, resulting in a profitable run of 581 performances.

Despite this success, Lerner and Loewe went their separate ways for the next few years, without the specific intention of working together again.[361] Both suffered turmoil in their personal lives, with Loewe's divorce from his wife Tina, and Lerner's divorce from the first of his many wives (an eventual total of eight). Lerner teamed up with Kurt Weill for *Love Life* the following year, and Loewe was absent from Broadway until 1951.

Although Weill's music for *Love Life* was pleasant and melodic, it produced no instant hits, and Lerner's uneven lyrics were not as fluent as those he wrote with Loewe.[362] In keeping with the times, the plot contained elements of fantasy and the choreography leaned toward ballet, but the plot, involving the breakup of a marriage, did not find substantial favour with audiences (252 performances).

The reasons behind Lerner and Loewe's disassociation during those years has apparently not been fully documented, although there is some evidence that their relationship suffered an acrimonious rupture. Whether Lerner intended to continue to work with Weill is uncertain, for that composer died in 1950. In any case, the team behind *Brigadoon* resolved their differences in time to write their least coherent effort, *Paint Your Wagon*, for the 1951 season.

Similar in context to *Oklahoma!*, with a rural theme surrounding the California gold rush, *Paint Your Wagon* is probably best known for the MGM movie version (which dared to allow Lee Marvin and Clint Eastwood to do their own singing; see Appendix). The film is probably better than the stage version, which suffered from a loosely assembled libretto, as well as music below the standard set by *Brigadoon*. Only "They Call the Wind Maria"[363] attracted substantial attention, although "I Talk to the Trees" and "Wanderin' Star" were also subsequently covered by a few recording artists.

The partnership was essentially dissolved after *Paint Your Wagon*,[364] not to be fully renewed again for five years. Lerner worked for MGM, notably on the lyrics for the Fred Astaire vehicle *Royal Wedding*, with its memorable "Dancing on the Ceiling" sequence, and the screenplay for *An American in Paris*.[365] Throughout this period, a number of people involved in the Broadway stage, among them Rodgers and Hammerstein and Noel Coward, were exploring the possibility of adapting as a musical the Shaw play *Pygmalion*, about a linguistics professor and a flower girl. All of these efforts were unsuccessful.

Although involved in other projects, Lerner and Loewe also examined the opportunities presented by Shaw's comedy as early as 1952. Over the next few years they completed five songs for inclusion in the play, should it ever become a reality.[366] Two were eventually included, and a third ("Say a Prayer For Me Tonight") later became part of the score for the film musical *Gigi*.[367] But despite this limited amount of progress, they recognized that the play still presented many obstacles, not least of which was the problem of how to inject music into an already familiar and very coherent script.

Perhaps the biggest impediment to turning *Pygmalion* into a musical was the essential nature of the play, in which the dialogue was the most important component. The comedy derives almost entirely from the conversations, leaving few logical places in which to interpose songs. Even less appropriate to the play were those staples of musical comedy, dances and choruses.[368] With a relatively small cast, such augmentation would distort its purpose and detract from the story.

Even worse, as Shaw wrote it, the play did not fit into that essential category for such productions, the love story. And in fact, the final version of *My Fair Lady* does follow Shaw's conception closely, with that one major exception.[369] Unlike *Pygmalion*, the musical concludes with a romantic relationship between the two lead characters.

In the years immediately after *Paint Your Wagon*, Lerner and Loewe could not develop a satisfactory method for adapting the Shaw play, and shelved the idea until 1954. That summer, Lerner approached Loewe once more, proposing a new approach in keeping with the tenor of the times. Lerner believed that developments in the theatre had allowed greater latitude in what a musical could and should be. He believed that what they had seen as problems might now be soluble.[370]

To say they solved the problems is without a doubt the most preposterous understatement ever made about musical theatre. Although proponents of *West Side Story's* position in history will probably disagree, *My Fair Lady* was "the most influential musical of the Fifties and one of the most distinguished productions of all time."[371] This is substantial praise indeed, but it is well deserved in view of the care with which the creators preserved the source. The way in which Lerner and Loewe adapted Shaw's original play resulted in perhaps the most faithful reworking of classic literature ever realized on the Broadway stage, done "with unerring intelligence, taste and style."[372] A side-by-side comparison of the play and Lerner's libretto bears this statement out. Much of the flavour of Shaw's dialogue is preserved in the musical version, as well as the overall sequence of events. "Lerner did not adapt *Pygmalion* as much as adopt it: not only Eliza and Higgin's lines, but virtually every character's is Shaw's script cut down, with music."[373]

Casting had a major effect on the success of the play. As Professor Henry Higgins, Rex Harrison brought to the production his experience in the Shavian milieu. His only major deficiency, his general lack of a singing voice, proved to be a charming asset, as he half sang, half talked his way through the role to create a whole new style of performing.[374] Stanley Holloway, a veteran of the English music hall scene, was the ideal choice for Alfred P. Doolittle, father of the flower girl, Eliza. Both Harrison and Holloway reprised their roles in the film version.

Fresh from her success in *The Boy Friend*, a very young Julie Andrews was outstanding as Eliza.[375] As she was British by birth, the accents required of the flower girl, both before and after Higgins' elocutionary training, flowed naturally from her lips. Her enormous vocal talent[376] suited the music perfectly. (When the film version was mounted, Andrews was passed over for the role in favour of Audrey Hepburn, whose singing ability was marginal.[377] To be fair, Hepburn captured the waif-like quality of Eliza perfectly, and did reasonably well with the accents required in the spoken dialogue.)

At 2,717 performances over a period of seven years,[378] *My Fair Lady* set a longevity record that stood until *Hello, Dolly!*, which opened in 1964, racked up 2,844. Since that date the record has fallen many times, but this is at least in part due to the rapidly expanding population and improved mass transportation that gives ever-increasing numbers of people ready access to the Broadway stage. For a show opening in 1956, the figures for *Lady* were extraordinary, and numerous road tours and foreign language versions subsequently spread its popularity all over the world.

The change in the ending of *My Fair Lady* has been the cause of some limited controversy, although taken in the spirit of the times, it was probably the correct choice. In *Pygmalion*, which certainly resonates more strongly in our present era, Eliza asserts her independence and leaves to escape the Professor's tyranny forever.[379] Shaw himself opposed the romanticized interpretation in *My Fair Lady*.[380] Although today's audiences may cringe in discomfort (or even disgust) when watching Eliza return to Higgins and forgive him in the movie version, in the atmosphere of 1956 this more romantic denouement was considered proper and necessary.

The outstanding success of *My Fair Lady* has engendered much debate over why it struck so resonant a chord among audiences. Despite the matter-of-fact depiction of class distinctions in British society, it is less realistic than *Oklahoma!*, and less emotional than *Carousel*. *On the Town* and *West Side Story* made much better use of dance, and it was left to shows like *Cabaret*, *Company* and *A Chorus Line* to create new forms.[381]

The answer lies elsewhere. In addition to the fine literary source, which was carefully preserved except for the ending, the libretto and score were perfectly matched and brilliant,[382] and the cast performed the British roles in as authentic a manner as possible. Another influential element is the essential strength of character represented in the figure of Eliza Doolittle, possibly a precursor of the women's movement to come in the next decade. In the final analysis, like *Show Boat* and *Oklahoma!* before it, *My Fair Lady* was exactly the right play for its time.

The music deserves special attention. The original cast album was phenomenally well received, making a hit out of virtually every song. The outstanding popular successes were "On the Street Where You Live," "I Could Have Danced All Night" and "I've Grown Accustomed to Her Face." Almost as well known is the comic tour-de-force, "With a Little Bit of Luck," introduced in Stanley Holloway's distinctive style. Holloway scored equally well with "Get Me to the Church on Time."

As Kern and Hammerstein discovered after *Show Boat*, one rarely follows a major hit with equal success. Lerner and Loewe's *Camelot* had much going for it: a delightful score, the same leading lady (Julie Andrews as Queen Guenevere), and a well-crafted interpretation of the Arthurian legend.[383] It even featured in the role of King Arthur the distinguished actor Richard Burton, who like Rex Harrison before him proved that one need not be a trained singer to put a song across well. And just to cover all the bases, the romantic Canadian baritone Robert Goulet (as Sir Lancelot) was entrusted with the most fervent love songs.

With *My Fair Lady* still in the middle of its phenomenal run, comparisons between the two shows were inevitable, and were largely unfair from a critical standpoint.[384] In a season that was to see some new trends developing, including *Bye Bye Birdie*, the gritty *Irma La Douce* and the comically satiric *How To Succeed in Business Without Really Trying*,[385] a romantic legend drawn from the tradition of *Brigadoon* was somewhat out of step. The comedy of *Camelot* was much more gentle than the sophisticated wit of *Lady*, although still very entertaining. Nevertheless, while the initial reviews were disappointing, the substantial advance ticket sales allowed time for the show's reputation to grow. Those who saw it early in its run were enthusiastic, and their word of mouth advertising helped propel it to a profitable 873 performances.[386]

Richard Burton left the cast fairly early in the run, and was replaced by Irish actor Richard Harris, who also appeared in the film version. Harris' vocal talents were better suited to Loewe's melodic style, and over the course of his career, he played King Arthur over 1,800 times.[387] However, the original cast album, which was the all-time best-seller of its day for sixty straight weeks, features Burton's subtle and more intimate renditions.

Sadly, *Camelot* is better known today for the overly long film adaptation that lacks much of the charm of the stage play. Despite a moody, evocative setting and some fine performances, the pace is slow and the relationships between the characters are indistinct, blurring the motivations that drive the plot. For example, one major problem was the casting of Vanessa Redgrave as Guenevere. In the stage version, with the young Julie Andrews playing opposite the much older Burton, it is easy to understand her attraction to the younger and more handsome Lancelot. But with Redgrave and Harris so obviously of the same generation, the point is lost. (See also Chapter Twenty.)

Camelot was Frederick Loewe's last major Broadway show,[388] although Lerner once more achieved slight recognition, teamed with Burton Lane to write the quirky *On a Clear Day You Can See Forever* (1965).[389] Lerner's earlier work was much more diverse, including a number of film credits, but Loewe's only major excursion away from the stage was the highly successful 1958 production of *Gigi*, based on the novel by Colette. This opulent film earned nine academy awards.[390] In style and appearance it is much like a Broadway musical, and the score rivals *My Fair Lady*.[391] The cast was uniformly excellent, with a young Leslie Caron in the title role and Louis Jordan as her suitor, and the standout supporting roles were the suave and elderly Maurice Chevalier and the wonderfully comic Hermione Gingold.

In the relatively innocent atmosphere of 1958, Hollywood was heavily censored, and in some quarters the plot, involving the training of a teenager to assume her place in a family of French courtesans, was feared to be too immoral for popular consumption.[392] It is a tribute to Lerner's skill that he handled the screenplay "without the suggestion of a smirk or a leer."[393] Somehow he turned a risqué plot into a gentle and comedic love story, and did so without offending the censors.

Lerner and Loewe attempted to capitalize on the film's success by mounting a stage interpretation in 1973, but it lasted only three months. The following year they wrote some material for the film *The Little Prince*, but other than these brief efforts, the composer was effectively retired. Lerner continued trying to duplicate his earlier triumphs with a half dozen Broadway productions, working with such luminaries as Leonard Bernstein, Burton Lane and Charles Strouse. All of these efforts were failures.[394] As with the teams of Rodgers and Hart and Rodgers and Hammerstein, it was largely the chemistry of his partnership with Loewe that produced masterworks.

The Lerner and Loewe canon is relatively modest in terms of numbers, with just three stage successes[395] and one outstanding original film, but in some ways it represents an era. Derivative rather than groundbreaking, the bookends (*Brigadoon* and *Camelot*) are escapist entertainment of a very high order, while the centrepiece of *My Fair Lady* stands alone as a major artistic achievement on every level. It is the quintessential Broadway classic.

EIGHTEEN
Other Voices

Although generally less prolific than Rodgers and Hammerstein in the 1940s and 1950s, a number of creative authors and composers helped shape these two very profitable decades of musical theatre. This chapter is necessarily incomplete, as this topic alone could fill a substantial book, but it includes the author's personal favourites.

***

The sad history of racial oppression in South Africa was movingly portrayed in the novel by Alan Paton, *Cry, the Beloved Country*. Kurt Weill's musical adaptation, *Lost in the Stars* (1949, book and lyrics by Maxwell Anderson), his last work before he died the following spring, was a tragedy at once daring and uncompromising in its treatment and exposure of the system of apartheid.[396] Although not commercially successful at the time (273 performances), it has since entered the permanent repertoire of the New York City Opera.[397] The title song is among Weill's finest creations, perhaps second only to "September Song."

***

Composer Jule Styne produced eight popular Broadway shows, and four are well known through their faithful film interpretations. A Londoner by birth, he moved to Chicago at the age of eight and began his career first as a youthful pianist, and later achieved modest success with his own dance band and by writing for films.[398]

His first Broadway hit was *High Button Shoes* in 1947,[399] with lyrics by Sammy Cahn. Next came *Gentlemen Prefer Blondes* (1949), which helped to establish Carol Channing's career, especially through her performance of the show's best known song, "Diamonds Are a Girl's Best Friend." Marilyn Monroe gave the tune a different but equally effective interpretation in the entertaining 1953 film version.

As *Blondes* did for Channing, *Bells Are Ringing* (1956) made a star out of Judy Holliday, who also played the role in the 1960 movie. Styne's scores are not as replete with well-known melodies as either those of Rodgers and Hammerstein or Lerner and Loewe, but each play produced at least one major hit, in this case, "The Party's Over." *Gypsy* came next (1959, see Chapter Sixteen), with two truly memorable tunes[400] and an excellent film version three years later. And *Funny Girl* (1964), based on the life of Ziegfeld star Fanny Brice, gave Barbra Streisand major exposure with her big hit "People," both on stage and in the 1968 movie.

Even Styne's lesser efforts, *Do Re Mi* (a 1960 satire on the music business) and the lightweight *Sugar* (1972), were reasonably successful at 400 and 505 performances, respectively. The latter show did not have a memorable score, but "Make Someone Happy" from *Do Re Mi* became a hit.

***

Among Frank Loesser's five successful shows, *Guys and Dolls* (1950) is the perhaps the finest,[401] and the best known. The literary source was the classic idiomatic Damon Runyon tale of gangsters, gamblers and Christian reformers entitled *The Idyll of Miss Sarah Brown*. Although originally planned as a serious romance,[402] the book by Abe Burrows is a comic masterpiece. Loesser wrote both the music and the lyrics, although like Stephen Sondheim, he started out by writing words for other composers, including Hoagy Carmichael, Burton Lane and Jule Styne.[403] He enjoyed considerable success in films before moving on to stage musicals.

Much of the appeal of *Guys and Dolls* is derived from the stereotypical characterizations and New York slang as adapted from the Runyon original.[404] Long before *The Sopranos*, Runyon turned criminals into sympathetic human beings, and Loesser managed to translate that feeling onto the stage. The music is excellent, and much of it was incorporated into the 1955 movie featuring Frank Sinatra and Marlon Brando. Unaccountably, however, that film omitted the smash popular hit from the stage version, "A Bushel and a Peck."[405]

***

Richard Adler and Jerry Ross produced only two major winners for the Broadway stage, and both were on somewhat unlikely themes. *The Pajama Game* (1954) involved union activities in a clothing factory, and

Damn Yankees (1955) dealt with baseball, surely a difficult topic to portray in the confines of a theatrical stage. Previous attempts that centred around the National Pastime had met with consistent failure. However, *Damn Yankees* was "such a clean hit that it broke the longheld jinx against shows dealing with baseball."[406]

The plot, of course, involves so much more than just a sports story. An ageing fan of the hapless Washington Senators strikes a bargain with the Devil, and leads his team all the way to the World Series against their hated rivals, the New York Yankees. Two of the cast members, Ray Walston[407] and dancer Gwen Verdon, built substantial careers on the quality of their performances, and both also appeared in the 1958 film version.[408]

Walston's portrayal of Satan[409] was humorously evil, with an appealing juvenile touch of frustration whenever being outwitted by a mere mortal. He delights in the evils of the world in the song "Those Were the Good Old Days,"[410] and his captive temptress (Verdon) almost stole the show with "Whatever Lola Wants."

Damn Yankees is a classic fantasy; after all, the thought of the Washington Senators ever beating the fabled Yankees is almost too improbable to entertain.[411] But it is a universally alluring tale, appealing to the underdog in all of us.

***

Perhaps the most unassuming musical play of 1960, *The Fantasticks* has since racked up the most impressive array of statistics in musical theatre history: over 40 years in continuous production, well over 10,000 additional productions world-wide, at least fifteen national touring companies, and a return of more than 10,000% on an original investment of $16,500.[412]

It almost didn't happen. When the show opened in the 150-seat Greenwich Village Theatre, initial reviews were unkind, and it would have closed in a week had not a small number of enthusiastic fans spread the word. But after receiving the Vernon Rice award for the best off-Broadway show, and with the success of the melody "Try To Remember,"[413] *The Fantasticks* (1960) settled into more than forty years of continuous performance, a first-run record that will probably never be eclipsed.

The story was freely derived from *Les Romanesques*, by Rostand, and involved a clever twist on the classic boy-meets-girl plot. Employing reverse psychology, the fathers of the two potential young lovers pretend to engage in a feud, hoping that their opposition to a romance between their children will drive them together. The arrival of a traveling carnival and its charismatic owner El Gallo (*Law and Order's* Jerry Orbach in an early role)[414] injects a surreal atmosphere of menace.

No description of the plot or its profound emotional impact does justice to this wonderful fantasy, and is therefore omitted here. Fortunately a film version was released in 2000, and although it is somewhat flawed, especially in its presentation of the pivotal song (see Appendix), it manages to capture the overall spirit that made this play such an astounding success. Unusual for an off-Broadway production, two songs achieved widespread popularity. In addition to "Try To Remember," the haunting "Soon It's Gonna Rain" is an unusual and deeply moving interpretation of the development of love.

***

As suggested in Chapter Sixteen, the year 1960 was something of a turning point on Broadway, with the last of the Rodgers and Hammerstein[415] and Lerner and Loewe shows[416] still in production, but representative of an earlier era. New trends were emerging, including the adaptation of unlikely literary sources and contemporary musical genres. For example, the very up-to-date *Bye Bye Birdie* satirized adolescent obsession with rock stars such as Elvis Presley, albeit sympathetically,[417] and the play enhanced several careers, including those of Dick Van Dyke and Paul Lynde. It also showcased the talents of singer and dancer Chita Rivera, who had first attracted considerable attention in a major supporting role in *West Side Story* three years earlier.[418]

In a much more serious vein, "*Fiddler On the Roof* defied the accepted rules of commercial success by dealing with persecution, poverty, and the problem of holding on to traditions in the midst of a hostile world."[419] The score by Jerry Bock effectively captured the ambiance of a Jewish village in pre-revolutionary Russia. Joseph Stein's book was a coherent and dramatic interpretation of the stories of Sholom Aleichem about Tevye the Milkman. It blended the themes of bigotry, racial prejudice, child-parent conflict and religious faith into a panoramic view of tragedy and hope.

This was no nostalgic view of rural life, as depicted in such shows as *Oklahoma!* The mood was bleak, with a set that conveyed the poverty and unrelenting struggle for survival of those times. Although pointedly sentimental, "the insistent cruelties of the story made its sentimentality believable."[420] In a complete break from the happily-ever-after tradition, the final plot resolutions are almost heartbreaking but realistic. The message is nevertheless one of hope: life goes on.

Another record-breaker, *Fiddler on the Roof* played 3,242 times over nearly eight years. While the score produced only one immediate commercial hit ("Sunrise, Sunset"), almost all of the music is well known today, especially the insightfully comic "If I Were a Rich Man" and "Matchmaker, Matchmaker."

***

Fiddler on the Roof was not the first successful musical of the 1960s to focus on a bleak theme. Lionel Bart's *Oliver!* (1963) translated Charles Dickens' novel *Oliver Twist* into an engrossing look at the abuses of children and the working poor in Victorian England. Bart wrote the book and composed both music and lyrics. Two years later, Mitch Leigh (music), Joe Darion (lyrics) and Dale Wasserman (book) also succeeded with an interpretation of the satiric tragedy *Don Quixote*, by Cervantes. Under the title *Man of La Mancha*, it produced the popular hit "The Impossible Dream" and earned a fine profit at 2,328 performances.[421] But the darkest musical of the 1960s was yet to come.

Cabaret (1966) "turned a sleazy Berlin nightclub into a metaphor for the decadent world of pre-Hitler Germany, with the floorshow numbers used as commentaries on situations in the plot."[422] Perhaps no other musical since *Pal Joey* had ever portrayed a less savoury collection of characters, but unlike that previous effort, the intent beneath the comedy was unrelentingly serious. At once a powerful indictment of anti-Semitism and a commentary on human degradation, *Cabaret* depicted young people as responding to life's injustices by indulging in hedonistic excess.[423]

The show achieved a startling authenticity through the imitation of Kurt Weill's musical styles and orchestrations, which were accurate for 1930s Germany.[424] Most chilling was the fervour of "Tomorrow Belongs to Me," as sung by members of the Nazi youth movement. Joel Grey's performance as the master of ceremonies defined the role, and he also appeared in the 1972 film version.[425]

***

Broadway did not lack traditional musical comedies in the 1960s. Such productions as *Funny Girl*, *Mame*, *You're a Good Man, Charlie Brown*,[426] and especially the controversial rock musical *Hair*[427] attracted large crowds. However, another revolution was on the horizon, the 1970 success of the Stephen Sondheim vehicle *Company*. But first, we take a brief look at the most atypical composer ever to grace Broadway with his talent.

NINETEEN
Milestones

The most modern and innovative composer for the Broadway stage in the mid 20th century was Leonard Bernstein. Classically trained and already renowned for his skills as a conductor[428] and composer of serious concert works, he brought to his stage musicals an operatic intensity and artistry that nonetheless rivalled the very best popular songs of the day.

Bernstein's education followed formal lines: an undergraduate degree, followed by studies in conducting under Fritz Reiner[429] at the Curtis Institute and later with Serge Koussevitsky. He first attracted attention when picked to substitute for conductor Bruno Walter at a performance of the New York Philharmonic on November 13, 1943.[430] At that time, he had already composed the first of his mature orchestral works.

It must have surprised devotees of the concert stage when, little more than a year later, his first Broadway production opened at the Adelphi Theatre for a run of 463 performances.[431] Even more amazing was the source of the show. Unlike other artistic musicals such as *Show Boat* and *Oklahoma!*, Bernstein's *On the Town* was not derived from a book or play. It came instead from the composer's own ballet, *Fancy Free*, upon which he had collaborated with choreographer Jerome Robbins.

On the Town in fact marked the first major appearance on Broadway of four highly influential personalities. In addition to Bernstein and Robbins,[432] Betty Comden and Adolph Green[433] contributed the book and lyrics. The story line was fast-paced and coherent, but the major share of attention was focused on the music and dancing, especially the contemporary harmonies and rhythms that were more typical of the concert medium than a stage musical.

Although the entire score was excellent, *On the Town* produced just one major hit, but it was to prove very durable. *New York, New York*[434] was among the most memorable of many tuneful tributes to that great city.[435] With a tip of the hat to the war effort (the principal roles depicted sailors), and a colourful New York setting, Bernstein's first musical struck a resonant chord with audiences, but he did not return to Broadway again until more than eight years later. On that occasion, the locale was New York once more, and Comden and Green provided the lyrics.[436]

Despite its apparent connection to *On the Town*, however, *Wonderful Town* (1953) was neither original with Bernstein or with the lyricists. They took over from Leroy Anderson and Arnold Horwitt, who had abandoned the project after a disagreement with the authors of the book. The new team stepped in just five weeks before rehearsals were scheduled to begin.[437]

Although Bernstein's score was technically superior and amazingly varied, embracing styles that ranged from simple ballads to aggressive 1930s-style swing, none of the tunes achieved popularity outside of the theatre.[438] With over 500 performances, however, the show was a commercial success, due as much to its style and wit as to the music. Perhaps with so little time to create the songs, and without a long-term affinity for the plot, Bernstein, Comden and Green did not have an emotional involvement in the project. Their talent and capacity for rapid work turned out a competent but eminently forgettable score. Nevertheless, the unmistakable Bernstein trademark is evident in the fresh harmonies, especially in the comic "Wrong Note Rag."

If *Wonderful Town* was a throwaway effort for Bernstein, his next project was anything but: an ambitious adaptation of the Voltaire satire *Candide*, with book by Lillian Hellman. Three lyricists worked on the songs. The first of them, John Latouche, died fairly early in the venture,[439] and Dorothy Parker and poet Richard Wilbur finished the job, with some input from both Bernstein and Hellman.

Bernstein's music was amazingly contemporary, employing many of the 20th century compositional techniques that were more normally reserved for opera, ballet or symphonies. His rhythmic treatments were especially exciting and attractive. For example, the most lyrical theme, a centrepiece of the overture, sounds on first hearing like a three-quarter time waltz, but is actually in an asymmetrical seven beats per bar. However, the sounds may have been too "arty" for the typical Broadway audience.[440] It "really did sound like an opera, not a musical,"[441] and there is some validity to the theory that the composer was more concerned with the music for its own sake than for its support of the show. (If true, it was an error he would correct when writing *West Side Story*.)

Sadly the enterprise failed, lasting only 73 performances over three months. Much of the blame was ascribed to Hellman's clumsy book, due partly to her inexperience in writing for the musical stage. Unsure of her own instincts, she accepted changes from her collaborators that are said to have weakened the story line.[442] It may also have been confusing to audiences, for unless the listener was familiar with Voltaire's novel, the play was somewhat incomprehensible.[443] In addition, *Candide* lacked any significant amount of dancing, at that time considered to be a staple in any Broadway show. The lyrics were also accorded their share of criticism, being seen as witty but somehow stilted and artificial. In the beginning, the eclectic score was the show's most valuable asset, containing everything from echoes of the 18th century to modern jazz and Latin rhythms. The overture has become a staple for the concert stage.[444]

The essential quality of *Candide* was recognized, if not by the general audience, then certainly by seasoned musicians and dramatists. The 1974 revival enjoyed much greater success at 740 performances,[445] largely because many revisions brought coherence to the entire production. The new book by Hugh Wheeler was much more streamlined and accessible, and the music was updated and freshened. The young Stephen Sondheim, who had declined to work on the project in 1956,[446] was employed to add some new lyrics. The new staging by Harold Prince gave the production all the excitement that the original version had lacked. "They combined to make *Candide* a rousing triumph and find for it a permanent place in the repertory."[447]

Critics differ regarding the overall influence of *Candide* on the future of musical theatre. There is no doubt that it was different from anything that came before, but it is debatable whether the formula has ever been repeated successfully. In some ways, *Les Miserables* was cut from the same cloth, although the music for that show was much more mainstream for its time than the cutting edge originality of Bernstein's score.

Candide attempted much, however, and its failure did not detract from its groundbreaking innovations and elevated artistic excellence and ambition. It may have failed initially, but like Sondheim's *Anyone Can Whistle* (see Chapter Twenty), it said to Broadway that anything is possible, and nothing is unthinkable.[448] And also like the Sondheim play, it was simply ahead of its time.

Bernstein's concurrent effort, *West Side Story*, clearly was not. Although based on the centuries-old drama *Romeo and Juliet*, by Shakespeare, it capitalized on the immediacy and context of cultural conflict on the streets of contemporary New York City. In returning to the setting of his first success, *On the Town*, albeit in a tragic rather than a comic mode, Bernstein and his collaborators substituted racial and territorial hatred between the newly emergent Puerto Rican gangs, and their more established Caucasian rivals, for the Montagues and the Capulets of the classic play.

The idea originated with choreographer Jerome Robbins, and was eventually realized in the book by Arthur Laurents, in his first successful attempt at a libretto. Initially considered by Robbins and Bernstein some years earlier, the Shakespearian-influenced project languished for lack of a suitable modern context. It was not until the onset of youthful gang wars in Los Angeles in the early 1950s that the idea of conflict between native-born and immigrant populations attracted widespread attention.

Bernstein himself had intended to write all of the lyrics, but deferred eventually to the less ornate poetry of Stephen Sondheim (see Chapter Thirteen), whose credits included scripts for the television series *Topper* and incidental music for the Broadway play *Girls of Summer*.[449] There is some dispute over which songs were exclusively Sondheim's, however, as in the early tryouts on the road, he and Bernstein were both credited for lyrics on the programs. The composer later removed his own byline in deference to the greater importance he accorded to his young associate's work.[450]

Romeo and Juliet had long been considered fair game for adaptation in many different forms by later authors, but these variations often departed from the original, especially in the denouement of the plot. Some 19th century versions, for example, sweetened the ending, and others added additional characters. Film versions took similar liberties, even including the admirable 1968 effort by Franco Zeffirelli, which was notable for casting principals of the proper age (Olivia Hussey at 15 and Leonard Whiting at 17).[451]

In retelling the plot of Shakespeare's play, *West Side Story* returns more closely to the original even than Zeffirelli's film, and certainly more than the typical nineteenth-century musical adaptations.[452] The credit belongs to Arthur Laurents for his skilful realization of the Bard's characters in modern terms. There is only one major deviation from the original source, as just one of the young lovers dies at the end of the musical, the Caucasian ex-gang member Tony. The Puerto Rican girl Maria (the Juliet character) survives, in order to deliver the final commentary on the tragedy of familial (in this case, read "racial") hatred. Otherwise the fundamental Shakespearian plot elements are mostly there.

The task of translating the story effectively into musical terms fell almost as much to Robbins as to Bernstein and Sondheim.[453] His choreography was undeniably artistic, closer to true ballet than to typical musical comedy dance routines, but entirely appropriate to the New York street gang members who performed it. Broadway experienced something entirely new in this vital and athletic dance form.

Whereas Agnes de Mille's dream ballet in *Oklahoma!* legitimised classical dance for the Broadway stage, Robbins' physically vibrant portrayal of macho strutting and posturing, and even of gang combat itself, breached the barriers of what dance could be used to portray. Dance became emblematic of attitude, and its artistry and vibrant symbolism served rather than detracted from the violent tension and tragedy of the plot.

West Side Story was a true milestone in the history of the musical, on a par with both *Show Boat* and *Oklahoma!* While Bernstein's position and influence as a 20th century composer extend far beyond his output for Broadway, it is the very accessibility of his stage music that made the public consider him contemporary rather than avant garde. Virtually every number in the show became popular, and most are considered permanent standards today.

West Side Story was Bernstein's last significant effort for Broadway, as he became increasingly more involved in his career as a pianist, conductor and symphonist. His last try, the 1976 collaboration with Alan Jay Lerner entitled *1600 Pennsylvania Avenue*, closed in just one week, although the fault lay more with a weak libretto (Lerner's) than with the music.[454] In total, Bernstein's reputation rests primarily upon one outstanding success, *West Side Story*, and one temporary failure, *Candide*. But even a hundred average musicals cannot equal a masterpiece, and Leonard Bernstein achieved not one, but two of the latter.

TWENTY
The Many Shapes Of Songs

Without a doubt, the most prevalent category of song in musical theatre is the love ballad, followed closely by the comic song. But there are many other types and subgroups, all contributing to the wide range of emotions that are so much more effective when carried on the wings of a melody. The following are just some of the less recognized varieties that may be found in the best of American musical theatre.

The Patter Song: Ever since Gilbert and Sullivan presented "I Am the Very Model of a Modern Major General" in *The Pirates of Penzance*, patter songs have been a staple of musical theatre. Sometimes they are sung, and sometimes they are in the form of rhythmic dialog. The tempo varies, and few go at the breakneck speed of "Modern Major General," but they all tend to have the same characteristics: clever lyrics and word play, plus a dynamic and almost breathless delivery.

Few songs of this type ever attain popularity outside of the theatre. One minor exception is Sondheim's classic patter song, "Getting Married" (from *Company*) and another is "Never Let a Woman in Your Life" (from the score of *My Fair Lady*). But the most familiar example is "Trouble" from *The Music Man*, delivered by Robert Preston in both the stage and film versions in declamatory style. Unlike the Gilbert and Sullivan example, "Trouble" has almost no melodic content. Like that famous model, however, it achieves its effect from an intense rhythmic drive.

The Metaphor Song: Metaphors and similes abound in literature and music, and range from amusing ("You're the Cream in My Coffee"[455]) to direct ("You Are Love"[456]). Others are much more subtle, and may be little more than fleeting images buried within the verses. One such example from "Try To Remember," calls up a lovely image, that of love as a tiny warm spark about to become a flame.[457]

Metaphors and similes are most often found in love songs, and a simile has a slightly different emphasis. Whereas the metaphor tells us that one thing *is* another ("you are love"), the simile compares one image with another. In "It Might As Well Be Spring," Oscar Hammerstein calls up imaginative visions of jumpy puppets and giddy babies to illuminate the feelings of young love.[458]

This type of song can be comic as well. Frank Loesser packed eleven similes into "If I Were a Bell" from *Guys and Dolls*, in which the young lady tries to convey how being in love makes her feel.[459] And in *South Pacific*, Oscar Hammerstein II gave the simile a clever reverse twist in his denial of anything to equal the charms of the feminine gender in the song "There is Nothin' Like a Dame."[460]

Comic similes and metaphors call up fanciful images, as with the uncertain suitor in the song "If This Isn't Love",[461] or the optimistic tone of "Life Is Just a Bowl of Cherries" from the eleventh edition of *George White's Scandals*. But the most touching are those that are closely associated with human emotions. Perhaps the most beautiful song of this type ever sung in musical theatre came from *Knickerbocker Holiday*. "September Song" uses the calendar as a metaphor for aging. [462]

In addition to containing the element of metaphor, "September Song" is also representative of the following sub-category.

The Age-related Song: The elements of bittersweet regret, of nostalgia, and of sadness at the passage of time all come together in the gentle melody that introduced *The Fantasticks* to off-Broadway audiences in 1960, "Try To Remember."[463] The same element of wistful reminiscence pervades the most popular song from the musical adaptation of the *The Fourposter*, entitled *I Do! I Do!* (also written by the authors of *The Fantasticks!*, Harvey Schmidt and Tom Jones). This was a remarkable play, for the cast consisted of just two people,[464] and the story covered their fifty years of married life, from their wedding to the day they move out of their home.[465] The song they share as they approach the end of their time together is "My Cup Runneth Over (with love)." [466]

Sometimes the sentiment is buried within an otherwise upbeat text. In "We Need a Little Christmas," composer and lyricist Jerry Herman concealed a slightly sad bit of longing for past youth in the second verse.[467] Nostalgia also figures in the atmosphere of *Gigi* (on film in 1958, on stage in 1973) in the song "I Remember It Well," and in a more subtle manner in *Camelot* (1960), both by Lerner and Loewe. In the latter show, a middle-aged King Arthur has become aware of the attraction between his much younger queen and the youthful and virile knight Sir Lancelot, and he wonders "How To Handle A Woman."[468] But the outstanding songs in this category came from *Fiddler On the Roof* (1964). "Sunrise, Sunset" perfectly captures the sadness of parents who see their children slipping away all too soon to begin their independent lives. And in the sadly comic "Do You Love Me?", two people reflect on their twenty-five year marriage, and for the first time take a really close look at their relationship.

Oscar Hammerstein II was perhaps unequalled in the diversity of his songs, and although he repeated some themes in different plays, he always seemed to give each new treatment a fresh approach. His best-known take on the age-related song came from *The King and I*. "Hello, Young Lovers" perfectly captured the fond memories of a widow, who sees in others the reflected memory of her own past happiness. The same mood persists in "An Ordinary Couple" from *The Sound of Music*. But Hammerstein was most adept at another category.

The What If Song: First included in the score of *Show Boat* (1927), this trademark Hammerstein device was a highly effective way of saying "I love you" without actually saying it (see Chapter Eight). The exquisite lyrics of "Make Believe" allowed the characters to hint to each other of their growing attraction without committing themselves. Hammerstein returned to the concept eighteen years later in the second of his efforts with Richard Rodgers, *Carousel*. In "If I Loved You," the characters Julie Jordan and Billy Bigelow come to terms with their love as if it didn't really exist, when both of them are in fact confirming that it does. Not "I love you," but "*if* I loved you"; the sentiment is somehow much more affecting and romantic when phrased this way.

The "what if" concept may or may not have originated with Hammerstein, but it certainly found its most eloquent expression in his hands, and other lyricists borrowed the idea. In *Brigadoon*, for example (1947), Alan Jay Lerner wrote "Almost Like Being In Love," conveying the same sort of sentiment. Frank Loesser gave it an ironic twist in the love-hate confrontation between Sarah Brown and Sky Masterson in *Guys and Dolls* (1950) entitled "I'll Know." Adler and Ross gave it a comic turn with "I'm Not At All In Love" (*The Pajama* Game, 1954). And Sheldon Harnick turned the idea upside down with the aforementioned "Do You Love Me?" in *Fiddler On The Roof*, a poignant duet between two people married for twenty-five years who have never said the words "I love you" to each other.

The "what if" song contains elements of approach-avoidance, as well as "what could have been." Hammerstein explores this aspect in *South Pacific* (1949), with "This Nearly Was Mine," a lament for lost love (although this one also belongs in the category that follows below). Then in *Flower Drum Song* (1958), he gives it a broad comic touch in "Don't Marry Me." Finally in *The Sound Of Music* (1959), he reverses the entire theme in a song between two people who aren't really in love at all ("How Can Love Survive").

The Denial Song: This category is somewhat related to the "what if" type, and includes such tunes as "People Will Say We're in Love" from *Oklahoma!* The essence of the message is to express the reverse of the actual words, as in "This Can't Be Love" (*The Boys From Syracuse*, 1938) or "It's Almost Like Being in Love" (*Brigadoon*, 1947). These three examples are positive, but there are gloomy and pessimistic ones, too. These songs focus on the reality that replaces fantasy in the cold light of day. One of the best examples was featured in *Bells Are Ringing* ("The Party's Over").[469]

Some denial songs seem to be something else when sung out of context. "Everything's Coming Up Roses" is, in both words and style, an upbeat and positive affirmation of faith in the future. But within the story line of the play *Gypsy* (1959), wherein a pushy stage mother drives her reluctant daughter toward an unwanted career on the stage, it comes across more like whistling in the dark.

The best denial song ever written in a comic vein has to be "It Ain't Necessarily So," from *Porgy and Bess*. Gershwin's slant on biblical tales comes across in the sly and devious preaching of the character Sportin' Life, but it has no subtext or reverse meaning like the examples cited above. Instead, it's direct and confrontational, a challenge to reject the teachings of the Bible. [470]

The Kid Song: There are many songs sung by and about children in Broadway musicals, but most of them more properly belong in other categories. For example, "Castle on a Cloud" (*Les Miserables*, 1987) is a classic yearning song (see below), and "The Wells Fargo Wagon" (*The Music Man*, 1957) is rhythmic comedy, almost a patter song. However, there are a few where the very question of being young is central.

Oscar Hammerstein was neither the first nor the only lyricist and author of musical theatre books to make good use of children in his productions, but examples from his work almost seem to define the concept.[471] He covered the age spectrum: teenagers in *Carousel* and *Flower Drum Song*, teens and pre-teens in *The Sound Of Music*, and infants and upward in *The King and I*. In some cases, the presence of young people is simply a routine part of the story, but in *Flower Drum Song*, Hammerstein focuses on a growing social issue. As sung from opposite viewpoints by both teenagers and adults, "The Other Generation" is a quintessential generation-gap song.

The show portrays families of Chinese immigrants living on the west coast of the United States. The topic of the lyrics is the difficulty of dealing with the differing values of old-world parents as they attempt to raise first generation Chinese-American children, who in turn are affected by the western culture in which they are now immersed. The kids are hip, the parents are square, and each group despairs of ever getting the other to see things their way.

Charles Strouse and Lee Adams tackled a similar issue in *Bye Bye Birdie* two years later with "Kids." They satirized both parents and children, the straight-laced attitudes of the former and the language, music, dancing, teen idol worship and mode of dress of the latter. "Kids" seems to be a fresh, clever and fundamentally comic approach to the problem of parent/child conflict, but in light of the decade just beginning then, it was a significant examination of the changing values and growing disaffection between the generations at the dawn of the protest era.[472]

There are differences between these two songs, of course, the most pronounced being the imposition of cultural influence on children of another race. But the theme is the same: value clash between generations, the one dependent upon but aching to break free of the other. "Kids" undoubtedly spoke to audiences in a louder voice (it is far more often sung today than "The Other Generation") but Hammerstein's exploration of the subject broke the ground. His was an era just beginning to feel the effects of the rock-and-roll revolution begun by Elvis Presley and others a few years before. Hammerstein can't have missed the influence it was beginning to exert.

Other kid songs are more likely to deal with the problems of growing up, such as "Sixteen Going On Seventeen" (*The Sound of Music*, 1959) and "Hello Twelve, Hello Thirteen, Hello Love" (*A Chorus Line*, 1975). Many also cross over into other categories. There are entire musicals that principally involve teenagers, such as *West Side Story* (1957) and *Babes in Arms* (1937), but the songs are not necessarily specific to the age group.

Musicals in which a younger child is the central figure are relatively rare. Two notable exceptions are *Oliver!* (1963) and *Annie* (1977), based on the Depression-era comic strip *Little Orphan Annie*. Several of the songs in *Annie* are sung by the children in the cast, but the outstanding comic tune is satirically delivered by the mean-spirited matron of the orphanage. "Little Girls" is an adult's take on the most annoying traits of the younger set. Another example of an older person's perspective on youth is much more positive and gentle: "Thank Heaven for Little Girls" (*Gigi*, on film in 1958, on stage in 1973).

There are even pseudo-kid songs ("I Won't Grow Up," from *Peter Pan*, 1954 and sung by a child-like but decidedly older Mary Martin). And one entire musical had a peripheral kid-based theme. The set for the high-tech *Starlight Express* (London in 1984, New York in 1987) was a combination electric train and Erector set.[473]

The Image Song: Some songs create powerful mental impressions, such as the sadly nostalgic "How Are Things in Glocca Morra" (*Finian's Rainbow*, 1947) and "Soon It's Gonna Rain" (*The Fantasticks!*, 1960). One of the most beautiful, "My Favorite Things," came from Rodgers and Hammerstein for *The Sound of Music*, with its vivid images of common but beautiful things in everyday life.[474]

Images need not necessarily be either beautiful or metaphorical. In "Seventy-six Trombones,"[475] Meredith Willson called up an entire marching band with nothing but notes and words and rhythm. And some songs evoke images through the power of their rhymes. In the Cole Porter song "I Love Paris," the composer suggests a year's worth of climate in the fewest possible words with the sibilant insistence of "drizzles" and "sizzles."[476]

There are many, many image songs in the Broadway lexicon, but perhaps none is as likely to evoke a smile as "We Need a Little Christmas" from *Mame*, which captures an almost universal spirit in its portrait of warm holiday gatherings in its images of candles, holly, carols and stockings.[477] It is the essence of what such songs strive to do.

The Yearning Song: Other than the straight love song, this type is probably represented more often than any other kind of ballad on Broadway. Examples wherein the sentiment is expressed in the title abound: "Wish You Were Here,"[478] "I'll Know,"[479] and "This Nearly Was Mine"[480] are just three from a very long list. Most often these songs deal with relationships, as in Sondheim's "Send In the Clowns," or "I Loved You Once in Silence" from *Camelot*. Meredith Willson handled it sweetly in Marian Paroo's longing for someone to sweep her off her feet ("My White Knight," from *The Music Man*).

Lerner and Loewe expressed the joyful side of yearning in *My Fair Lady* with "On the Street Where You Live," and Hammerstein did it in *The Sound of Music* with the kid song "Sixteen Going On Seventeen," where the desire is as much for maturity as for someone to love. And a yearning song need not always be for a lost or absent loved one, as in the poignant plea of "Lost in the Stars," with its fear that God has withdrawn to abandon His people.[481] Sometimes the object isn't fully defined, as in "Look To the Rainbow"[482] from *Finian's Rainbow*, or it can be for a place, perhaps unobtainable, as in Rodgers and Hammerstein's "Bali Ha'i."[483]

Comic yearning songs are uncommon, but they do exist. The best example is from *Guys and Dolls*, "Luck Be a Lady," which expresses a more complex set of emotions than seems immediately apparent. The protagonist Sky Masterson has pinned everything on the roll of the dice: his reputation, his promise to the one he loves, and ultimately her love for him.[484]

To sum up the genre, one song embodies both the expectation of love and the more abstract craving for something to make life worthwhile. In the first act of *Beauty and the Beast*, Belle longs to break free of her confining and provincial village. Underlying her words is the desire for adventure and excitement, but also for someone with whom to share life.[485]

TWENTY-ONE
Another 'Sixties Revolution

On the night of April 4, 1964, a visitor to the Broadway theatre district of New York City had a wonderful choice of musicals to attend. The newest runaway hit featured Barbra Streisand at the Winter Garden Theatre. *Funny Girl* had opened just nine days earlier, but had already captured rave reviews for the fine songs by Jule Styne and Bob Merrill, an engaging story (based on the life of comedienne Fanny Brice), and the wide range of talents displayed by its star.

Still going strong at the St. James Theatre, *Hello, Dolly!* showcased Carol Channing in her most memorable role, and at the Imperial, Lionel Bart's British import *Oliver!* attracted much favourable attention, not least for its Tony Award-winning set. This revolving masterpiece of interlocking mechanics fully evoked the atmosphere of Dickens' Victorian England, while allowing rapid and seamless transitions between scenes.

At the 54th Street Theatre, *What Makes Sammy Run* captured the spirit of the times in its portrait of a hard-driving opportunist, determined to succeed at the expense of anyone who got in his way, even his best friends. For a less jaundiced view of the business world, the comedic satire *How To Succeed In Business Without Really Trying* was in its third year at the 46th Street Theatre.

The discerning theatregoer, however, might have taken a chance on a premier that night, a new musical just opening at the Majestic Theatre. One would likely not question such a reasonable choice, given the credentials of the show's creators, especially the composer/lyricist. Stephen Sondheim's first solo effort, *A Funny Thing Happened On The Way To The Forum*, had been the surprise hit of the 1962 season. His work as lyricist for Leonard Bernstein's *West Side Story* and Jule Styne's *Gypsy* had already established him in the forefront of Broadway's new cadre of young talent.

Sondheim's latest offering, *Anyone Can Whistle*, benefited from a fine, experienced cast, headed by the multi-talented Angela Lansbury. Also included were Lee Remick and Harry Guardino. The plot was, by 1960s Broadway conventions, unusual and convoluted, with a book created by

Arthur Laurents, who was then best known for his collaboration with Bernstein and Sondheim on *West Side Story*. But the plot was of relatively less importance than the way in which Laurents and Sondheim treated it. Therein lay the true innovation of *Anyone Can Whistle*.

In short, the story involved the Mayor (Lansbury) of a small town that lay poised on the verge of bankruptcy, ironically because of the simultaneous success and failure of its one industry. This company manufactured a product that could never wear out. Since people need not ever buy a replacement, the company failed for lack of repeat orders.

In an era that was infamous for the phrase "planned obsolescence,"[486] by which products were often produced with deliberately limited life spans to ensure future sales, this satiric jab was well targeted, but it may have been too subtle. (In fact, *Anyone Can Whistle* was from start to finish a clever and cerebral series of parodies, not only in subject matter, but also in its musical construction.)

The Mayor and townspeople devise a simple plan to rescue their situation: they engineer a fake miracle. Hoping to attract multitudes of tourists to bolster the economy, they construct an ever-flowing stream of supposedly healing water that pours from a rock. Among the visitors are a delegation of mental patients, brought by a nurse (Remick) who plans to discredit the "miracle" by proving that the water has no beneficial effect on her patients. The plot is further complicated by a patient who is mistaken for a psychiatrist, and who becomes romantically involved with the nurse, but this is peripheral to the main point.

The play draws a parallel between insanity and unconventionality, suggesting that to be normal, and therefore sane, is to conform to society's prevailing modes of behaviour. This theory, promoted by psychiatrist R. D. Laing, suggests that mental illness equates to nonconformity and unconventional or individualistic conduct.[487]

The social commentary that Laurents and Sondheim were attempting to present proved to be somewhat elusive to the audiences who attended during its short nine-day run. In retrospect, *Anyone Can Whistle* has received much critical attention and analysis, and has been successfully revived several times. The convoluted murkiness of the central and peripheral themes doomed it during the initial presentation, but have imparted to it a certain cult status in the years that followed.[488]

Anyone Can Whistle was a product of its times, and very much on the cutting edge, but was therefore not immediately comprehensible to the average theatre patron.[489] They were accustomed to the more conventional forms of musicals, especially the large subgroup labelled musical *comedy*, that filled most Broadway houses to capacity. Even the star, Angela Lansbury, nearly abandoned the role before opening night.

In the final analysis, the wonder is not that *Anyone Can Whistle* failed, but that it almost succeeded. Stylistically it is a wonderful achievement, full of clever musical satire and effective theatrics. Indeed, there was considerable praise for the music, lyrics and staging. Perhaps, however, its creators simply attempted to achieve too much within the confines of a single evening's diversion.

In 1964, audiences were hardly prepared for such probing explorations into the human psyche, under the guise of entertainment. It was also simply too complex to be grasped on a single hearing (a criticism that might be levelled at most subsequent Sondheim creations). To study the score, however, is to appreciate that Laurents and Sondheim gave us much to ponder in their perceptive analyses of human nature and emotion.

In his later musicals, Sondheim continued with varying degrees of success to explore the inner workings of individuals, and of social institutions and society as a whole, in ways that had hitherto been the province of dramatic theatre, but not of musical theatre. In so doing, he extended and expanded upon a tradition that was born almost a half century before, in the personality, books and lyrics of a man whom Sondheim himself credited with an inordinate amount of influence upon his career, Oscar Hammerstein II.[490]

To understand the influence the elder man exerted, not only upon Sondheim but upon the entire genre of modern musical theatre, is to understand the maturing process of the form that he inaugurated with his first major success, *Showboat*. If Stephen Sondheim initiated a revolution in the concept and execution of the Broadway musical, beginning in the 1960s, it was no more important than the similar groundbreaking effort by Hammerstein in 1927. And most important, while both were products of their times, they were also blueprints for the future.

TWENTY-TWO
Imagination And Exploration

The works of Stephen Sondheim exhibit a scope and variety unlike those of most other music theatre specialists. Whereas there is a unity and consistency among the productions of Rodgers and Hammerstein, Lerner and Loewe, and even so diverse a composer as Andrew Lloyd Webber, each new Sondheim musical promises surprises and innovation.

Sondheim's plays are unique among theatre pieces, and new ones are instantly recognizable by anyone thoroughly familiar with his approach to musical drama. They are intellectual and complex, and the songs especially are so filled with meaning that they are almost impossible to appreciate fully on one hearing. Happy endings are rare, and the characters he and his collaborators portray must frequently wrestle with the consequences of their own actions.[491] In this regard, the plays are reflective of modern life and society.

Follies (1971) employed a tried-and-true convention, that of a musical about a musical,[492] but there the similarity to earlier productions in the same format comes to an end. The plot revolves around a reunion of the cast members of a Ziegfeld-like revue, but instead of concentrating upon the 1930s superficiality of such shows, it explores instead the contrast between the realities of life and the artificiality of the theatre.[493] In contrasting reality with the illusion of reality as seen on stage, *Follies* explored musical theatre as a metaphor for human existence.[494]

As in *Company*, the characters are essentially jaded and disenchanted with life,[495] and the atmosphere is often bleak. Interestingly, the show contains no truly memorable tunes,[496] which suggests how far removed musical theatre of the early 1970s was from the ambience of the 1930s. As with all mature Sondheim musicals, the songs are as much responsible for furthering the story as the spoken dialog. The lyrics require the audience to devote careful attention to every word, without which the essential plot lines may be lost.

To summarize the plot is to do a grave disservice to what is so much more than a story. One comes away from *Follies* feeling totally immersed in the lives and emotions of the characters. It isn't hard to identify with one of its most intense songs, "Losing My Mind."

Having created two essentially gloomy and introspective musicals in *Company* and *Follies*, Sondheim and Harold Prince next turned their attention to a period piece set in Sweden at the turn of the century, with a distinctly old-fashioned romantic emphasis. Structurally innovative[497] and relatively small in scope, *A Little Night Music* is perhaps best known for the inclusion of "Send In The Clowns" in the score. It was filmed in 1977 with Elizabeth Taylor in a lead role. Despite the talents of Diana Rigg, Hermione Gingold and the acclaimed stage actor Len Cariou (who would be featured in the role of Sondheim's *Sweeney Todd* on stage two years later), the film fails to capture the spirit of the original. In fact, the only film versions of Sondheim's musicals that make sense are those of the actual stage plays themselves[498] (see Appendix).

Of all the Sondheim musicals, *A Little Night Music* is perhaps the most approachable (at least in the stage version), and the most easily grasped in one exposure.[499] On the surface it presents a portrait of romance, sexual tension and intrigue, not uncommon themes in the theatre, and in this respect it succeeded well. However, a deeper meaning was intended,[500] and if Sondheim and Prince had indeed set out to reveal a more intricate analysis of human emotions as per their two previous efforts, their efforts did not come across well. But both the score and dialog are, at least on the surface, approachable and appealing, making *A Little Night Music* a popular success.[501]

Sondheim's next creation, *Pacific Overtures* (1976), fared less well with audiences at only 193 performances. However, it is worthy of attention for what it tried to do, and for the spirit of authenticity that the composer's research imparted to it. The project was ambitious in the extreme, a dramatic 120-year history of the nation of Japan from its isolationist past to an international economic power. This play is perhaps the most faithful realization of an Oriental culture ever to appear in musical form, due mostly to Sondheim's intensive research into authentic music, and his interpretation of Kabuki, Japan's ancient style of theatre.[502]

The presentation of Oriental themes and settings had frequently proved enticing and attractive when cloaked in various musical forms, including opera (*Madame Butterfly*), operetta *(The Mikado)* and traditional musical comedy (*The King And I* and *Flower Drum Song*, and more recently in *Miss Saigon*). Although initially uninterested in the project or its topic, Sondheim embarked upon exhaustive study into Oriental culture, both academic and through travels to Japan, and came away highly enthusiastic.[503]

In some respects, *Pacific Overtures* is a predecessor of the trend toward political correctness that characterized much of American thought and preoccupation near the end of the twentieth century. In its essentially anti-American stance, it encourages the sort of self-critical examination of historical events that so often moves unrealistically out of context, and even results in revisionist history.[504]

The play was attacked on many fronts ("racist, loathsome, disgusting, pseudo-liberal"[505]) and an examination of the merits of this point of view is beyond the scope of this book. But musically it is startling, from its use of traditional Japanese instruments to the formality of sentence structure that gives it a distinctly Oriental flavour.[506] And the sets were similarly authentic and effective.

As with most Sondheim plays, there are no "hit tunes." In fact, the musical was a moribund form in 1976. *Pacific Overtures* is the only play in this form that Stanley Green lists in his "Show By Show" chronicle for the entire calendar year.[507] And it is notable that Green considered it worthy of mention, considering its commercially unsuccessful run of only 193 performances.

Having attempted much on the artistic level, and having failed so definitely both in terms of critical and monetary reward, it would not have been surprising had Sondheim and Prince chosen a more conventional subject for their next collaboration. Instead they elected to create a serio-comic tragedy, a melodrama, a pulp fiction type of story that was totally unlike anything Broadway had ever seen before: *Sweeney Todd, The Demon Barber Of Fleet Street.*

TWENTY-THREE
Two Hits And A Miss

Sweeney Todd was different from anything Sondheim had ever attempted, and was essentially different from anything ever tried before in a musical play. With courage approaching that of Bernstein with *Candide* or Hammerstein with *Carmen Jones*, he skirted the perimeter of operatic tragedy, and gave the stage two of its most memorable characters.

The plot is rooted in a popular penny dreadful serial entitled "A String of Pearls" by Thomas Peckett Prest, first published in England in *The People's Periodical*. It was adapted as a melodrama in 1847 by playwright George Dibdin Pitt, and received numerous interpretations thereafter, mixing comedy, satire and horror in a crude form of entertainment that found much favour in Victorian England. The characters were one-dimensional caricatures, and the action was deliberately exaggerated beyond believability.[508]

Stephen Sondheim chose to treat the subject seriously, eschewing melodrama and creating a classic tragedy out of the venerable plot. Comic elements abound, of course, but not at the expense of the nature of the story. Musically it represents yet another departure from the norm, one that would set the pattern for such future successes as *Les Miserables*. In every important respect, *Sweeney Todd* is an opera, and has been recognized as such by its inclusion in the repertoire of major opera companies. The dialog is almost entirely sung ("through-composed"), and the text and score are a unified whole.

The contrived plot line revolves around revenge and mayhem. The principal character is a barber named Benjamin Barker, now known as Sweeney Todd to conceal his former identity. He is a falsely convicted felon who has returned to London from a decade and a half of exile in Australia. His intention is to wreak vengeance upon the judge who sentenced him, and who subsequently seduced Todd's wife during his incarceration. The plot is further complicated by a romance involving Todd's daughter, who has become a ward of the lecherous judge, and a young sailor who was instrumental in Todd's return to England.

The other principal character, Mrs. Lovett, is the proprietor of a meat pie shop. In the mid nineteenth century, food service entrepreneurs were not always scrupulous about the source of their ingredients. Mrs. Lovett sings of the questionable components of one of her competitor's products ("The Worst Pies In London"), suggesting that the main ingredient is feline in origin.[509]

When Todd fails to carry out his plans to kill the judge, his dementia degenerates into a killing spree. His victims are the customers of his barbershop, and through a simple but cleverly designed mechanism (provided by the wonderful sets of Eugene and Franne Lee), the corpses are deposited below into Mrs. Lovett's pie shop. The characters' entrepreneurial symbiosis is revealed in the centrepiece comic duet, "A Little Priest," surely the finest homage to cannibalism ever to appear on stage.

In Sondheim's hands, *Sweeney Todd* is a tragedy of Shakespearian proportions. Todd's wife, whom he at first believes to be dead, is actually insane as a result of her treatment by the Judge. Inevitably, and at first unrecognized by her husband, she dies by Sweeney's own hand. Nor do Todd and Mrs. Lovett escape in the end, and the audience's sympathies are strangely drawn to the mad barber, in spite of his horrific actions.

The background of the play is the darkness and oppression of the Industrial Revolution, which in some ways is Sondheim's real target, his "attack on the cannibalizing effects of the Industrial Revolution on a Brechtian, vermin-infested London."[510] This is reflected in the gloomy, almost overpowering set, and in the style of the musical accompaniment that is often dark and heavy. The play does not spare the audience's sensibilities; Todd's razor strokes across his victims' throats are startlingly realistic, the blood welling convincingly from deep simulated slashes.

The dialog (mostly sung) is rich in content and imagery, and as in any other opera, careful attention by the listener to the lyrics is essential to an understanding of all its nuances. Sondheim succeeds in painting all of the major characters in multifaceted detail. And the inclusion of a chorus to comment upon the action is one of the most effective uses of the technique in modern theatre,[511] echoing the device introduced by Rodgers and Hammerstein in *Allegro* decades earlier.

Like the music, the poetry of the lyrics is complex and intricate, with witty and wonderful rhymes interspersed among the lines in such a way as to emphasize the meaning.[512] The eloquent and multifaceted manipulations of language are reminiscent of Cole Porter, but whereas that earlier composer tended toward the comic and ironic, Sondheim is more often macabre and even ghoulish.

The reactions of audiences afforded this play immediate notoriety, which undoubtedly contributed to its respectably long run. Offended by the gore and cannibalism, some attendees walked out in protest, although most recognized its intent and appreciated its technical and musical excellence.

Critics were not kind to the play, objecting especially to the sympathy it evokes for the murdering protagonist, and the implication that there is a little bit of Sweeney Todd in all of us.[513] In fact, it seemed to reviewers that the murderer is glorified at the expense of the victims, and that the portrayal of the degradation and corruption of Victorian life somehow trivializes its reality. Whatever the validity of these arguments, audiences found *Sweeney Todd* generally to their liking, in spite of some truly vitriolic attacks in the press. It lasted 557 performances, a substantial success for such a dark and forbidding undertaking.

How does one follow "the most grisly musical ever presented for a commercial Broadway run"?[514] Sondheim's next effort, entitled *Merrily We Roll Along*, was a return to the Broadway of earlier and simpler times, and it bombed![515] Critics had long been of the opinion that Sondheim was incapable of writing an essentially positive, entertaining musical, without resorting to the psychological introspection, and especially the dark cynicism, that characterized much of his earlier work.[516]

Apparently they were right. The faults are delineated in a short chapter of Joanne Gordon's book, *Art Isn't Easy*,[517] the brevity of which serves to point out that the art of Stephen Sondheim cannot survive when it is essentially imitative of others. Neither strongly attacked nor praised, *Merrily We Roll Along* was mostly ignored by audiences and critics alike, although the score is lovely[518] and the story is quite charming.

Perhaps the play's characters, made up of creative artistic types drawn from Sondheim's own milieu, were too far removed from the audience's experience. (The composer himself has said that the only truly autobiographical song he ever wrote was "Opening Doors" from the closing scenes of *Merrily*.[519]) Or perhaps it simply suffered not from its own shortcomings, but from being unlike what audiences expected from him. Fortunately it survives in an excellent original cast recording, and is occasionally revived.

Sondheim may have been disenchanted with Broadway, at least temporarily, and he made one fundamental change in his modus operandi by ending the association with Hal Prince that had resulted in his previous six musicals. His new collaborator was James Lapine, a director and playwright with a relatively short but impressive resume of New York productions. With Lapine, Sondheim returned once more to his own large and very personal corner of the theatrical world, that of innovation and invention. He emerged in 1984 with a stunningly literate and innovative production that lasted 604 performances and captured the 1985 Pulitzer Prize: *Sunday In The Park With George*.

The inspiration for the play is perhaps the most unconventional source imaginable, being neither literary nor dramatic. It was instead the visual art of the mysterious French artist who developed the style known as pointillism, wherein tiny dots of paint are used to create an overall, light, impressionistic effect. The specific painting in question is entitled *A Sunday Afternoon On The Island Of La Grande Jatte*,[520] by Georges Seurat.

Seurat was a strange and peculiar artist who, in the tradition of such personalities, died young (31) under puzzling circumstances.[521] Although the first act centres around his character, Sondheim's music is not really about him or even the painting, but about the creative process itself. He explores what an artist is, what he does, and how creative personalities relate to the world and those with whom he comes into contact.[522]

These issues are of course fundamental to the concerns of musicians as well as visual artists, and therefore *Sunday In The Park With George* is probably the composer's most personal statement. Whereas minute particles of paint were the tools of Seurat's expression, Sondheim's bits and pieces were the musical motives, the individual structural forms, and the combinations of the elements of music (tones, harmonies, rhythmic fragments) that combine to make the whole.

A Sunday Afternoon On The Island Of La Grande Jatte is a painting of extraordinary detail, comprised of countless tiny dots of paint, all carefully chosen to contribute to the massive whole. The amount of time and work involved in its creation is almost beyond comprehension, and in that way, the work is analogous to Sondheim's own achievement in organizing a highly complex musical around it.[523]

The story is told in two parts. Act One deals with the artist Seurat, his relationships (especially with his mistress/model) and his struggle to complete the epic painting upon which the play is based. The act concludes with a remarkable tableau in which the characters become the painting itself. The second act moves forward in time to deal with Seurat's great-grandson, a sculptor facing the same sort of challenges as his forebear. "Sondheim was examining ideas, not characters."[524]

With a substantial year-and-a-half run, *George* established not only a new concept of musical theatre, but also created (or perhaps found and identified) a whole new segment of the audience: literate, intelligent, and willing to be challenged. And challenge them Sondheim did, but in a totally new and unexpected manner, in an extraordinary production called *Into The Woods*.

TWENTY-FOUR
Into The Woods

At one and the same time, *Into the Woods* (1987) is perhaps Sondheim's most entertaining and also his darkest musical, rivalled in the latter category only by *Sweeney Todd*. Sondheim's woods represent the fears and challenges that beset us all, the dark recesses not only of the world but of the soul, into which we venture with trepidation, but which cannot be resisted.

The medium Sondheim and author James Lapine chose for their vehicle was a familiar and approachable one: children's fairy tales. By adapting material already very well known to audiences, they set out to build a complex but highly entertaining exploration into the human psyche. The stories they selected to interpret are classic: *Jack And The Beanstalk; Little Red Riding Hood; Cinderella;* and *Rapunzel* ("…let down your hair"). To this seemingly unrelated mix they added an original fairy tale conceived by Lapine in the same style, *The Baker And His Wife*.

The play begins with an almost Disney-esque atmosphere, in a fairy tale set that predicts delightfully the familiar stories that one expects to unfold. The entertaining songs are among the composer's most melodic, and the audience is initially drawn into a world in which the problems the characters face seem not too serious, given the comic treatment they initially receive. But Sondheim and Lapine have something much more sinister and revealing in mind than a simple interweaving of bedtime stories.

All of the elements of classic scary children's tales are there, in a potpourri of witches and giants, quests and curses, suspense and menace. But as the first act evolves, the psychological complexity of the characters' relationships and the revelation of the flaws in their individual personalities begin to lift the play above the level of simple story-telling. As the individual tales meld and intertwine into a single unified script of trickery and deceit, the authors explore themes of maturity, dependence and the relationships that arise between parents and their children.[525]

In the opening sequence, the characters are introduced in a mood of dissatisfaction with their lives. Everyone wants something ("I wish…").

Remaining faithful to the original stories, Cinderella wants to go to the ball, Jack and his mother dream of riches, and Little Red Riding Hood, in a seemingly altruistic but basically greedy counterpoint to the others, wants to take bread, and practically everything else that the baker has made, to her Granny in the woods. (Much humour is derived from Red's voracious appetite.)

But the most profound wish is that of the Baker and his Wife: they yearn to have a child, but she is barren, the result of a Witch's spell. These two people are, in fact, the central motivating force around which all of the other characters' actions rotate. The first act concerns their desire to have the curse lifted.

The Witch promises that the Baker and his Wife will at last conceive a child, provided they embark upon a quest. She presents them with a list of treasures and charges them to enter the woods, collect the items, and bring them to her within three days. Her motivation for the request seems vague at first, although it later becomes apparent that she needs these ingredients to mix a potion that will return her to her former beauty. The four items are a white cow, a red cape, a skein of yellow hair and a golden slipper.[526]

Sondheim and Lapine are relying on the audience's familiarity with the fairy tales to identify these items with the other characters.[527] The authors then create a mosaic of adventures whereby all achieve their wishes. Cinderella attends the ball and marries the prince. Jack sells the cow and plants the beans and grows the beanstalk and slays the giant and captures the treasure. Most important, the Baker and his Wife deliver all of the items to the Witch, aided by another character, the Mysterious Man, although along the way they lie and cheat to steal the items they need.

The play oscillates between broad humour, reminiscent almost of *A Funny Thing Happened On The Way To The Forum*, and stark reality along the lines of *Sweeney Todd*. But amid the humour, an underlying menace casts a shadow over even the most innocent activities. The Red Riding Hood sequence is especially graphic, with the leering and anatomically correct wolf a metaphor for pedophilia. After Red's rescue from the wolf's clutches (she and Granny are violently sliced from the creature's belly, mercifully enacted in silhouette in highly comic fashion), she sings of her loss of innocence.

Some of the action is as grim as the original Grimm.[528] Milky White the cow dies (and is brought back to life by the Witch to make her potion); Rapunzel (she is actually the Witch's daughter) is cast out into the desert, and her prince is blinded; the giant that Jack kills lands with a tremendous crash in the back yard; the Mysterious Man (yet to be identified precisely, although the audience is beginning to get a clue) also dies; and pigeons peck out the wicked stepsisters' eyes.[529]

At the end of the first act the Witch feeds the four items to the cow and milks her, thus obtaining the magic potion that breaks the spell. The Witch is transformed from old and ugly to young and beautiful, although in true fairy tale fashion, her powers are now taken away. The Baker's Wife becomes pregnant. Rapunzel's tears heal her prince's eyes and they return from exile in the desert. In other words, it appears that all of the heroes and heroines are finally going to live happily "ever after" (a song cue, if you've ever heard one!). But the audience leaves for the intermission with an inescapable feeling of foreboding, for as the first act concludes, an ominous note intrudes on the celebration: another beanstalk is growing.

Sondheim and Lapine demand much of an audience. The plot of *Into The Woods* is intricately manufactured and extremely fast-moving, making it essential that every line of dialog, every lyric, be assimilated and examined for totality of meaning. A single attendance at this musical is rarely enough; it requires repeated exposures for the entire plot to be absorbed.

In the second act ("Once upon a time… later"), the characters must come face to face with the consequences of their actions. As before, the mood swings from humour to menace. The two princes, now married to Cinderella and Rapunzel, betray the "happily ever after" theme with their roving eyes (including a dalliance by Cinderella's prince with the Baker's Wife in the woods). Having grown bored with the wives they once courted so eagerly, they now discover and lust after other fairy tale characters, Snow White and Sleeping Beauty, in an hilarious reprise of the song "Agony."

Most ominous of all, the slain giant had a wife, and she's mad! As she goes on a rampage, the characters try to escape from the destruction of their world, and must come to terms with their own responsibility for what has happened. They cast about blindly for somewhere to place the blame, primarily on each other (in the song "Your Fault"), but finally manage to join forces and conquer the giant through cooperation.[530]

The conclusion of the play is strangely in contrast to the previous frenetic pace. The characters have finally achieved a state of maturity, an acceptance of reality, and even a sense of optimism. In a mood of quiet reflection, the survivors sing of the folly of their dissatisfaction, and the realization that their covetous wishes have brought about their own destruction.[531]

And yet the final line of the play is a plaintive call that brings the story full circle: "I wish…"

The work of Stephen Sondheim is a logical extension of that of Oscar Hammerstein II, although in a much darker vein. Like his mentor, Sondheim addresses the fundamental questions of humanity with wit and wisdom, and manages to entertain as well. But in Sondheim, the intellectual stretches that challenge his audiences have taken the American musical theatre out of the realm of pure entertainment, and into the far reaches of philosophy. And that is art. [532]

TWENTY-FIVE
Of Death And Opera

Prior to 1927, light musical theatre in America consisted of burlesque, vaudeville, revue, operetta and musical comedy, and the emphasis was, for the most part, positive and upbeat. The weightier themes were left to opera. *Show Boat* changed that by introducing the concept of the musical *play*, as opposed to the musical *comedy*. Despite the romance and amusement to be found in that Kern/Hammerstein production, the overriding themes of racial prejudice, abandonment, courage and success in the face of considerable odds dominated the plot and the mood.

With the shift in emphasis to escapist entertainment and satire in the 1930s, and always recognizing the single atypical example of *Porgy and Bess* (1935), comedy dominated musical theatre at least until *Pal Joey* (1940). And even in that pivotal show, with its ultra-realistic look at the seamy side of society, humour prevailed.

There is, however, an almost linear plot development that connects Kern and Hammerstein's masterpiece with the first of the Rodgers and Hammerstein classics sixteen years later, leapfrogging over the aberrant 1930s. The tragic figure in *Show Boat*, the mulatto entertainer Julie La Verne, fades from the lives of the rest of the cast in order to give Magnolia Hawks a chance at success. The impression is left that she would decline into alcoholism from that point on, but it was not until *Oklahoma!* that Oscar Hammerstein finally introduced the absolute finality of death as a crucial element in the plot of a musical.

The character of Jud Fry is that of a homicidal stalker, a concept far ahead of its time in musical theatre in 1943. The scene in which he dies by his own knife at the hands of Curly McLain was certainly one of the most shocking and unexpected plot twists in a genre better known for untainted happy endings in pre-World War Two America.

One may argue that Gershwin and Heyward did it first, for Porgy killed Crown in the climactic scene of the last act of *Porgy and Bess*.[533] The circumstances are similar, even to the identical choice and ownership of the murder weapon, but the operatic *Porgy* was a very different vehicle from *Oklahoma!*, which was much closer to the musical comedy tradition. Whether Hammerstein deliberately appropriated the idea from Gershwin is not important. He used it in a very different context, culture and society, and in a play that audiences had expected to be essentially positive and uplifting. *Oklahoma!* ultimately had that affirmative ending, and as in *Porgy*, the tragedy of the character's death was muted by his portrayal as evil or corrupt.

Death as a contributory theme appeared again in Rodgers and Hammerstein's second work, *Carousel* (see Chapter Thirteen). With the demise of Billy Bigelow, in the aftermath of an attempted robbery, Hammerstein explored elements of character and the complexity of human actions in a more ambiguous way than in *Oklahoma!* Certainly Bigelow is a disreputable individual, but a sympathetic one nonetheless. The same might be said about Jud Fry,[534] but whereas there is an element of redemption about Billy Bigelow's concern for his daughter, Fry goes to his grave as the result of his own actions, and that's that!

But in the typical musical comedy of the mid 20th century, and even in those that aspired to be musical dramas, death as a plot device was usually avoided. The comic gangsters in *Guys and Dolls*, for example, are hardly reminiscent of murderous characters such as Al Capone and Legs Diamond in the prohibition years. The battling divorcees of *Kiss Me, Kate* may have wanted to kill each other, but it would have put a definite damper on the play if it had happened. And Annie Oakley shot straight, but no one died as a consequence. Such was the prevalent atmosphere of Broadway in the 1940s and early 1950s.

And then in *The King and I*, Hammerstein again used death to illuminate character. The King of Siam, for all his autocratic nature, stubbornness and pride, is seen as a very human person who strives to be better. He dies at least in part because of his own failure to come to terms with the dichotomy inherent in his own personality. His death is the essential denouement. No other ending would have been so powerful, nor so correct.

After *The King and I*, the 1950s musical theatre soldiered on with its formerly light-hearted air, through *Paint Your Wagon*,[535] *Wonderful Town*, *Can-Can*, *Kismet*, and *The Pajama Game*. Death is comic in the stylized Hell of *Damn Yankees*, and not a factor at all in *My Fair Lady*, the very sentimental *The Most Happy Fella*, or *L'il Abner*. *Bells Are Ringing* and even *Candide* also dealt primarily with life. Perhaps then the contrast of a grim plot resolution was one factor that made *West Side Story* so revolutionary when compared with concurrent shows. As in *Oklahoma!*, where Curly kills Jud Fry in self defence, Tony kills Bernardo, the brother of his beloved. Tony's own death at the conclusion of the play is a senseless but inevitable tragedy, in the context of the racial hatred and gang warfare that precipitated it.

Perhaps no musical play, no matter how serious its intent, could survive without humour. The wonderfully silly flight of first love in the song "I Feel Pretty," and the satirical cop-baiting parody of "Gee, Officer Krupke," played a constant counterpoint to the growing dread of conflict in *West Side Story*. Dark humour also pervades "America" (its subject the plight of Hispanic immigrants in New York), and without it, the story would have been too unrelentingly bleak to provide good entertainment.

As the 1960s gathered steam, Broadway turned once again satirical, as in *How To Succeed in Business Without Really Trying*, and introspective with Sondheim's successful *Company*. Comedy and romance, the latter admittedly laced generously with cynicism, prevailed. On the serious side, the climactic death of Bill Sykes in *Oliver!* (1963) is dramatic in the same vein as Jud Fry's murder, but unlike Billy Bigelow's passing or that of the King of Siam, it has little to do with explaining his character. Even amid the darkness of *Fiddler on the Roof* (1964), optimism survives, as do all of the principal characters.

Sinister influences became more common in musical theatre with the success of *Man of La Mancha* (1965, set amid the Spanish Inquisition) and *Cabaret* (1966, Nazi-era Germany), but comedy filled most of the houses. The new trend established by Stephen Sondheim gathered speed, and while *Hair* and *Oh, Calcutta!* tested the limits of what was acceptable in mainstream theatre, *Godspell* and *Jesus Christ Superstar* gave the Christian gospel a gaudy and thoroughly contemporary (if sometimes somewhat irreverent) flavour.

Those were unsettling years, overshadowed as they were by unrest at home in North America and the unfortunate involvement of the American military in Viet Nam. Amid a series of revivals, only some of which were even moderately profitable,[536] Broadway sought to recapture some of its past, but as the 1970s gave way to the 1980s, other influences came to be felt. Stephen Sondheim's idiosyncratic approach redefined the musical, but was not duplicated successfully by other native composers and lyricists. The big hit of 1980 was *42nd Street*,[537] not exactly a revival, but a stage version of the classic 1933 film. And foreign influences were more strongly felt than ever.

Death, when treated at all, was used for shock effect, as in the murders committed by *Sweeney Todd* (1979), or comically, as by the carnivorous plant in *Little Shop of Horrors* (1982). But amid the gore and glee, a revolution of immense influence arrived with the play *Evita* (1979), which wasn't American, wasn't a comedy, and wasn't even a musical in the time-honoured sense.

If the Broadway concept of musical theatre is said to be a purely American development, other countries soon embraced the genre and gave it their own particular slant. Many musicals had been exported from Broadway, especially to England, but beginning with the importation of *Oliver!* in 1963, the tide began to flow ever so slightly in the opposite direction. The trend exploded in the 1980s with the ubiquitous influence of Britisher Andrew Lloyd Webber.

Taking its cue from the political climate of the Western Hemisphere in the post-Eisenhower 1960s, *Evita* examined a "Latin American dictator and the streetwalker he makes his wife,"[538] Juan and Eva Peron, as seen in retrospect through the eyes of the revolutionary terrorist Che Guevara. The power wielded by Eva Peron and the adulation she received from her people are seen in stark contrast to the minimal amount of good she did for her country. Upon her death at age 33 from cancer, she is portrayed as being venerated almost as a saint.[539]

Although the fact of her death drives the plot, the influence of the play *Evita* went far beyond the story. It was a British production, a substantial success in London before being transplanted to Broadway, and was in almost every respect an opera rather than a musical. In the manner of Sondheim's slightly earlier *Sweeney Todd*[540] (these two shows opened in New York just six months apart), it was entirely sung, but since it preceded *Sweeney* abroad by a year, Webber gets the credit for the instigating the trend for transformation of musicals into popular operas in the English language.

And then came *Les Miserables* (1987)[541], another import (this time an English adaptation of a 1979 French production) that attempted to capture the sweep and scope of Victor Hugo's immense novel of post-revolutionary France. This substantial effort intertwined the themes of courage, honour and duty with a total of five pivotal deaths, each of which was used to advance the plot and to comment upon aspects of humanity.

Les Miserables employs two dramatic deathbed scenes, two deaths in battle, and a suicide, all employed as important turning points in the plot. First comes the sad passing of the unwilling prostitute Fantine, driven to her disgrace and destruction by her dismissal from her job in a factory owned by the protagonist, fugitive Jean Valjean. When Valjean discovers that his lack of compassion has led to her shame and final illness, he is driven by remorse to assume the care of her daughter. This decision, along with the concurrent discovery of his true identity by the policeman Javert, forces him to abandon his position as factory owner and mayor of the town in order to go into hiding with the child in another city.

Two deaths in battle are among the most emotional scenes in the play. Amid the revolutionary uprising of the French students, the young girl Eponine is first to die of wounds inflicted by the authorities. But the fact of her death, coming as it does during her selfless sacrifice for the man she loves, illuminates her character and affects the subsequent actions of the other combatants, especially the student Marius, who is later to become the husband of Fantine's daughter.

In like manner, the much younger boy Gavroche is shot while trying to retrieve weapons for the older students. Gavroche is a hero of the revolution, having exposed the spy Javert, who has infiltrated the enemy lines. The child's death is more tragic even than the two that preceded it, given his tender years and his valiant belief in their cause.[542]

The suicide of Inspector Javert is central to the whole theme of *Les Miserables*, and requires some background explanation. Jean Valjean's crime, for which he spent many years in prison, was the theft of a small amount of food for his sister's starving family. Under the severe penalties imposed by the law, the motivation for the crime had no bearing upon the imposition of a jail sentence as punishment. Javert views all of humanity in terms either black or white, and all criminals as unredeemable, no matter how trivial their crimes may be. When Valjean breaks his parole and goes into hiding, Javert becomes obsessed with his recapture, and pursues him relentlessly.[543]

At the time of the students' revolution, Javert infiltrates their lines and is exposed by Gavroche and captured. Expecting death at their hands, he is instead rescued by Valjean, who then releases him. Javert is at first unable to conceive that the man he considers a criminal has spared his life. He is forced to examine the entire premise of his career as defender of the law, and must confront the consequences of his erroneous evaluation of Valjean's character. Unable to live with the subsequent loss of his personal honour, or with the error inherent in his philosophy, he takes his own life.

The final deathbed scene, of course, is that of Valjean himself, during which he is judged and found worthy, through his selfless sacrifice on behalf of others. In his final redemption there is seen the triumph of honour, courage and responsibility that made Victor Hugo's novel such a powerful statement on the essential goodness of humanity.

Ironically, *Les Miserables* disappointed its backers in the initial run, attracting at first only marginal support and some very critical reviews. The music was generally recognized for its quality, but the plot was condemned for its somewhat confusing and abrupt changes of scene.

For example, after Valjean is released from prison, he is unable to find work and resorts to stealing, this time from a church. When taken once more into custody, he is defended and forgiven by the clergy, and is then given financial aid to re-establish his life. But when next he appears, he has suddenly been transformed from a penniless fugitive into a prosperous factory owner and mayor of another town.[544] This and other quick plot twists apparently confused the reviewers, and they reported their displeasure accordingly.

The criticism is not unwarranted, for *Les Miserables* attempts the near impossible task of compressing most of the major elements of Victor Hugo's expansive story into a single evening's entertainment. But this complaint fails to take into account the intelligence of theatre audiences, or of the popularity of the original 19th century novel. In point of fact, the narrative is very well known, even to modern readers, and those already familiar with the plot had no difficulty following the musical.[545] Enthusiasm for the production grew, and in spite of the unfavourable press, *Les Miserables* began to play to full houses. In the years since, productions have been mounted in dozens of countries and languages, attesting to the universality of the tale.

Sondheim's *Into the Woods* (1987) was similarly fatal to a number of its characters and for the same purpose, that of examining morality. At once a dark comedy and a tragedy, *Into the Woods* examined individual and collective motivations in a sympathetic but by times pessimistic acceptance of human frailty (see Chapter Twenty-four). Whereas *Les Miserables* is ultimately a tribute to valour and honour, *Into The Woods* is pragmatic, probably more realistic, and ultimately bleak.

The creators of *Les Miserables* next borrowed from the theme of the Puccini opera *Madame Butterfly*, updating it to Viet Nam at the time of the American withdrawal, in *Miss Saigon* (1991). As in their earlier show, the entire script was sung in recitatives and arias. The concept of a clash between cultures was a familiar one to audiences, having been explored on different levels in such lighter shows as *South Pacific* and *Flower Drum Song*, but the treatment also held up a mirror to America's motives in the Viet Nam conflict.

Corrupt elements of Vietnamese society and the irresponsible behaviour of American military personnel were broadly painted against the tragic effects of the war on the general population, especially its most defenceless members, its women and children. The twin tragedies of economic and societal breakdown and of the fate of mixed-race babies[546] culminated in the most dramatically effective suicide in popular theatre history, that of the young Vietnamese mother, Kim. With no hope that her child will enjoy any sort of stable future in his homeland, she sacrifices herself so that her son may be taken to America to live with his soldier father.

Death as a dramatic device will no doubt always be a staple of theatre,[547] although thankfully not a ubiquitous one. Nevertheless it is a powerful demonstration of the developing maturity of the musical theatre genre over the course of the twentieth century.

AFTERWORD

If Broadway struggled through a scattered and unfocused search for identity in the 1970s and 1980s, the succeeding decade saw it coming back together again. Handsomely mounted revivals brought back the golden years: *Grease* and *Show Boat* in 1994, *The King and I* and *A Funny Thing Happened on the Way to the Forum* in 1996, among numerous others. New ideas surfaced, such as the translation to the stage of Disney cartoons (*Beauty and the Beast* and the startlingly innovative *The Lion King*), and old concepts in new dress, such as *Victor/Victoria* in 1995, brought new life to the theatre.[548]

Not all of musical theatre adopted the operatic approach toward the turn of the 21st century, as evidenced by the outstanding success of a more traditional style in *The Producers* (2001),[549] a high-kicking chorus girl musical satire in the time-honoured tradition of the revue. And the varied approaches of Andrew Lloyd Webber continue to find favour, some operatic (*Evita*, *Aspects of Love*, and to some extent *The Phantom of the Opera*)[550], some technologic (*Starlight Express*) and some wonderfully unconventional (*Cats*, 1982, and *Song and Dance*, 1985).

It will be history's task and pleasure to evaluate the success of these efforts, and to determine their eventual influence. For now, the revitalization of the American musical theatre in all its many forms predicts a secure and stable future for the form.

APPENDIX
Broadway On Film

The medium of film has made American musical comedies and dramas available to much larger audiences than have ever been inside a Broadway theatre. Unfortunately, Hollywood can rarely resist the temptation to make "improvements" in the material. As a result, film versions of successful musicals range from faithful and excellent (most often when under the control of the original creators, and/or with original cast members) to garbled and distorted shadows of the theatre productions.

To be fair, Broadway has also been notably unsuccessful in adapting film musicals to the stage.[551] Most such efforts have been failures, although two stand out as excellent, both taken from Disney animated features: *Beauty And The Beast* and *The Lion King*. *42nd Street* (1980), a stage version of film's "definitive backstage musical,"[552] was one of very few successful attempts. Such promising vehicles as *Seven Brides for Seven Brothers*,[553] *Gigi*, and *Singin' in the Rain* could not make the transition.[554]

Following is a list of most of those filmed musicals which, in the author's admittedly somewhat biased opinion, come reasonably close to capturing the essence of the original stage productions, or succeed in their own right despite changes.

ANNIE (1982, 1999): This 1977 stage musical has been filmed twice, first for theatres and subsequently by the Disney studios in 1999 for television. The 1982 theatrical version was almost universally panned by critics for a variety of reasons, and while some of their criticism was justified, the movie deserves a second look.

The stage play was based upon a vintage comic strip (*Little Orphan Annie*), and had a highly successful run on Broadway of 2,377 performances, the third longest-running musical of the 1970s[555]. While the plot was fairly conventional, and nothing about the production was considered innovative, the music is undeniably attractive. One of the tunes, "Tomorrow," enjoyed great popularity.[556]

Unfortunately and in true Hollywood fashion, the play was considerably altered for the screen. The music was diluted and rearranged, and some songs were dropped entirely, most notably the wonderfully evocative tribute to New York, "N.Y.C." Unaccountably, "Tomorrow" was postponed until late in the film, whereas the stage play used it early and with charming effect to paint the portrait of an orphan hoping for a better future.

Other changes distracted the audience from the main story line, especially the unrealistic and improbable rescue at the end, wherein Annie is plucked by gyrocopter from the top of an inexplicably open railroad lift bridge. Hollywood too often becomes enamoured with chase scenes and special effects, but not all films benefit from their inclusion. In this case, they should simply have told the story, and left the gimmicks out.

Nevertheless, the 1982 movie version has redeeming qualities, especially some of the performances. Albert Finney strikes just the right note as the hard-hearted industrialist Daddy Warbucks,[557] and young Aileen Quinn's portrayal of Annie is polished and affecting. Miss Quinn was one of the main targets of the critics, however.[558] In retrospect, this view was unfair. The film makers chose to emphasize the comic strip heritage of the material, including the way in which the character of the little orphan girl was portrayed. Miss Quinn not only closely resembled the cartoon child in appearance, her performance was well within the off-the-wall spirit of the entire production.

Two more examples of this somewhat surreal interpretation are Carol Burnett's outrageous performance as a drunken, man-hunting Miss Hannigan, matron of the orphanage, and Bernadette Peters' caricature of a dim-witted blonde con artist. Both are burlesque in the purest sense of the word. In addition, the portrayals of Franklin and Eleanor Roosevelt brought many smiles to those old enough to recall them.

The 1982 film cannot be excused for the damage done to the score, however, and in the 1999 television version, the Disney studios wisely chose to revert to the original stage play as their model, rather than to remake the previous movie. Most of the music is restored, including a production-number treatment of "N.Y.C." More significantly, the score is presented in the same sequence as in the stage version, restoring the emotional flow and impact of the original.

This time, most of the action is indoors. Except for an effective recreation of 1930s New York City, complete with vintage automobiles and expansive street scenes, this version is very close to a stage play in atmosphere. The production numbers, especially "I Think I'm Gonna Like It Here" as staged in the foyer of the Warbucks mansion, are easy to visualize as theatrical rather than cinematic.

There is only one jarring note, stemming from the studio's laudable but misguided attempt at political correctness. Whereas the principal characters in the first film version were exclusively Caucasian, this time the orphan group has a mixture of races. Regrettably, the inclusion of just *one* black child and *one* Oriental calls attention to an undoubtedly unintended appearance of tokenism. This small problem aside, having representation from races other than white is commendable.

The casting of the very talented black Broadway actress Audra McDonald for the role of Grace Farrell, Daddy Warbucks' secretary and Annie's champion, presents a very different problem. Given her vocal talents and the tenor of *present* times, she was an excellent choice for the role. It is sad that the question of her race is unavoidable in a period story such as this.

Throughout the film the unspoken attraction between the Farrell and Warbucks characters is subtly handled, and in the concluding scene, he presents her with an engagement ring. In the 1990s, such an interracial coupling would not seem out of place, and again, the studio's approach to the issue of race is commendable. However, in this particular case it is so historically inaccurate as to be ludicrous.

The era of the Great Depression in which the play is set began in 1929, just two years after *Show Boat*, with its revolutionary treatment of miscegenation between blacks and whites (see Chapter Eight). However powerful the message of that play, society in general was still heavily segregated, in fact in the south and de facto in much of the north. Whereas the film emphasizes and depends upon the Depression-era milieu, the prospect of an interracial marriage among American society's elite in those years is just too unbelievable to accept. However admirable the intent, this distortion of historical reality does a disservice to all those who sacrificed much to remedy the abuses of those prejudiced years.

The 1999 film version of Annie is otherwise quite faithful to the stage production, with a finely realized score, a stage-like appearance to the sets, and admirably balanced performances. The interpretation is less outrageous and cartoon-like than the 1982 movie, and therefore the characters are closer to reality and somewhat more accessible. In addition, the unavoidable sentiment surrounding a homeless orphan is, if not downplayed, at least not overplayed. The young actress who plays Annie, Alicia Morton, is more subdued than Aileen Quinn, and also more affecting, and Kathy Bates' style as Miss Hannigan makes the character more human and somewhat more sympathetic than Burnett's.[559]

In an interesting historical salute to the stage play, the original stage Annie, Andrea McArdle, appears in the Broadway play-within-a-play sequence of "N.Y.C."[560]

ANNIE GET YOUR GUN (1950): This MGM production is reasonably faithful to the original, although Betty Hutton's performance as Annie Oakley is a bit too broad and comic to be taken seriously. While undeniably funny, it is almost a caricature of itself. "Hutton's frenetic style and frontal attack on the songs divest the character of necessary warmth and make her seem a mite mechanical."[561] Judy Garland was originally signed to do the role, and actually filmed a few scenes before being forced to withdraw.[562] Had she remained, it would probably have been a very different film, with a more believable and sensitive heroine.

Nevertheless, the performances of Irving Berlin's music are of high calibre, making the movie worth seeing (unless you are of Native American ancestry, in which case you will be sorely and justifiably offended). This is probably the composer's most varied score, ranging from wildly comic ("You Can't Get a Man With a Gun") to beautiful ballads ("The Girl That I Marry" and "They Say It's Wonderful").

BEAUTY AND THE BEAST (1991): The order is reversed here, as the Oscar-nominated animated film[563] preceded the Broadway play by three years. It is tempting to surmise that when the Disney studio made this impressive feature, they were already anticipating the 1994 Broadway version, because the film was assembled almost as if it were a stage play.[564] And when the play was mounted, the live actors very much resembled the animated characters,[565] even those whose personas are essentially human, such as the heroine Belle and her father. The villain, Gaston, is larger than life on screen, and was similarly overwhelming on stage.

Many of the characters in the film were anthropomorphic (a candelabra, a clock, even a chest of drawers), necessitating elaborate costumes for the live actors, and probably great discomfort for some of them as well. Complex special effects were required to realize fantasized scenes that were easy to accomplish with animation. Much attention was given in the press to the technical ingenuity of the flaming candelabra, but the mesmerizing mid-air transformation of the Beast into the Prince was mechanically just as challenging. Perhaps the most cartoon-like aspect of the stage play, other than the costumed figures, is the extended and visually impressive centrepiece production number, "Be Our Guest."

In both of its incarnations, *Beauty and the Beast* is a dramatic and effective retelling of the classic fairy tale, with a finely crafted plot and suspense-building pace. The score from the film (music by Alan Menken, lyrics by Howard Ashman) was adapted almost note for note, but with some additional songs.[566] When Disney re-released the film in 2002 in large screen Imax format, one of the songs exclusive to the Broadway version, "Human Again," was inserted, along with a new animated sequence.

BELLS ARE RINGING (1956): This one works well, mostly because Judy Holliday reprised her own stage success,[567] and they didn't mess with the music, written by Jule Styne, with lyrics by the team of Betty Comden and Adoph Green. Other than that, the production seems somewhat pedestrian, and not up to director Vincent Minnelli's usual standard.[568]

BRIGADOON (1954): The producers had sense enough to leave this one mostly alone, and in some respects it is nearly as charming as the stage version, although they can't be forgiven for omitting a great comic song, "My Mother's Wedding Day." The story is preserved nearly intact, and an ethereal air of fantasy surrounds the 18th century Scottish village, standing out in stark contrast to the jarring atmosphere of 20th century New York near the end of the film. The overall ambiance is, however, to some extent wooden and unconvincing.

According to the story, the village minister made a pact with his creator, in which Brigadoon was enchanted, protected forever from the wickedness of a changing world by a spell to put the villagers into a long, long sleep at the end of every day. To shelter the inhabitants from evil, the village would vanish each night, not to return for a hundred years. Each new day for Brigadoon would be a hundred years later for the rest of the world, keeping the town in secluded isolation.[569]

Such an idyllic miracle could not continue if the villagers were exposed to the passing centuries, so in order to preserve their unique paradise, the townspeople may never journey beyond the confines of the town. But a rejected suitor, Harry Beaton, angry at the marriage of the woman he loves to another, tries to leave Brigadoon. This precipitates Agnes de Mille's spectacular chase ballet, during which Beaton is killed and the miracle is preserved.

Perhaps the major problem with the film is what would normally be considered an asset: it seems almost as if it is confined to a stage. This is especially true in the chase ballet. Without an overview as would be provided by the theatre, the relative positions of the characters are unclear, and Beaton's inability to escape seems artificial. The camera fails to capture the broad picture, in spite of the wide-screen CinemaScope print, and the element of dance inherent in the original conception is vaguely ill defined.

Stage productions do this sort of thing well, as perhaps no movie can without losing the intimacy inherent in a musical. A comparable scene occurs in *Beauty and the Beast*, wherein a stylised ballet portrays wolves chasing the heroine's father, and later attacking the Beast himself. It worked on stage, and it also worked especially well in the animated version, but it would take outstandingly innovative direction to capture the same spirit in a live-action film. *Brigadoon* understandably fell short here.

Despite a talented cast and some fine dancing, somehow the film never really comes alive.[570] It is as if the producers couldn't decide whether to make a realistic movie or to film a stage play. The sets are obviously artificial, with painted backdrops that don't look real, but don't really look like stage scenery either, and the action wavers from too realistic to too ethereal.

Nevertheless, the film of *Brigadoon* offers some fine entertainment, especially Gene Kelly's slightly goofy song-and-dance version of "Almost Like Being In Love." To anyone who has never seen the stage play, the movie will suffice.

BYE BYE BIRDIE (1963): This one was nearly left out of the list, as it distorts the original by turning it into a tour de force for Ann-Margaret. The basic story and some of the gags survive, although the plot was made somewhat sillier and more contrived (the hyperactive turtle is a little hard to take). The music (what's left of it) is well done,[571] although they should have resisted the impulse to "improve" it. The stage version of "Kids!" is much better than the filmed one, for example. Only two significant members of the Broadway cast made it into the film, Dick VanDyke as the male lead and Paul Lynde as the long suffering father.[572]

In one respect, Ann-Margaret is miscast for the role of Kim MacAfee, the naïve teenager who is smitten with rock star Conrad Birdie. She is too seductive, too brash and blatant,[573] which somehow dims the satire intended by the original. However, her featured song "How Lovely To Be a Woman" is a wonderful spoof of how teenagers see themselves.[574] You won't see much of Broadway in the film, but it is fun.

CABARET (1972): On rare occasions, Hollywood made substantial changes to a Broadway musical and still managed to produce a successful and artistically satisfying result. Such is the case with *Cabaret*. Although much different in many ways from the stage version,[575] it still captured the decadence of 1930s Germany, especially through the demonic performance of Joel Grey as the androgynous master of ceremonies.[576] Also effectively portrayed is the menace of the growth of Nazism. Even with about half of the score being the same, *Cabaret* the movie is virtually a different creation from *Cabaret* the stage musical, but both are worthy efforts in their own respective fields.[577]

CALL ME MADAME (1953): With the original stage star (Ethel Merman) in the cast, and the story and music left mostly alone, it works! (Why can't Hollywood always do it this way?) However, you have to be a Merman fan to enjoy it. "For those unfortunate enough to remain unresponsive to the lady's particular brand of scenery-chewing, sock-it-to-'em tactics, the experience must, indeed, have been a painful one. For the film was Merman, and Merman was the film."[578]

CARMEN JONES (1954): This unique opera/musical works on many levels, although at times it seems somewhat artificial. Bizet's music frequently sounds strangely out of place in the black context, although in some songs it is startlingly powerful, and Pearl Bailey's performance is outstanding.[579] Overall the movie is fairly successful, although when viewed from the perspective of contemporary American life, the characters too often come across as stereotypes.[580]

CAROUSEL (1956): Beautifully filmed but somewhat distorted from the stage version, this ambitious Hollywood effort gave away part of the plot by showing Billy Bigelow in Heaven much too early. However, the voices are strong and the score is almost intact. Two scenes are especially effective, the amazingly athletic dance sequence all over the roof and dock of a Maine seaport,[581] and the magnificent dream ballet, danced principally by a very young Susan Lucky.[582] The plot works, but if you've ever seen the stage version, the changes will annoy you.

Gordon MacRae accepted the role of Bigelow after Frank Sinatra pulled out, reportedly because he refused to film each scene twice, once for the new wide-screen CinemaScope 55 and once for regular format.[583] Some of the early Sinatra footage survives, and as with the substitution of Betty Hutton for Judy Garland in *Annie Get Your Gun*, his presence would have given the character a much more disreputable, unfeeling nature, appropriate to the plot.[584] MacRae seems at times almost too nice for the part.

CATS (1998): Not a movie in the traditional sense, this production is a faithful filming of the original play. The performances are excellent and the stage ambiance is authentic, but the scope and power of this innovative musical are muted and constrained by the small screen.

CHICAGO (2003): Innovative and evocative, this Oscar-winning film reinterpreted the Broadway original through the judicious and imaginative use of current film techniques. The best of the stage play's music benefits from fine performances and the immediacy of the camera, especially "All That Jazz," "When You're Good To Mama," "Mister Cellophane" and "Razzle Dazzle." Some scenes are essentially theatrical (the wonderful puppet sequence, for example) while others, such as Richard Gere's metaphorical tap dance, are strictly cinematic. As entertainment, *Chicago* the movie is superb.

DAMN YANKEES (1958): This one transplanted some of the original cast onto film, and told the story well. The music (by Richard Adler and Jerry Ross) comes through almost unscathed, and is especially effective when sung by Ray Walston as the Devil. Gwen Verdon portrays a 172-year-old temptress, the role she created on stage, and displays a "marvellous gift for zany comedy, combined with… exuberant eroticism… in the dance numbers."[585] There's even enough baseball footage to attract sports-minded moviegoers.

EVITA (1979): Andrew Lloyd Webber's 1978 examination of the life of Eva Peron was among the first of the operatic musicals to hit Broadway in the last quarter of the 20th century. In choosing to film it in the through-sung style of the original stage play, director Alan Parker created "the world's longest music video."[586] Pop diva Madonna, in the lead role, demonstrated vocal equipment equal to the task, but didn't quite manage to create the persona nor evoke the sympathy for the charismatic Eva Peron that made the Broadway production so compelling. The film is both visually and structurally interesting, however, and is even by times spectacular.

THE FANTASTICKS (2000): Fans of Joel Grey, the androgynous master of ceremonies in *Cabaret*, will applaud his affecting performance in this imperfect but still captivating version of off-Broadway's most famous long-running production. The story is well told, and the photography, using some of the Arizona locations first seen in *Oklahoma!*, is stunning. The film was not released for five years, and then only after re-editing by Francis Ford Coppola. Some of his revisions are questionable, however, especially the elimination of the long version of "Try To Remember" to open the show, if indeed that alteration was Coppola's responsibility. This and other deleted scenes are available on the DVD, and may suggest that the original director, Michael Ritchie, had a better handle on what made this celebrated musical, at over forty continuous years, the longest-running New York production ever.

FIDDLER ON THE ROOF (1971): Why, oh why, didn't they cast the original stage Tevye (Zero Mostel)? Chaim Topol looks the part, and is very effective in the scenes with his wife Goldie ("Do You Love Me?") and with his children, but his overall performance slows everything to a crawl. If you're patient with introspective emotion, his interpretation is wonderful, but Mostel's more exuberant approach on stage made for better contrast with the darker elements of the plot. Also missing is the original dramatic choreography of Jerome Robbins.[587]

On the plus side, the story is very powerfully told, and most of the music survived the transition to film. The children are all effectively played, although in appearance they could not possibly have been from the same family, or even the same ethnic heritage. The on-location shooting (in Zagreb in the former Yugoslavia) and some innovative directing lift the film above the ordinary. Especially effective are the freeze-frame scenes where Tevye considers how to react to his children's rebellious actions.

FINIAN'S RAINBOW (1968): The fantasy atmosphere survives, as does the message about tolerance, and Fred Astaire is a standout in the cast. The music (by Burton Lane and E. Y. Harburg[588]) is well done, as is the choreography, but try to find the wide screen version, or you'll miss the scope of it. Unfortunately, the whole concept seems dated, even including the satire on racial bigotry.[589] It's fun and entertaining, but doesn't capture the immediacy of the plot that stabbed audiences in their collective conscience in 1947.

FLOWER DRUM SONG (1961): Didn't anyone in the casting department realize that people of Japanese, Korean and Polynesian descent don't all look Chinese? Otherwise it's only okay, with some songs out of order (especially "The Other Generation") and/or cut, thus losing part of their effectiveness. Jack Soo's comic performance rescues several of the scenes, and Miyoshi Umeki is ideally cast as the shy young immigrant who arrives to fulfil an arranged marriage. It's nicely filmed, but somewhat patronizing toward the west coast Chinese community.[590]

42nd STREET (1933): This is an outstanding example of the very few movie-first, stage-play-later successes.[591] As the grip of the Depression came increasingly to be felt, motion pictures began to mount their campaign to compete with and even to supplant live entertainment. Six years after the advent of sound motion pictures, Hollywood had finally conquered most of the technical difficulties of filming large-scale musicals, and this one is the best of that era. With a fine score by Harry Warren and innovative camera work that made the dancing sequences (staged by Busby Berkeley) come alive, this fine film still entertains today.

The lead roles (Ruby Keeler and Dick Powell) are well cast, and the goofy story line, "laced with sardonic lines, is often funny, and it is forthright in its unglamourized look at life behind the footlights."[592] In a style to rival the stage presentations of Ziegfeld, *42nd Street* ends in a grand spectacle, a tribute to Broadway itself.[593] The startling camera angles, including the overhead shots that became his trademark,[594] established Berkeley at the top of his craft.

Although the 1980 stage version could not reproduce the effects that made the movie so memorable, the music survived, helping to make it one of the few motion picture musicals ever to withstand translation to the stage.

A FUNNY THING HAPPENED ON THE WAY TO THE FORUM (1966): Too many quick scene changes and a frantic pace substitute for the subtle humour of the stage version, although the music (by Stephen Sondheim) is okay (what's left of it), and it features the talents of a very young Michael Crawford as the dim-witted hunk. You'll probably enjoy it, unless you've seen the stage original, which had a smoother story line and much more style and wit. But it is one of very few filmed records of Zero Mostel's comic style, and worth a look for that alone. But overall, it "tries too hard, comes off forced."[595] Notable is one of the last appearances on screen by silent film star Buster Keaton.

GENTLEMEN PREFER BLONDS (1953): Marilyn Monroe and Jane Russell are in top form,[596] and enough of the Jule Styne/Leo Robin score survived to make this movie greatly entertaining. The dance sequences (by Jack Cole) were similarly well done, but the effort loses steam at the end.[597] Watch it for the music, the dancing and the girls.

GIGI (1958): This Lerner and Loewe film masterpiece should have been a natural for a stage interpretation, but it failed miserably in 1973, not because the material was weak, but because the adapted script lacked polish and imagination,[598] proving that even the finest, most familiar shows cannot survive a deficiency of loving attention. The film is included in this list because it represents the talents of two men whose best work on Broadway (*Brigadoon*, *My Fair Lady* and *Camelot*) epitomized an entire era, and shows their skill to good advantage.

GOOD NEWS (1947): Much of the original score and a believable college atmosphere make it enjoyable, although twenty years after the stage production, this interpretation borrows too much from the style of the 1940s. Nevertheless, the music and staging are both exciting, as is the quality of the acting, and younger audiences probably didn't notice the difference. The tunes "Lucky in Love" and "The Varsity Drag" are among the few truly durable standards from 1920s musicals. (An earlier version of this show, somewhat primitively filmed in 1930, is believed to be unavailable.)

The adaptations from stage to screen are of relatively minor importance, such as changing the pivotal college class from Astronomy to French to accommodate a new song (the "French Lesson," a duet between the male and female leads). The style of the added material is more in keeping with 1947, and is therefore much different from the 1927 score. That doesn't detract from the story, however, partly because the new musical numbers are so well done. Overall, both the good humour and Roaring Twenties atmosphere come through in an entertaining if somewhat forced manner.

GUYS AND DOLLS (1955): This film features fine choreography by Michael Kidd, and hilarious recreations of the gangster patois, a la Damon Runyon, the journalist who originally created the characters. Frank Sinatra is typecast with his perfect New Jersey accent, and who would have thought Marlon Brando could sing? But the standouts are the adenoidal Vivian Blaine and Stubby Kaye, reprising their Broadway roles.

The most romantic music in the play is assigned to the character Sky Masterson, and the choice of Brando for that part is intriguing. Because of its vocal demands, Frank Sinatra would have seemed a more natural choice.[599]   Surprisingly, Brando delivers the songs, especially "Luck Be a Lady," with competence[600] if not ease. (Hollywood too often made ill-advised changes in quality material in order to accommodate the actors chosen for specific roles. However in this case, reverse casting of Sinatra and Brando as Masterson and Detroit respectively would almost certainly have weakened the film.)

GYPSY (1962): This adaptation comes close, with the score and story intact, although one longs for the intensity of the original Broadway star (Ethel Merman) in the role of Mama Rose. The choice of Rosalind Russell was simply a misguided one, in terms of both personality and singing ability. Her "big song, 'Everything's Coming Up Roses,' gets nowhere near the surging confidence and faith exuded by Merman. Her 'Rose's Turn' is a game effort to crystallize the mother's heartbreak and defiance, but it lacks the intended emotional impact."[601]

This view is not a universal one, however. Critic Clive Hirschhorn offers the opinion that "where Merman had been volcanic, Rosalind Russell… was merely dynamic, with Miss Russell accurately conveying Rose's unflagging energy and zeal, her almost frightening ambition and, at the same time, the enthusiasm, warmth and humour that made it feasible that her children loved her while being frustrated by her."[602]

In the role of Gypsy Rose Lee, Natalie Wood is unquestionably exquisite. A tiny actress, she successfully portrayed both the waif-like child and the adult stripper, and lent to the latter a charming blend of naïveté and seductiveness. The songs were well done, and the production captured much of the gaudy atmosphere of burlesque.[603]   The Technicolor photography is superb.

HOW TO SUCCEED IN BUSINESS WITHOUT REALLY TRYING (1967): Great fun! Unfortunately some of the songs from the stage version were dropped, but the clever satire survived intact, even if Bob Fosse's original choreography and direction didn't. In another example of the resurrection of a former star in a revised medium, crooner Rudy Vallee acquits himself well a half century after his initial success and subsequent obscurity, in the same manner as Buster Keaton in *A Funny Thing*.

INTO THE WOODS (1987, released in 1990): A masterpiece! This is not a Hollywood movie.[604]   Filmed on stage with the original cast, this multiple Tony winner (see Chapter Twenty-four) will show you the genius of Sondheim as it should be seen. A word of caution: the plot is so complex that it requires great concentration, or better yet, a review of the fairy tale sources before viewing the film. It's an unsettling look deep within the human psyche, told through the medium of familiar children's stories, and is by turns delightful, scary and disturbing. The play features Bernadette Peters, whose work in several Sondheim musicals brought his female characters dramatically to life, equalled perhaps only by Angela Lansbury. Overall, the cast is well matched and evenly talented.

Stephen Sondheim's musicals do not fare well when removed from the stage. An example is *A Little Night Music* (1977), a noble attempt that somehow misses the boat (and proves once and for all that Elizabeth Taylor, for all her dramatic talent, should never have attempted a singing role). Keeping *Into the Woods* on the theatrical boards was the only intelligent way to translate it onto film.

THE KING AND I (1956): Fortunately, Rodgers and Hammerstein retained control of this vehicle, and saw that it was filmed faithfully, making it the best realization of their work in the motion picture medium.[605] Yul Brynner is as magnificent on film as he was on stage. With interior settings that replicate the feel of a stage, this may be as close as a film ever came to reproducing the atmosphere of Broadway, prior to Sondheim's *Sweeney Todd*.

Deborah Kerr's interpretation of a strong and independent Anna Leonowens provides a powerful counterpoint to Brynner's autocratic magnificence, and represents the best of her work.[606] Although her songs were dubbed by the accomplished mimic Marni Nixon,[607] the timbre of their voices is well matched, and the synchronization is excellent.

The sets rival those used on stage, with a convincing opulence appropriate to a 19th century Oriental kingdom, but it never interferes with the narrative. "The book permits us to enter into the complex mind of the king and into the feelings of an intelligent woman puzzled, intrigued, and deeply irritated by this man."[608] Best of all, the movie retained all of the familiar elements from the Broadway production, among them the music, the ballet sequence, and the children's march.

KISMET (1955): Operetta revivals on film were in fashion in the 1950s, with such works as *The Merry Widow*, *The Vagabond King* and *The Desert Song*,[609] among others. In addition, the crossover operetta/musical *Show Boat* received its third film treatment in 1951,[610] and the new *Rose Marie* (1954) was the first musical filmed in the CinemaScope process.[611]

In appearance, *Kismet* is perhaps the best of these efforts, with an opulent and colourful setting[612] and lavish costumes. The score is excellent, adapted from the 19th century Russian composer Alexander Borodin. The pacing is somewhat uninspired, however, and lacks the excitement of the stage version.

KISS ME, KATE (1953): This is Cole Porter at his best, thanks to a faithful transplant of song and story.[613] The dancing sequences are among the finest ever filmed, choreographed by Bob Fosse and featuring his own on-screen performance. The cast is well chosen, with the voices of Kathryn Greyson (in her best film role[614]) and Howard Keel in top form, although Greyson's performance lacked some of the fire that characterized the role on stage.[615] Unlike in some earlier filmings of Porter's musicals, the Broadway score was retained almost in its entirety, and was well executed.

THE LION KING (1994): In another of the very rare examples of a successful Broadway realization of an original motion picture, *The Lion King* is as different in appearance on stage from the animated version as *Beauty and the Beast* was similar. Whereas that earlier cartoon was filmed almost as if it were a stage play, the animated *Lion King* portrayed the openness of a vast primitive landscape, and anthropomorphic animals reminiscent of the ground-breaking 1942 Disney hit, *Bambi*.[616]

In the Broadway version, the staging and stylised costumes gave the entire production a completely different atmosphere. Such contrivances as the immense giraffe dominated the stage, although the other animals were blends of human shapes and beast-like masks, allowing the actors more freedom for the elaborate choreography. Whereas *Beauty and the Beast* was notable for the faithful similarities between movie and stage, *The Lion King* was a radical departure, unlike anything ever seen before on Broadway (although vaguely reminiscent of *Cats* in atmosphere).

THE MUSIC MAN (1962): This film is as close as you can come to transferring the stage to an open air setting, and is rivalled in authenticity perhaps only by *My Fair Lady* and *The King and I*. The music is faithfully and accurately performed,[617] and the story is told in the same sequence. Robert Preston defined the role of Prof. Harold Hill on stage, and was really the only reasonable choice for the film. Shirley Jones was certainly competent as Marian the Librarian, but why, oh why did Hollywood constantly ignore the talented Barbara Cook, the wonderful soprano who created the role? Catch a very, very young Ron Howard, lisping his way through "The Wells Fargo Wagon."

A misguided 2003 remake for television is inferior in almost every respect to the 1962 original. Like Yul Brynner as the King of Siam, Robert Preston *was* Prof. Harold Hill, and despite his vocal talents, Matthew Broderick's low-key interpretation fails to capture the character's brash con-man persona. Unless a unique performance such as Preston's can unquestionably be improved upon, a remake should not be attempted. One might as well repaint the *Mona Lisa*.

MY FAIR LADY (1964): They gave this famous musical the Hollywood treatment in the extreme, but the opulence works beautifully, mostly because they didn't tamper with the story, and Rex Harrison, in his original stage role, is perfect. The drawing-room atmosphere that worked so well on stage is reproduced here as well. Even the exterior street scenes have a theatre-like quality to them, although some reviewers feel this works to the disadvantage of the film.[618]

Audrey Hepburn is ideal in both appearance and manner as a waif-like Eliza Doolittle, but her attempts at singing the songs, several of which are preserved as "Special Features" on the DVD version, reveal why the filmmakers wisely chose voice mimic Marnie Nixon to dub the tunes.[619] When the film was cast, the producers believed that they needed the proven box-office draw that Hepburn provided, and therefore turned down Broadway's original Eliza, Julie Andrews, for the role.[620] (Andrews subsequently beat out Hepburn for that year's Best Actress Oscar for *Mary Poppins*: poetic justice, indeed.)

OKLAHOMA! (1955): At seven million dollars, it was the most expensive film ever made up to that time,[621] produced by Rodgers and Hammerstein and very faithful to the stage version, including Agnes de Mille's innovative ballet. Even the sets captured the flavour of the stage version.

Much of its success reflects the intelligent choices made by the team that created it on Broadway. For the role of Laurey, for example, Rodgers chose the then-unknown Shirley Jones,[622] whose blend of innocence and considerable vocal talents made the character both attractive and believable. The rest of the cast was similarly well chosen, especially Rod Steiger as the unlikeable Jud Fry and Charlotte Greenwood as Aunt Eller. Greenwood's unique dancing style, including especially a head-topping lateral kick step that is all the more impressive considering her height, earned her many character parts in movie musicals. Agnes de Mille adapted her own choreography from the stage version.

With almost all of the score retained, the music is entertaining and well staged, although the affected western accents sometimes seem too coy and overdone ("medder" for "meadow" and "purty" for "pretty," for example).[623] Shot in the then-new 65-millimeter Todd-AO process, the backgrounds are magnificently colourful.

OLIVER! (1968): This Oscar winning interpretation of the British import fully captures the spirit and atmosphere of the stage play, although without the wonderful revolving stage that attracted so much attention on Broadway. As Fagin, Ron Moody comes very close to the wonderful interpretation created by Clive Revill in the New York presentation.

PAJAMA GAME (1957): This stylish and exuberant film is well done,[624] and is mostly faithful to the stage original.[625] Some of the Broadway cast is present, including especially John Raitt in his only starring role on film. However, movie veteran Doris Day was chosen as the female lead instead of Janis Paige, who starred on Broadway. "Day… gives the best musical performance of her career. By now she had demonstrated her skill as a dramatic actress, but except for *Love Me or Leave Me* in 1955, she had not been given a role for years that made good use of her musical talent.[626]"

The fine choreography by Bob Fosse is not constrained by the movie screen.[627] The film also benefits from imaginative camera work, "proof that it was possible to transfer a Broadway hit to the screen almost intact without its becoming stage-bound in the process."[628] The score is well done, with a standout being the comic tango, "Hernando's Hideaway."

PAL JOEY (1957): Although undeniably entertaining, this misguided effort distorted the premise of the original by transforming the lead character into a "flippant nice guy."[629] It would have been left out of this list except for the excellence of the Rodgers and Hart score.

The problem is similar to what was done to *Bye Bye Birdie*, wherein the concentration upon the image of a principal performer, in that case Ann-Margaret, imposed a change of focus on the entire production. Having cast Frank Sinatra in the lead role, "Columbia removed most of the bite and turned Joey Evans from an opportunistic heel into a brash, 'ring-a-ding-ding' Sinatra-type swinger with a soft spot he tries to conceal."[630]

The movie isn't as offensive as the stage version either, since the plot was toned down and the language and lyrics were sanitized, losing much of the impact of John O'Hara's libretto. In Dorothy Kingsley's screenplay adaptation, Joey Evans comes across as too sympathetic, a sort of tarnished saint instead of an immoral sinner.[631]

Nevertheless, Sinatra does justice to the music, as does vocalist Jo Ann Greer, who dubbed the songs for female lead Rita Hayworth. The sets, costumes and photography are similarly well done, but aside from the score, the entire film is but a pale reflection of that controversial musical of 1940.

PORGY AND BESS (1959): Except for some very low quality pirated versions, this classic is not available on either tape or DVD, which is a pity. It "caught the teeming intensity of life in the black Charleston slum, and extracted every ounce of melodrama from the story of the crippled Porgy and his doomed love for Bess."[632] The music won Academy Awards for arrangers Andre Previn and Ken Darby.[633] The overall production is a bit slow and laboured,[634] but the atmosphere is authentic and reasonably true to Gershwin's conception. It deserves to be re-released, if only for its historic significance, as many people are familiar with the rich score, but not in the context of the drama that inspired it.

SHOW BOAT (1936): This is a wonderful interpretation of the pivotal musical, with an excellent cast[635] and almost all of the story line intact, although the ending is just a bit muddled, with several plot elements resolved too quickly and unconvincingly.[636] Charles Winninger, who created the role of Cap'n Andy on stage, is at his surprisingly athletic best in the "play-within-a-play." The music is authentically realized, considering the technical limitations of the era.[637] Paul Robeson defined "Old Man River" for all time, and Kern and Hammerstein gave him another song that wasn't in the stage version, "Ah Still Suits Me."[638]

The camera work also set the standard for those years, as did the imaginative staging and the excellence of the art direction.[639] The entire cast was competent, but the outstanding performance was by Helen Morgan as the mulatto Julie La Verne, reprising her Broadway role.

Showboat was first filmed in 1929, but that version is apparently lost. Strangely for a movie based on a musical, it was begun as a silent film, and then modified with just a partial sound track, a la *The Jazz Singer*. Some of the Kern/Hammerstein score was retained, but it was augmented by spirituals such as "Deep River."[640]

The story was remade again in 1951, but you should avoid this one, unless you've first seen the 1936 version for authenticity. The butchered story line will confuse and annoy you. In trying to "improve" it, Hollywood destroyed much of what the original libretto set out to do. But it is undeniably beautiful, in splendid Technicolor and with fine vocal performances. William Warfield delivers a wonderful "Old Man River," a worthy successor to Robeson's effort. (See Chapter Eight for additional information.)

THE SOUND OF MUSIC (1965): Okay, it's got every Rodgers and Hammerstein cliché: cute kids, young love, triumph over adversity, religious symbolism, a cruel potential stepmother, an almost-thwarted romance, etc., etc. But how well it works! Rodgers himself oversaw the production. He dropped only one song (sadly, the clever "How Can Love Survive?") and added a couple of nice new ones.[641] Julie Andrews is perfect as Maria, and an aristocratic Christopher Plummer (as Baron Von Trapp) can even sing (well, sort of). The actual events of Maria Von Trapp's life story are not too realistically portrayed, but the stage version was to blame for that, and the story line of the film is nearly identical. Be sure to catch voice mimic Marnie Nixon[642] as Sister Sophia, in a rare appearance on film. And bring two or three handkerchiefs.

SOUTH PACIFIC (1958, 2001): In the first version, the cinematographers got carried away with technical experimentation, adding outrageous colours to many of the scenes without really heightening the emotional effect. Instead, they detract from the exoticism and magic they were intended to impart.[643] In the song "Bali Ha'i," for example, the beach scene is overlaid with green and purple filters, and the beauty of the island[644] during the tender love song "Some Enchanted Evening" is buried within yellow fog. [645]

Otherwise, the Pacific locations are attractive, and Rodgers and Hammerstein made sure that the story and music stayed intact. But once again, a magnificent stage actress, in this case Mary Martin, was excluded from the film version; too old for the part, they said. (Hadn't anyone considered makeup?)

In the remake for television, *South Pacific* seems somehow bland by comparison. The 1958 version was sometimes criticized for the overly silly antics of the sailors and too much sentimentality, but it had many strongly entertaining moments, especially when provided by Ray Walston as Luther Billis. The new version is beautiful and sometimes more dramatically satisfying, but does not represent a great leap forward.

STATE FAIR (1945): Never a stage production, this Rodgers and Hammerstein film is included here for its similarity to their Broadway productions and for the engaging score,[646] including especially the song "That's For Me." Somewhat in the manner of *Oklahoma!*, *State Fair* "had a contemporary setting, but its rose-colored, picture-postcard view of American life placed it squarely in the tradition of the period musical."[647] The plot originated with a non-musical 1933 movie. (The 1962 remake is "third rate Americana,"[648] capitalizing on the popularity of young stars Pat Boone, Ann-Margaret, Pamela Tiffin, and Bobby Darin. It has few of the qualities of the original.)

SUNDAY IN THE PARK WITH GEORGE (1986): Fortunately, Hollywood didn't get its hands on this one either. Once again, Bernadette Peters interprets Sondheim with style and panache in this on-stage filming. Equally skilful is Mandy Patinkin, a multi-talented stage-film-TV actor and singer who first came to widespread attention for his role as Inigo Montoya in the cult classic *The Princess Bride*.

SWEENEY TODD (filmed in 1979, concert version 2001): Like *Into The Woods* and *Sunday In The Park With George*, this is another original cast presentation filmed on stage with authentic theatre sets. Not for the squeamish, the performances by Angela Lansbury and Len Cariou are quintessential Sondheim. The concert version is also excellent, with greater immediacy in the camera work, but the drama sometimes seems muted by the minimal staging.

WEST SIDE STORY (1961): "Though (choreographer) Jerome Robbins had to be thrown off the set for his annoying perfectionism, his dances are all there."[649] So is the wonderful Sondheim-Bernstein score, Arthur Laurents' book and an authentic New York setting. Long and sometimes too loud, but very effective and affecting, this is another three-handkerchief Oscar winner. Marnie Nixon dubbed Natalie Wood's songs in a near perfect imitation of that actress's vocal quality, and with a most convincing Hispanic accent.

***

Hollywood is perhaps a victim of its own fecundity. By attempting too often to reproduce Broadway on film, it understandably falls short more often than it succeeds, but filmmakers should be credited for their occasional masterpieces, such as *The Music Man*, *The King and I* and *My Fair Lady*. Better that they tried often and failed, than that they tried too rarely and missed giving us films that bring Broadway musicals to those who may never have the opportunity to see them on stage.

GLOSSARY

The following definitions are specific to the topics addressed in this book, and are not all-inclusive.

Aria: A melody sung by a soloist in an opera or other musical stage presentation, normally melodic and often virtuosic. In the traditional opera, the aria serves as commentary, rather than as an advancement of the plot, although this distinction is not always observed. See *recitative*.

Boards: A slang term to identify stage presentations, as in "on the boards," sometimes used to distinguish live plays from films or television.

Book: The overall package of plot, dialog and characterization, and the pattern by which these elements are combined and interrelated in a stage musical production. The music and lyrics are treated as separate elements. The actual dialog and lyrics are combined into the working script, called the libretto.

Broadway: A term widely applied to theatrical productions of a dramatic or comedic nature, musical or otherwise, that are presented in large-scale theatres in New York. The name refers to the major thoroughfare that bisects that city's entertainment district. See *off Broadway*.

Burlesque: A humorous theatrical production emphasizing sex, satire and ridicule, usually presented as a series of individual skits. See *revue* and *vaudeville*.

Chorus: A musical selection in an opera or other stage production that is sung by a group, usually with more than one voice per part. Also the group that sings the selection. See *aria* and *recitative*.

Concept Musical: A show written around a thematically explanatory staging plan, in which all of the elements are integrated and focused upon a central idea, rather than an overall plot.

Libretto: The entire text of an opera or other musical stage production. See *book*.

Lyrics: The words of a song.

Minstrel Show: A performance of humour, music and variety presented by actors in blackface makeup, imitative of a white person's view of Negro culture, especially of the last half of the 19th century.

Off Broadway: A term applied to theatrical productions of a dramatic or comedic nature, musical or otherwise, that are presented in smaller houses peripheral to the main theatre district in New York. See *Broadway*.

Opera: A musical drama, usually with orchestral accompaniment, and usually with all of the dialog conveyed in song. See *aria, recitative* and *chorus*.

Operetta: A musical drama, usually with orchestral accompaniment, and usually of a comic or romantic nature, in which the narrative is normally conveyed in a mixture of song and spoken dialog. See *opera*.

Princess Musical: A series of intimate theatrical productions, written by the team of Jerome Kern, Guy Bolton and P. G. Wodehouse, that broke with the European tradition and created a uniquely American style. They were named after the small Princess Theatre in New York that first hosted these presentations.

Recitative: A somewhat melodic imitation of speech, sung by a soloist in an opera or other musical stage presentation. The style is rhythmically free, in imitation of the natural inflections of spoken dialog. A recitative normally advances the plot or narrative, and most often is paired with and precedes a related aria (which see).

Revue: A theatrical production, usually on a grand scale, in the form of a variety show loosely connected by a general theme or plot, and emphasizing feminine beauty in a more refined manner than burlesque. See *burlesque* and *vaudeville*.

Score: The body of music for a theatrical production, referring specifically to the melodies and orchestrations, but by extension applied also to the lyrics.

Through-composed (through-sung): A theatrical production in the "Broadway" format in which most or all of the dialog is presented melodically through arias, recitatives, choruses, etc., in the manner of grand opera.

Vaudeville: A variety show presentation of comedy, music and specialty acts directed toward general audiences, and downplaying the sexual content and elaborate displays inherent in burlesque and revue (which see).

BIBLIOGRAPHY

Beauty and the Beast. Milwaukee, Wisconsin: Hal Leonard Publishing Corporation, 1991.

Block, Geoffrey. *Enchanted Evenings*. New York: Oxford University Press, 1997.

Bordman, Gerald. *American Music Theatre: A Chronicle*, 2nd Edition. New York: Oxford University Press, 1992.

Broadway Gold. Winona, Minnesota: Hal Leonard Publishing Corporation, 1982.

Broadway Platinum. Winona, Minnesota: Hal Leonard Publishing Corporation, 1982.

Flinn, Denny Martin. *Musical! A Grand Tour*. New York: Schirmer Books, 1997.

Garebian, Keith. *The Making of West Side Story*. Oakville, Ontario: Mosaic Press, 1995.

Gordon, Joanne. *Art Isn't Easy: The Theater of Stephen Sondheim*. New York: Da Capo Press, Inc., 1992.

Gottfried, Martin. *Balancing Act*. New York: Kensington Publishing Corp., Pinnacle Books Div., 2000.

Green, Stanley. *Broadway Musicals Show By Show*, Fifth Edition. Milwaukee: Hal Leonard Corp., 1996.

Hirschhorn, Clive. *The Hollywood Musical*. London: Octopus Books Ltd., 1981.

Katz, Ephriam. *The Film Encyclopedia*. New York: Perigee Books Div. Of The Putnam Publishing Group, 1979.

Kimball, Robert, and Alfred Simon. *The Gershwins*. New York: Atheneum, 1973.

Lees, Gene. *Inventing Champagne, The Worlds of Lerner and Loewe*. New York: St. Martin's Press, 1990.

Maltin, Leonard. *Leonard Maltin's Movie & Video Guide*, 2002 Edition. New York: New American Library, 2001.

Martin, Mary. *My Heart Belongs*. New York: Warner Books, Inc., 1976.

Martin, Russell. *Beethoven's Hair*. New York: Broadway Books, 2000.

McBrien, William. *Cole Porter*. New York: Alfred A. Knopf, 1998.

Mordden, Ethan. *Coming Up Roses, the Broadway Musical in the 1950s*. New York: Oxford University Press, 1998.

Mordden, Ethan. *Make Believe, the Broadway Musical in the 1920s*. New York: Oxford University Press, 1997.

Mordden, Ethan. *Rodgers & Hammerstein*. New York: Harry N. Abrams, Inc., 1992.

My Fair Lady. New York: Penguin Putnam Inc., 1980.

Pygmalion. New York: Penguin Putnam Inc., 1980.

Rodgers, Richard. *Musical Stages*. New York: Random House, 1975.

Secrest, Meryle. *Somewhere For Me, A Biography of Richard Rodgers*. New York: Alfred A. Knopf, 2001.

Secrest, Meryle. *Stephen Sondheim, A Life*. New York: Alfred A. Knopf, 1998.

Sennett, Ted. *Hollywood Musicals*. New York: Harry N. Abrams, Inc., 1981.

Sheward, David. *It's a Hit*. New York: Watson-Guptill Publications, 1994.

Solomon, Brian. *The Heritage of North American Steam Railroads*. Pleasantville, NY: The Reader's Digest Association, Inc., 2001.

ENDNOTES

Introduction

1 "On the Street Where You Live" (Lerner and Loewe: *My Fair Lady*).

2 "Somewhere" (Bernstein and Sondheim: *West Side Story*).

3 There are various reasons why most Baroque operas are rarely performed today, and shallowness of plot ranks high among them.

4 The next time you watch a *Law and Order* episode, "Try To Remember" that Jerry Orbach was the Narrator and also the character El Gallo in the original 1960 production of *The Fantasticks*.

5 "Oh, What a Beautiful Mornin' " (Rodgers and Hammerstein: *Oklahoma!*).

6 *The Jazz Singer* of 1927 is generally credited as being the first film with an integrated sound track, although it contained only the songs and one extended spoken exchange between the lead character and his mother. The remainder was silent, and used frames of printed text to convey the dialog. Earlier primitive attempts to provide sound with recordings on disks were largely unsuccessful, as they were difficult to synchronize with the film.

7 If you don't believe this, call to mind the two most famous traditional wedding marches. The "Here Comes the Bride" theme is by Wagner, and the other one is Mendelssohn's.

8 A few examples: *I Do, I Do* is a musical version of *The Fourposter*, *The Most Happy Fella* was adapted from *They Knew What They Wanted*, and perhaps most famous of all, *West Side Story* is an updated *Romeo and Juliet*.

9 Not content to leave well enough alone, Hollywood tried again in 1951. While undeniably beautiful in Technicolor, and benefiting from the impressive vocal talents of Kathryn Grayson and Howard Keel, this remake of *Show Boat* garbles the plot and buries the emotional power of the original.

10 Bordman, p. 591.

11 *Cinderella* (Rodgers and Hammerstein).

12 *Gigi* (Lerner and Loewe).

13 It is questionable whether a concert presentation of a more traditional musical, such as *My Fair Lady* or *West Side Story*, would be equally effective.

14 Andrew Lloyd Webber's through-sung *Evita* actually preceded *Sweeney Todd*, opening in London in 1978, although it followed Sondheim's 1979 play on Broadway by six months.

15 One longs, however, for the perfection of Angela Lansbury's characterization of Mrs. Lovett in the stage version, and for the startling special effects when the Demon Barber slices his first victim's throat.

16 *Miss Saigon* is the product of the same team that created *Les Miserables*, Claude-Michel Schonberg and Alain Boublil.

Chapter 1

17 Green, p. 3.

18 Solomon, p. 29. Sadly, southern railroads were decimated during the ensuing war years, a factor that slowed reconstruction and limited the growth of the economy in the region.

19 Bordman, p. 1.

20 Green, p. 3.

21 Bordman, p. 7.

22 Then as now, the acting profession offered little long-term financial security for the majority of its adherents.

23 Bordman, p. 7.

24 Flinn, p. 81.

25 Bordman, p. 19.

26 Green, p. 3. Estimates for the cost of production ranged between $25,000 and $55,000, an extraordinary amount for those times and comparable to the inflated dollar amounts that are spent on the lavish productions on Broadway today.

27 Flinn, p. 82.

28 Professional song pluggers in the employ of publishers promoted the tunes of each current hit in the 1920s and 1930s, but as the recording industry flourished, phonograph records became far more influential. With the advent of the original cast album in the 1940s, entire scores quickly became familiar to audiences. This resulted in much greater attendance at the plays themselves, as well as sales of sheet music and records. Today it is common for cast albums to be on sale in theatre lobbies for promotional purposes.

29 Flinn, p. 82.

30 Even more than New York, the city of Boston was once known for a strict code of censorship regarding art and literature. The phrase "Banned in Boston" was therefore a powerful form of advertising for licentious material, and was an almost certain guarantee of success for a play or a novel. By attracting interest in other cities and towns, it generated an effect directly opposite that which was intended by the censors: widespread popularity and greater dissemination of the supposedly morally objectionable material.

31 Despite being fully covered by their tights, which were made of pink silk that appeared flesh-coloured to the audience, the dancers were frequently described in the press as being at least partially nude.

32 While *The Black Crook* is often cited as the prototype Broadway musical, it is more accurate to view it as a precursor of burlesque (see Chapter Three).

33 Flinn, p. 82.

34 Bordman, p. 19.

35 Flinn, p. 87.

Chapter 2

36 Technically, the word is the plural form of "opus," which simply means a "work," in this case a musical composition. Therefore an opera is a compilation of compositions (an example of a plural word that is now considered singular).

37 Kislan, p. 13.

38 The composer Christoph Willibald Gluck is generally credited with promoting this movement, which was subsequently embraced by Mozart and others.

39 In the film *Amadeus*, the Mozart character refers to his opera *The Magic Flute* as a "burlesque."

40 The element of satire, a component of much drama in almost any era, came close to defining the typical American musical of the 1930s, and enjoyed a strong resurgence in the 1960s.

41 Flinn, p. 54.

42 Kislan, p. 14.

43 Flinn, p. 54. This factor of integration of music and story later played a vital role in the success of the innovative musicals staged at the Princess Theatre in New York in the early 20th century, and in such subsequent productions as *Show Boat*. See Chapter Five.

44 Whether it is nobler to attract the public purse through satire or by sexual exploitation is a topic best left to philosophers.

45 Kislan, p. 19.

46 Bordman, p. 13.

47 The immensely popular Al Jolson is perhaps best known for his blackface routines, widely popularized by the first sound film, *The Jazz Singer*, in 1927.

Chapter 3

48 No pun intended, although the standards of what constituted female beauty leaned decidedly toward the plump and ample in those years. Today's anorexic starlets and models would have been totally out of the running.

49 Flinn, p. 85.

50 Flinn, p. 100.

51 Kislan, pp. 41-2.

52 Radio became an economic haven for many displaced vaudeville performers, such as George Burns and Gracie Allen.

53 Flinn, p. 99.

54 Kislan, p. 85.

55 Miss Brice was best known to wartime radio audiences as the voice of the irrepressible Baby Snooks. She was effectively (if somewhat inaccurately) portrayed by Barbra Streisand in the 1960 Styne-Merrill musical *Funny Girl*, as well as in a quality film version in 1968 and a less successful movie sequel, *Funny Lady*, in 1975.

56 Flinn, p. 106.

57 Rodgers' first major success came with the *Garrick Gaieties* of 1925, an outstanding example of this type of revue.

Chapter 4

58 It is significant that the life span of the operetta as a dominant form of legitimate musical theatre in the United States coincided almost exactly with that of burlesque, each preceding and contributing to the development of mature, essentially American musicals.

59 Flinn, p. 89.

60 Kislan, p. 97.

61 Secrest, *Somewhere For Me*, p. 67.

62 Bordman, p. 133.

63 Maltin, p. 72.

64 Sheward, p. 21. The integration of plot with music became an important characteristic of the Princess Theatre musicals, and later a hallmark of Rodgers and Hammerstein. The trend back toward opera eventually came full circle in the late 20th century, with the through-sung musicals of such creators as Andrew Lloyd Webber (*Evita*), Schonberg and Boublil (*Les Miserables* and *Miss Saigon*), and Stephen Sondheim.

65 Bordman, p. 391. It should be noted that one of the two authors of *Rose-Marie*, Oscar Hammerstein II, was also responsible for the book and lyrics of *Oklahoma!*

66 Flinn, p. 92.

67 In fairness, Friml's second most popular work, *The Vagabond King*, was set in France. But the almost equally popular play, *The Firefly*, had an American story line.

68 Among the three authors who contributed to the book and lyrics was Oscar Hammerstein II.

69 While the 1954 version preserved much of the music of the original, the story was first given two silent film treatments, in 1919 and 1927.

70 This story idea resurfaces with amazing regularity, most recently in the Disney movie *The Princess Diaries*, in which Broadway star Julie Andrews has a major non-singing role.

71 Flinn, p. 94.

Chapter 5

72 Following the widespread economic collapse that began in late 1929, the North American financial system experienced only limited recovery until World War Two, when

the demand for military equipment and personnel spurred industrial growth and solved the unemployment problem.

73 Secrest, *Somewhere For Me*, p. 26.

74 Pronounced "Wood-house."

75 Kislan, p. 117.

76 Flinn, p. 141.

77 Bordman, p. 203.

78 Flinn, p. 139.

79 Green, p. 23.

80 Kislan, p. 115.

81 Flinn, p. 143.

82 Secrest, *Somewhere For Me*, p. 28.

83 Bordman, pp. 319-20.

84 Flinn, p. 150.

85 Green, p. 24.

86 Although mounted in the somewhat larger Longacre Theatre instead of the Princess, this play was produced by the same management team, and is grouped with the Princess Musicals for historical purposes.

87 Flinn, pp. 154-5.

88 This year saw two productions which have remained in the repertoire almost continuously ever since. *Good News*, with its campus setting and several hit songs in the score, is a frequent choice for high school and college productions. And the redoubtable *Show Boat* enjoyed three film versions and a very successful run in Toronto and New York in the 1990s.

89 Although "A Pretty Girl" was from a revue, and not a book musical, it predicted the type of songs with which Berlin would later achieve lasting fame.

Chapter 6

90 Solomon, pp. 72-3.

91 Flinn, p. 166.

92 Bordman, p. 352.

93 Flinn, pp. 166-7.

94 Katz, p. 529.

95 Flinn, p. 167.

96 Martin, p. 44.

97 In the so-called "Swing Era" of the 1930s and '40s, the big bands of such musicians as Tommy Dorsey and Benny Goodman were among the very first performing groups in the United States in which members of the black and white races performed side by side. Many other bands, such as Glenn Miller's organization, were restricted to white membership, although the popularity of all-black bands such as those of Jimmy Lunceford,

Count Basie and Duke Ellington suggested a wider appreciation for their talents among the record-buying public, regardless of their racial background.

98 Mordden, *Make Believe*, p. 184.

99 Flinn, p. 168.

100 Green, pp. 43, 54.

101 Bordman, p. 242.

102 *Sunny* was not the first musical in which all three major elements (book, lyrics and score) were created by native-born Americans, but it is nevertheless a turning point, employing the talents of three such highly talented personalities on the cusp of their maturity.

103 His most effective and best-remembered tune from *Sunny* was "Who?", later to become a substantial hit recording for the Tommy Dorsey Orchestra in the Swing Era.

104 Mordden, *Make Believe*, p. 107.

105 A Russian immigrant of Jewish heritage, Berlin's career as a stage composer spanned over half a century and produced a huge body of musical standards, topped by the ubiquitous "White Christmas."

106 The best known of these white ensembles was the Original Dixieland Jass Band, and this early alternative spelling of "jazz" probably reflects the pronunciation of that word in the Negro dialect of the times. The exact origins of the word are somewhat obscure and in dispute.

107 History repeated itself in the mid 1950s, when Elvis Presley's successful recordings injected black vocal stylings into mainstream pop music, coincidentally helping to establish the new genre of rock and roll.

108 Bordman, p. 400.

109 Gershwin's first show was *La La Lucille*, written in 1919 when he was just twenty years old.

110 Green, p. 44.

111 Mordden, *Make Believe*, p. 109.

112 Their first effort, *Poor Little Ritz Girl*, opened in 1919, although aside from the clever title, it attracted little attention.

113 Kislan, pp. 91, 93-94.

114 Virtually all such American-influenced efforts were comedies, not dramas.

Chapter 7

115 In addition to his revues, Florenz Ziegfeld was the producer of several successful book musicals.

116 Bordman, p. 422.

117 Secrest, *Somewhere For Me*, p. 68.

118 Green, p. 55: "still another variation on the outlaw-in-disguise theme of such previous offerings as *Naughty Marietta* and *The Desert Song*."

119 When Ziegfeld moved *Rio Rita* to another theatre to make room for his production of *Show Boat* in December, it was still attracting substantial audiences.

120 Bordman, p. 423.

121 Katz, p. 643. Keeler was born in Halifax, Nova Scotia in 1909, and first appeared in a Broadway chorus line at age 14. She is best remembered for her role in the pivotal film about Broadway, *42nd Street* (1933), in which she played a girl picked from the chorus line to replace an injured star.

122 This self-styled "King of Jazz" was among the most popular recording artists of the day, leading an ensemble that featured such talents as Bing Crosby, the Dorsey Brothers and Bix Beiderbecke. Whiteman's orchestra presented the premier of Gershwin's *Rhapsody in Blue* in 1924, and was the centrepiece in the first Technicolor film musical, also entitled *The King of Jazz* (1930).

123 Green, p. 56.

124 Bordman, p. 424.

125 Mordden, *Make Believe*, p. 113.

126 Bordman, p. 427.

127 Sheward, p. 27.

128 This is especially true when the budget is limited, as appropriate costumes and sets are generic to the age group in question.

129 *Dearest Enemy* ran for 286 performances, and *Peggy-Ann* for 333.

130 Bordman, p. 431.

131 Book by Paul Gerard Smith and Fred Thompson.

132 Green, p. 59.

133 Hirschhorn, p. 357.

134 Green, p. 59.

135 Book by Hammerstein and Otto Harbach, music by Emmerich Kalman, Herbert Stothart and Robert Stoltz.

136 Bordman, p. 435.

Chapter 8

137 Mordden, *Make Believe*, p. 128.

138 Hammerstein's attention to the conventional book musical was occasionally diverted by innovative experiments, however, most notably the adaptation of Bizet's opera *Carmen* in 1943, with an all-black cast and under the title *Carmen Jones.*

139 Green, p. 60.

140 Rodgers and Hammerstein perfected the device of the musical soliloquy, an expansion of the dramatic soliloquy employed centuries earlier by such playwrights as Shakespeare to allow the audience to share a character's innermost thoughts and feelings. The "Soliloquy" from *Carousel* is the prototype for this device in musical theatre. In a rudimentary sense, two tunes from *Show Boat*, "Bill" and "Can't Help Lovin' Dat Man,"

accomplish the same end, although not in the extended form that made the *Carousel* experiment so innovative.

141 Block, p. 37.

142 Although the term "Negro" is now rarely used to describe persons of African descent, and in the modern perspective is considered by many to be derogatory or condescending, it is employed here in its historical context, just as it was used by Hammerstein. Even more inflammatory today is his use of the word "nigger" in the dialog and the song "Old Man River," but it must be considered within the perspective of the reconstruction years, and also of 1927 when the libretto was written. Hammerstein chose his language carefully, so as to be realistic and historically accurate, but used it in a manner that managed to convey subtly his own outrage at the innate racism of the times.

143 It is ironic that Jefferson is often credited with the "all men are created equal" phrase that was such a major foundation stone in the establishment of the United States (see Chapter Two).

144 He wrote both the music and the lyrics.

145 Secrest, *Somewhere For Me*, pp. 360-1.

146 Those who would revise history may be well intentioned, but their efforts often achieve results diametrically opposed to what they intend. In the case of *Show Boat*, the protesters should have had more faith in theatre audiences to place the play in its historical context, and to recognize it for what it was, an appeal for the abolition of prejudice. This same sort of misguided censorship has resulted in an unfortunate pattern of book-banning, exemplified by the removal from school libraries of such powerful anti-racist books as Harper Lee's *To Kill A Mockingbird* because of the historically accurate language they contain.

147 Block, p. 25.

148 Flinn, p. 516.

149 Robeson's militant civil rights activities were decades in advance of the movement that finally produced positive changes in the segregation laws of the United States in the 1950s and 1960s. His sympathy for communism also drew much unfavourable attention, and adversely affected his career.

150 Winninger was also a member of the original stage cast in 1927. His skill at physical comedy was featured in other films throughout the decade, including *Babes In Arms* (1938).

151 Flinn, p. 178.

152 Flinn, p. 181.

153 Green, p. 68.

154 509 first run performances.

155 Flinn, p. 183.

Chapter 9

156 Block, p. 40.

157 *Sweet Adeline* (1929), *Music in the Air* (1932), and *Very Warm for May* (1939).

158 From *Roberta*.

159 From *The Cat and the Fiddle*.

160 From *Sweet Adeline*.

161 Both from *Music in the Air*.

162 Green, p. 74.

163 The Technicolor process was in its infancy and very expensive, and was therefore initially reserved only for movies that could guarantee a strong box office.

164 Bordman, p. 451.

165 Included in the score was the perennial favourite, "Night and Day."

166 Some multi-talented stars, such as George Burns and Gracie Allen, began in vaudeville, then made a smooth transition to movies and eventually to television.

167 Radio provided employment for many vaudeville and revue performers, such as Ed Wynn, Jack Benny and Fanny Brice, whose "Baby Snooks" character was immensely popular. In an odd twist, the ventriloquist act of Edgar Bergen and Charlie McCarthy was similarly successful, despite the fact that radio did not provide the visual impact of a talking dummy. Bergen's talents for comedy and voice characterization were his stock in trade.

168 Bordman, p. 490.

169 Trivia buffs should note the presence in the original cast of Vivian Vance, later to become Lucy Ricardo's sidekick Ethel Mertz in the *I Love Lucy* series on television.

170 The song "I Get a Kick Out of You" contains the word "cocaine," but because of pressure from censors it is often changed, most commonly to "perfume from Spain." Cocaine was at one time widely available without prescription, and was even an ingredient in such products as soft drinks. It was outlawed only after its addictive qualities became understood.

171 McBrien, p. 169.

172 McBrien, p. 167.

173 McBrien, p. 170.

174 Green, p. 78.

175 It may not be grammatically correct, but "I Got" is the correct original phrase, not the more literate "I've Got."

176 Bordman, p. 476.

177 Green, p. 74.

Chapter 10

178 Flinn, p. 187.

179 Kimball and Simon, p. 36.

180 Bordman, p. 316.

181 Block, p. 61.

182 Grofe is best known for his symphonic tone poems on American themes, the *Mississippi Suite* and the immensely popular *Grand Canyon Suite*.

183 Block, p. 61.

184 The Russians Stravinsky, Prokofieff, Shostakovich and Rachmaninoff wielded considerable influence, and Maurice Ravel's work (somewhat in the impressionistic style of DeBussy) injected a French flavour, tending to overshadow indigenous North American efforts.

185 Block, p. 60.

186 The somewhat chaotic atmosphere surrounding the creation of the *Rhapsody* relies heavily on anecdotal evidence, but it is acknowledged that Grofe completed the orchestration barely in time for the performance, and that Gershwin played the solo piano part from memory, as he had not yet committed it to paper.

187 Block, p. 61.

188 Flinn, p. 193.

189 Kimball and Simon, p. 173.

190 Block, p. 63.

191 It is hard to imagine that Heyward, with his innate sympathy for and understanding of the culture of his subjects, could not have been uneasy with such a minstrel show type of interpretation.

192 Flinn, p. 194. There is also evidence that George did not consider himself sufficiently skilled to attempt the project at that time, and was already contemplating further study in preparation.

193 Kimball and Simon, p. 173.

194 Green, p. 91.

195 From *George Gershwin*, edited and designed by Merle Armitage (London: Longmans, Green and Co., Ltd., 1938), as quoted by Kimball and Simon, p. 174.

196 Flinn, p. 196.

197 Block, p. 65.

198 Bordman, p. 494.

199 Broadway came full circle with the use of recitative and aria in the last quarter of the 20th century in operatic musicals such as *Sweeney Todd* (Sondheim) and *Les Miserables* (Schonberg and Boublil), and even Andrew Lloyd Webber's *Evita*.

200 Block, p. 65.

201 Bordman, p. 495.

202 Flinn, p. 200.

203 Green, p. 91.

204 Flinn, p. 200.

205 Hirschhorn, p. 279. Witness Frank Sinatra's climactic performance of "Ol' Man River" in the 1946 film, *Till the Clouds Roll By*. If you can ignore the highly fictionalized story of Jerome Kern's life, this film is a tribute to that composer's talent, and features

wonderful performances by Judy Garland, Kathryn Grayson, Angela Lansbury, Dinah Shore and others.

206 Ira returned to Broadway without his brother for the 1936 edition of *Ziegfeld Follies* (music by Vernon Duke).

207 Flinn, p. 207.

Chapter 11

208 Bordman, p. 495.

209 The other two are "My Romance" and "Little Girl Blue." The waltzes of Richard Rodgers have been favourably compared to those of Johann Strauss Jr.

210 Hirschhorn, p. 167. The two songs were the title tune and "Where Or When."

211 The most notable versions are by Bobby Darin, Ella Fitzgerald, Louis Armstrong and Frank Sinatra.

212 Weill addressed the tragedy of racial conflict in South Africa in this adaptation of Alan Paton's novel *Cry, the Beloved Country*.

213 Mary Martin, pp. 83-4.

214 *Dubarry Was a Lady* (408 performances), *Panama Hattie* (501 performances), and *Let's Face It!* (507 performances), respectively.

215 Despite the patriotic fervour of many motion pictures during World War Two, relatively few stage plays capitalized on the theme.

216 *Too Many Girls* (1939, 249 performances) and *By Jupiter* (1942, at 427 performances the longest running Rodgers and Hart musical).

217 Secrest, *Somewhere For Me*, pp. 39, 101.

218 Kislan, p. 135.

219 Secrest, *Somewhere For Me*, p. 181. A more reasonable figure would be half that total, as Rodgers probably wrote slightly less than a thousand songs in his entire life.

220 As defined by Meryle Secrest in *Somewhere For Me*, "A male rhyme… has its accent on the final syllable, while a female rhyme has the accent on the penultimate syllable," p. 34.

221 Rodgers, pp. 27-8.

222 Flinn, p. 216.

223 Rodgers, p. 204.

224 Flinn, p. 216.

225 Rodgers, p. 204.

226 Shakespeare himself borrowed this one from a predecessor, Plautus.

227 Based on *The Taming of the Shrew* and *Romeo and Juliet*, respectively.

228 Flinn, p. 216.

229 Green, p. 112.

230 Bordman, p. 523.

231 Block, p. 104.

232 Green, p. 112.

233 Block, p. 104.

234 Green, p. 111.

Chapter 12

235 Secrest, *Somewhere For Me*, p. 240. The failures were: *Rainbow* (1928, 29 performances); *The Gang's All Here* (1931, 23 p.); *Free For All* (1931, 15 p.); *East Wind* (1931, 23 p.); *Three Sisters* (1934, 45 p.); *Gentlemen Unafraid* (1938, cancelled on the road before New York); *Very Warm For May* (1939, 59 p.).

236 Rodgers, p. 207.

237 Flinn, p. 211.

238 Rodgers, p. 9.

239 Bordman, p. 401.

240 Rodgers, p. 20.

241 Flinn, p. 211.

242 Bordman, p. 404.

243 Flinn, p. 219.

244 After *By Jupiter* in 1942, Rodgers and Hart's only other collaboration was a revival of *A Connecticut Yankee*, concurrent to *Oklahoma!*, for which the team wrote some new music. Hart was frequently confined to hospital during this period, the only times when he was sober enough to do quality work.

245 Rodgers, p. 207.

246 Flinn, p. 218.

247 Kislan, pp. 139-40.

248 Rodgers, p. 216.

249 Flinn, p. 219, quoting Oscar Hammerstein II.

250 The understated manner in which the chorus finally appeared is also significant. Hammerstein disguised it within the women's preparations for a rural social event.

251 It is interesting to examine the use of the term "musical comedy" within the context of *Oklahoma!* It had become the fashion to call all musicals "comedies" in the 1930s and early 1940s, excepting only such works as *Porgy and Bess* for which new terms, in that case "folk opera," were coined. But *Oklahoma!* required that a new and more encompassing definition be created, one that became much more common later in the century: "music drama."

252 Rodgers, p. 218.

253 Sheward, p. 67.

254 Rodgers, p. 219.

255 Flinn, p. 220.

256 Bordman, p. 535.

257 Secrest, *Somewhere For Me*, p. 121.

258 It seems almost ironic that less than a century after *The Black Crook's* accidental success with a ballet troupe, the concept would return to its original intention: an artistic statement integral to the plot.

259 "Slaughter On Tenth Avenue."

260 Bordman, p. 534.

261 Sheward, p. 67.

262 Green, p. 119. In *Somewhere For Me*, Meryle Secrest specifies 2,248 (p. 256), also supported by Bordman, p. 536.

263 Bordman, p. 536.

Chapter 13

264 Secrest, *Stephen Sondheim, A Life*, p. 37.

265 Secrest, *Somewhere For Me*, p. 241.

266 Hammerstein's mother had died when the young man was fifteen, and she was probably much less influential on her son than his assertive father.

267 The King's limited affection for his children, especially the youngest, is touched upon briefly. But having so many of them, it is obvious that he knows none of them well, with the exception of the first-born son, the Prince, who is to inherit the throne.

268 Green, p. 184.

269 *The Sound Of Music* purports to be biographical, and in fact is loosely based upon the lives of the Trapp Family Singers. However, the play takes so many liberties with events and personalities that most of what is seen on stage, and especially in the film version, is fiction.

270 Secrest, *Somewhere For Me*, p. 276.

271 This plot element is nevertheless close to a Christian view of the hereafter, and would supposedly have been foreign to someone of Judaic background like Hammerstein.

272 Secrest, *Somewhere For Me*, p. 276.

273 Bordman, p. 546.

274 Secrest, *Somewhere For Me*, p. 355.

275 *Broadway Platinum*, p. 16, from *The Sound of Music* (1959) by Rodgers and Hammerstein.

276 It's tempting to speculate that his Jewish background influenced this attitude, although concrete evidence supporting this theory is not extant.

277 *Broadway Gold*, p. 72, from *The King and I* (1951) by Rodgers and Hammerstein.

278 Secrest, *Somewhere For Me*, p. 345.

279 The craft of criticism carries with it a tremendous responsibility, in that audiences are often unwilling to take a chance on something new that supposedly knowledgeable columnists have denigrated. However, some very worthwhile productions have survived on the strength of word-of-mouth advertising even after poor reviews, notably those two phenomenally successful efforts, *The Fantasticks*, and *Les Miserables*.

280 Secrest, *Somewhere For Me*, p. 354.

281 There may also have been some element of whistling in the dark, given the threat of nuclear annihilation present during the cold war.

282 Secrest, *Stephen Sondheim, A Life*, p. 115.

283 *Broadway Platinum*, p. 149, from *Oklahoma!* (1943) by Rodgers and Hammerstein.

284 Laurents also provided the book for *West Side Story*, and is cited by Sondheim as having a powerful influence upon his work.

285 Read "stripper."

286 Playwrights often borrow freely from each other, and ideas are frequently recycled.

287 It is no surprise that Sondheim collaborated, although only once, with Richard Rodgers after Hammerstein's death. He wrote the lyrics for the Rodgers production *Do I Hear a Waltz?* (with a book by Arthur Laurents), which opened on Broadway in 1964 for a modest 220 performances. At the time, however, Sondheim was already beginning work on his own revolutionary approach that resulted in *Anyone Can Whistle* (1965).

288 Gordon, pp. 13-14.

289 Gordon, p. 112.

290 Gordon, p. 301.

Chapter 14

291 Green, p. 122.

292 *Cabin in the Sky* was profitable in 1940, but on a modest scale at 156 performances. The film version, director Vincente Minelli's first major assignment, has been released on tape, and provides a fascinating insight into Hollywood's early treatment of black cultural themes.

293 Bordman, p. 540.

294 Flinn, p. 228.

295 Bordman, p. 540.

296 "If I Loved You", "June Is Bustin' Out All Over", etc. Again, the power of the original cast album to manufacture hit tunes proved to be contributory to the popularity of the stage play.

297 *My Fair Lady*, p. 188.

298 *Broadway Platinum*, pp. 20-1, from *Gigi*, by Lerner and Loewe.

299 Mordden, *Rodgers & Hammerstein*, p. 95.

300 Bordman, p. 559.

301 Mordden, *Rodgers & Hammerstein*, pp. 95-96.

302 While this number would have been substantial two decades earlier, the cost of mounting a Broadway musical had risen considerably. At 2,212 first-run performances, *Oklahoma!* had set records to which other shows now had to aspire. *Carousel* lasted a substantial 890, but Allegro was not considered a hit by the standards of the day. Nor did it produce a memorable score.

303 Flinn, p. 234.

304 358 performances. Like *Allegro*, the story was original with Hammerstein, not adapted from another literary source, and was somewhat contrived and unsatisfying.

305 Secrest, *Somewhere For Me*, pp. 294-5.

306 Based upon a novel by John Steinbeck, it may ultimately have been unsuited to musical treatment by anyone, no matter how skilled.

307 The films over which Rodgers and Hammerstein retained control are the most faithful to the stage conceptions, and most successfully realised as entertainment. The best of these is *The King and I*, which could almost be a stage play itself in mood and setting, followed closely by *Oklahoma!* and *The Sound of Music*. *Carousel* was partially out of their hands, and was subtly distorted, and *Flower Drum Song* also suffered too many changes from the original.

Chapter 15

308 The two men worked together briefly in 1919 and 1920; see Chapter Twelve.

309 *State Fair* was an original film musical, released in 1945 and remade in 1962. It has been argued by some that this motion picture was much less successful as a musical than their first two stage productions, but perhaps that is only in contrast to the overwhelming popularity of *Oklahoma!* and *Carousel*.

310 An original television production for the CBS network.

311 Hard on the heels of *Oklahoma!*, *Carmen Jones* enjoyed a substantial run of 503 performances on Broadway, and was dramatically filmed in 1954.

312 Notice especially their productivity during the last days of Hammerstein's life: one major television event and two full-scale Broadway musicals in less than three years.

313 Secrest, *Somewhere For Me*, p. 305.

314 *Oklahoma!, Carousel, State Fair.*

315 His first major success, *Show Boat*, was based on the Edna Ferber novel by the same name. Hammerstein's skill at narration is not in question, nor is the dramatic power of his plot development. It is rather his ability to fashion innovative story ideas that is open to discussion.

316 *The Boy Friend* is notable for Julie Andrews' first appearance on Broadway, two years before her monumental success in *My Fair Lady*.

317 Green, p. 187.

318 Secrest, *Somewhere For Me*, p. 369, quoting Alan Brien.

319 Gordon, p. 26.

320 Gordon, p. 35.

321 Gordon, p. 36.

322 Bordman, p. 669

323 Green, p. 229.

324 *Company* was one of only two musicals to return a profit that season. The other was *Applause*, by Charles Strouse and Lee Adams.

Chapter 16

325 Green, p. 125.

326 Bordman, p. 543.

327 Flinn, p. 243.

328 Green, p. 129.

329 On the plus side, the cast included Pearl Bailey and Juanita Hall, and the score contained the subsequent standard "Come Rain or Come Shine."

330 Bordman, pp. 551-2.

331 Secrest, *Somewhere For Me*, p. 278.

332 "Doin' What Comes Natur'lly"; "The Girl That I Marry"; "They Say It's Wonderful"; "Anything You Can Do"; and more.

333 Bordman, p. 555.

334 "How Are Things in Glocca Morra?"; "If This Isn't Love"; "Look To the Rainbow"; "Old Devil Moon"; etc.

335 Bordman, p. 557.

336 Green, p. 134.

337 Secrest, *Somewhere For Me*, p. 364.

338 "Another Op'nin' Another Show"; "Why Can't You Behave?"; "Wunderbar"; "So In Love"; etc.

339 Bordman, p. 566.

340 Green, p. 144.

341 Bordman, p. 579.

342 Flinn, p. 341.

343 Mordden, *Coming Up Roses*, p. 58.

344 Lees, p. 63.

345 Bordman, p. 581.

346 Green, p. 165.

347 Bordman, p. 592.

348 Green, p. 166.

349 Bordman, p. 598.

350 Green, p. 168.

351 Flinn, p. 252.

352 Green, p. 177.

353 In what surely must rank as the least astute decision ever made by musical comedy actors, the role was declined both by Gene Kelly and Danny Kaye, among others.

354 Green, p. 182.

355 Sheward, p. 154.

Chapter 17

356 Flinn, p. 340. Lerner worked with composers Kurt Weill and Burton Lane, for example, between *Brigadoon* and *My Fair Lady*.

357 Lees, p. 4.

358 Bordman, p. 540.

359 Lees, p. 46.

360 Sheward, p. 94.

361 Lees, p. 52.

362 Bordman, p. 563.

363 Pronounced "Mar-EYE-uh."

364 Lees, p. 63.

365 Hirschhorn, pp. 319, 324.

366 Block, p. 230.

367 "The Ascot Gavotte" and "Just You Wait."

368 Lees, p. 89.

369 Bordman, p. 598.

370 Lees, p. 93.

371 Green, p. 168.

372 Bordman, p. 597.

373 Mordden, *Coming Up Roses*, p. 154.

374 Sheward, p. 138. The problem of poor singers or non-singers in musicals was not a new one. The music for Anna in *The King and I* was carefully crafted with a limited range to accommodate Gertrude Lawrence's tendency to sing flat. But in *My Fair Lady*, the question of to sing or not to sing became moot. Harrison's dramatically modulated sing-speak worked just fine.

375 Bordman, p. 598.

376 Miss Andrews commanded a four-octave range in her youth, and only slightly less in her maturity.

377 Miss Hepburn tested for the singing sequences, but the producers wisely chose to have voice mimic Marnie Nixon dub her songs. See Appendix for more information.

378 Mordden, *Coming Up Roses*, p. 151.

379 Hammerstein established this element of female independence in *Show Boat*, with the strength of character shown by Magnolia Ravenal and her daughter Kim.

380 Block, p. 231.

381 Mordden, *Coming Up Roses*, p. 152.

382 Sheward, p. 138.

383 Based on *The Once and Future King*, by T. H. White.

384 Bordman, p. 619.

385 Green., pp. 188, 190, 196.

386 Bordman, p. 619.

387 Lees, p. 317.

388 The composer died in 1988, having outlived the much younger lyricist by nearly two years.

389 Despite a short run (280 performances), it was considered worthy of filming, but the 1970 version starring Barbra Streisand was only marginally successful.

390 Sennett, p. 255.

391 "Gigi"; "The Night They Invented Champagne"; "Thank Heaven for Little Girls"; "I'm Glad I'm Not Young Any More"; "I Remember It Well"; etc.

392 How times have changed!

393 Sennett, p. 255.

394 Block, pp. 243-4.

395 *Paint Your Wagon* is purposely omitted here.

Chapter 18

396 Bordman, p. 570.

397 Green, p. 144.

398 Bordman, p. 559.

399 727 performances.

400 "Everything's Coming Up Roses"; "Let Me Entertain You."

401 Proponents of his later work, *The Most Happy Fella* (1956) will probably disagree.

402 Green, p. 148.

403 Bordman, p. 564.

404 Flinn, p. 421.

405 Bordman, p. 576.

406 Green, p. 167.

407 TV's original *My Favorite Martian*.

408 Novels, operas, plays and even musicals (e.g., *Cabin in the Sky*) have given this Faustian theme many serious and comedic interpretations.

409 His name in the play is Mr. *Apple*gate. Get it?

410 Example: "That glorious morn Jack the Ripper was born…"

411 Mordden, *Coming Up Roses*, p. 101.

412 Green, p. 189.

413 Bordman, p. 617.

414 Orbach's acting and vocal talents were on display in such hits as *Chicago* and *42nd Street* before his success as Lenny Briscoe.

415 *Flower Drum Song* and *The Sound of Music*.

416 *My Fair Lady* and *Camelot*.

417 Green, p. 188.

418 Bordman, p. 616.

419 Green, p. 209.

420 Bordman, p. 638.

421 Beware of the 1972 movie version, perhaps the most execrable assassination ever perpetrated by Hollywood on Broadway.

422 Green, p. 219.

423 Kislan, p. 182.

424 Bordman, p. 651.

425 The plot lines in the stage and film versions are very different. See Appendix.

426 Based on the "Peanuts" cartoon characters of Charles Schultz.

427 Without much story line, but celebrating the sexual revolution, protest movement and hippie culture of the times, it lasted a substantial 1,750 performances.

Chapter 19

428 Especially in a long-term post with the New York Philharmonic.

429 Reiner was permanent conductor of the Chicago Symphony for many years.

430 Bordman, p. 545.

431 Green, p. 126.

432 Robbins' twelve substantial hits included such diverse titles as *The King and I* and *Call Me Madame*.

433 Both accomplished actors, Comden and Green were also included in the cast of *On the Town*.

434 Not the same as the *Theme from New York, New York*, the movie tune popularized by Liza Minelli and especially Frank Sinatra in the late 1970s.

435 Regrettably, most of the Bernstein-Comden-Green score was left out of the popular and successful 1949 film version, which starred Frank Sinatra and Gene Kelly and was dramatically shot on location (a major first for musicals, which were usually confined to the somewhat artificial surroundings of studio back lots).

436 But not the book, which was the work of Joseph Fields and Jerome Chodorov.

437 Green, p. 165.

438 Bordman, p. 585. *Wonderful Town* lasted for 559 performances.

439 Green, p. 172.

440 Some have called the music pretentious, but that might be true only in the context of a typical Broadway musical. *Candide* aspired to be something more.

441 Mordden, *Coming Up Roses*, p. 175.

442 Bordman, p. 602.

443 Mordden, *Coming Up Roses*, p. 175. The same sort of criticism was later levelled at *Les Miserables*, especially by first-night critics, casting doubt on their own background knowledge of great literature.

444 Bordman, p. 602.

445 Green, p. 239.

446 Secrest, *Stephen Sondheim, A Life*, p. 120.

192

447 Bordman, p. 681.

448 Mordden, *Coming Up Roses*, p. 170.

449 Bordman, p. 605. Sondheim's credentials were both literary and musical, the latter benefiting from his studies with composer Milton Babbitt.

450 Mordden, *Coming Up Roses*, p. 239.

451 Maltin, p. 1165.

452 Block, p. 257, paraphrasing Guernsey, ed., *Broadway Song and Story*, p. 43.

453 Green, p. 175.

454 Bordman, p. 688.

Chapter 20

455 From *Hold Everything* (1928), by DeSylva, Brown and Henderson.

456 From *Show Boat* (1927), by Kern and Hammerstein.

457 *Broadway Platinum*, p. 71, from *The Fantasticks* (1960), by Jones and Schmidt.

458 *Broadway Platinum*, p. 112, from *State Fair* (1945) by Rodgers and Hammerstein.

459 *Broadway Gold*, pp. 60-1, from *Guys and Dolls* (1950), by Frank Loesser.

460 *Broadway Gold*, p. 98, from *South Pacific* (1949), by Rodgers and Hammerstein.

461 *Broadway Platinum*, p. 4, from *Finian's Rainbow* (1947), by Harburg and Lane.

462 *Broadway Platinum*, p. 78, from *Knickerbocker Holiday* (1938) by Weill and Anderson.

463 *Broadway Platinum*, p. 71, from *The Fantasticks* (1960) by Jones and Schmidt.

464 It takes an uncommonly good play and an unusually talented pair of actors to hold an audience's attention without the usual trappings of choruses, dancing and extravagant sets. *I Do! I Do!* was such a play, and the actors, Robert Preston and the wonderfully talented Mary Martin in the twilight of her career, were perfectly cast. It ran for 560 performances.

465 Green, p. 220.

466 *Broadway Platinum*, pp. 54-5, from *I Do! I Do!* (1966), by Jones and Schmidt.

467 *Broadway Gold*, p. 107, from *Mame* (1966), by Jerry Herman.

468 This is one more example of the inept casting that detracted from the film version of *Camelot*. The song worked on stage because of the age spread between Richard Burton and Julie Andrews, an element that was missing in the movie (see Chapter Seventeen).

469 *Broadway Platinum*, pp. 234-5, from *Bells Are Ringing* (1956), by Styne, Comden and Green.

470 *Broadway Gold*, pp. 199-200, from *Porgy and Bess* (1935), by Gershwin, Gershwin and Heyward.

471 Young children appeared infrequently on the Broadway stage prior to World War Two.

472 It is probably unfair to say that Strouse and Adams stole the "Kids" idea from Hammerstein, but they cannot have escaped being influenced by it. The similarities are

too pronounced. *Flower Drum Song* must have touched a nerve. While not as successful as such Rodgers and Hammerstein productions as *Oklahoma!* or *Carousel*, it had a respectable first run of 600 performances.

473 Green, p. 276. This extravagant spectacle had a computerized mechanical set that was in almost constant motion, with shifting ramps and a huge suspension bridge that combined into various patterns for the roller-skating cast. It is said to have been so expensive that even a full house could not pay for the cost of staging it.

474 *Broadway Platinum*, pp. 13-4, from *The Sound of Music* (1960), by Rodgers and Hammerstein.

475 From *The Music Man* (1957).

476 *Broadway Gold*, pp. 78-9, from *Can-Can* (1953), by Cole Porter.

477 *Broadway Gold*, pp. 106-7, from *Mame* (1966), by Jerry Herman.

478 From *Wish You Were Here* (1952), by Logan, Kober and Rome.

479 From *Guys and Dolls* (1950), by Frank Loesser.

480 From *South Pacific* (1949), by Rodgers and Hammerstein.

481 *Broadway Gold*, pp. 133-4, from *Lost In the Stars* (1949), by Weill and Anderson.

482 From *Finian's Rainbow* (1947), by Lane and Harburg.

483 *Broadway Platinum*, pp. 94-5, from *South Pacific* (1949), by Rodgers and Hammerstein.

484 *Broadway Gold*, pp. 63-4, from *Guys and Dolls*, by Frank Loesser.

485 *Beauty and the Beast*, p. 22, by Menken and Ashman.

Chapter 21

486 Perhaps no product was more vilified in the 1960s than the American automobile. Although powerful, flashy and overhyped, these "supercars" often expired very soon after their meagre warrantee periods, setting the stage for the Japanese invasion of the North American car market.

487 Gottfried, p. 190.

488 Gordon, p. 28.

489 Bordman, p. 635.

490 Secrest, *Stephen Sondheim, A Life*, p. 142.

Chapter 22

491 Bordman, p. 664.

492 *Babes In Arms*, *A Chorus Line*, etc. also used this format.

493 Green, p. 232.

494 Gordon, p. 76.

495 Green, p. 232.

496 The list of Sondheim hits from his stage plays is remarkably short: "Send In The Clowns," and "Good Thing Going" are the only two that have been recorded with any

great success by popular stylists. Frank Sinatra's versions of these two are distinctive and affecting. However, Sondheim's work in other genres, such as the songs for the film *Dick Tracy* that were sung by pop diva Madonna and earned him an Academy Award, have brought his work to the attention of many who have never seen one of his stage plays.

497 Green, p. 237. Every song in the show is in some form of triple meter, and the overture is sung by a quintet, rather than played by an orchestra.

498 *Sweeney Todd, Sunday In The Park With George,* and *Into The Woods* have all been produced in the filmed-on-stage format.

499 Others, notably *Into The Woods*, are so complex as to require several viewings, even by the most attentive theatregoers.

500 Gordon, p. 154.

501 600 first-run performances.

502 Green, p. 245.

503 Gordon, p. 174.

504 The temptation to interpret history in terms of present-day values reached the height of absurdity in 1992, with the 500th anniversary of Christopher Columbus' first voyage of discovery to the new world. Vehement critics sought to hold him personally responsible for the deaths from European diseases suffered by the native population, as if Columbus should have known it would happen, and should have stayed home. Ridiculous! Only through hindsight can ethical responsibility be assigned to his voyage of discovery.

505 Gordon, p. 175. Ms. Gordon provides an excellent analysis of the political turmoil surrounding the production, as well as an insightful analysis of its musical and dramatic structure.

506 Stylistic speech is vital to authenticity, as with the slang in *Guys and Dolls*.

507 Green, p. 245.

Chapter 23

508 Gordon, p. 207.

509 Gordon, p. 219.

510 Green, p. 253. There are also many parallels between the original story of *Sweeney Todd* and the literary crusades of Charles Dickens.

511 Gordon, p. 230.

512 Bordman, p. 697.

513 Gordon, p. 251.

514 Green, p. 253.

515 Sixteen performances.

516 Bordman, p. 708.

517 Pp. 255-261.

518 It includes Sondheim's "other" hit (with "Clowns"), "Good Thing Going."

519 Secrest, *Stephen Sondheim, A Life*, p. 328.

520 This monumental work measures a full 120 by 81 inches, or ten by nearly seven feet! It's composition is highly detailed, and the colour dots cause it to shimmer with an almost palpable light.

521 Secrest, *Stephen Sondheim, A Life*, p. 327.

522 Gordon, p. 264.

523 Gordon, p. 265.

524 Bordman, p. 716.

Chapter 24

525 Gordon, pp. 301-302.

526 Gordon, p. 306.

527 It is curious, however, that a golden slipper was substituted for the more traditional one made of glass.

528 In a tribute to those original frighteners of generations of children, the Sondheim/ Lapine tales are as dark and foreboding as the Brothers Grimm at their worst.

529 Sometimes one must work hard to remember that so optimistic a soul as Oscar Hammerstein II was Stephen Sondheim's mentor!

530 Gordon, p. 314.

531 Gordon, p. 314.

532 Gordon, p. 337.

Chapter 25

533 Bordman, p. 535.

534 Lerner and Loewe explored the same territory in *Brigadoon* (1947), wherein the dissatisfied suitor Harry Beaton threatens the safety of his enchanted village, but is accidentally shot and killed. Beaton is portrayed as sympathetic, despite the peril his actions impend for the townspeople.

535 The peripheral deaths in this musical are presented more for emotional effect or as plot contrivances, rather than to comment upon the human condition.

536 Even the venerable *Oklahoma!* played only 293 performances in 1979.

537 3,486 performances.

538 Bordman, p. 700.

539 Green, p. 254.

540 This pioneering work had little spoken dialog, depending primarily upon the lyrics to carry the story line.

541 Music by Claude-Michel Schonberg, English lyrics by Herbert Kretzmer after the original French text by Alain Boublil and Jean-Marc Natel.

542 At the author's third attendance at *Les Miserables*, in the spring of 2001, the power of this scene, and of theatre in general to move an audience, was amply demonstrated. As the youthful actor portraying Gavroche descended from the barricade, a shot was fired,

seeming to tumble him to the ground. He struggled to crawl toward the discarded firearms, and with exquisite timing at the sound of the next shot, his body convulsed, drawing an involuntary gasp from the audience. With unusual restraint for such a young performer, he reacted somewhat less to the next shot, and even less to the next, gradually subsiding into a most realistic simulation of death. As the scene played out, crying could be heard among members of the audience, for whom the scene was, in an emotional sense, not just drama but very real.

543 This plot device by Victor Hugo also served as the source material for the television series *The Fugitive*, and for the Harrison Ford movie of the same name.

544 Some attendees reported not recognizing the mayor as the same man from the previous scene.

545 Although other factors may have been at work, this does not speak well for the level of education of the reviewers, and is one more example of the folly of underestimating the power of public opinion.

546 The plight of the ostracized offspring of Vietnamese women and American servicemen served as part of the motivation for the second act. Rejected by their own people and abandoned by their absent fathers, these children were left to grow up in orphanages with little hope for meaningful futures. In a scene set in the United States, films of these children formed a backdrop to a fundraising effort on their behalf. Their very existence was portrayed as an indictment of American involvement in that tragic war.

547 The killing of Bambi's mother in the Disney cartoon classic no doubt traumatized a whole generation of people now in late middle age.

Afterword

548 Of significant importance was the recent revitalization of the theatre district in New York, transforming it from seedy to respectable once more.

549 Music and lyrics by Mel Brooks, book by Brooks and Thomas Meehan.

550 1979, 1990 and 1988, respectively.

Appendix

551 Flinn, p. 520.

552 Maltin, p. 480.

553 Bordman, p. 710.

554 Flinn, p. 520.

555 Green, p. 247.

556 This song quickly became a perennial choice for auditions by kid performers, and was probably responsible for ending many budding careers before they began. The melodic line is technically quite difficult, especially for young voices. The range is not extreme (an octave and a fourth), but there are a number of unsympathetic skips, especially the

descending major 7th that occurs at the end of the first full phrase. It's an open invitation to disaster for any child (or adult!) with insecure pitch.

557 The original Depression-era comic strip often contained some very pointed satire. Consider especially the choice of the name "Warbucks," a not-too-subtle jab at combat profiteers.

558 One awards ceremony named her the worst actress of the year, a cruel and ill-conceived attack on a very young performer. Even if true (which, in the author's opinion, is not the case), the blame should have been aimed at the director and not the actress, who at such an early age bore little of the responsibility for the interpretation of the character.

559 Compare especially the performances of the song "Little Girls" in both films.

560 Fans of *Sex and the City* should note that one of the juveniles who played Annie during its run on Broadway was Sarah Jessica Parker.

561 Sennett, p. 273.

562 The reasons why she left the film are variously reported as ill health and/or unreliability. Her scenes have been preserved, and are available commercially as part of the DVD version of the film. They reveal an actress with considerable skill and undeniably superior vocal talent. However, she appears to be physically drained, supporting the contention that her poor health was the primary reason for her replacement. At the time, her growing addiction to drugs, partially a result of the studio's attempt to control her weight, was not public knowledge.

563 *Beauty and the Beast* was the first full-length animated film to be so honoured.

564 Maltin, p. 98.

565 Green, p. 297.

566 Tim Rice provided the lyrics for some of the new material, as Howard Ashman had died shortly after completing work on the film.

567 Hirschhorn, p. 370.

568 Sennett, p. 329. If you want to see Minnelli at his best, the 1944 film musical *Meet Me in St. Louis* is a good place to start. This movie also showcases the extraordinary voice and acting talent of a slender and exquisite Judy Garland, who subsequently became Minnelli's wife.

569 Bordman, p. 557.

570 Sennett, p. 276.

571 By Charles Strouse and Lee Adams.

572 By replacing Chita Rivera with Janet Leigh, the Hispanic element was deleted, along with the wonderful comic song, "Spanish Rose."

573 Sennett, p. 331.

574 This sequence also belies the supposed innocence of the character, however. It is a strip tease in reverse, with the character getting dressed in a seductive manner that almost contradicts the satire of the lyrics.

575 Sennett, p. 351.

576 Grey reprised his Broadway role.

577 Flinn, p. 504.

578 Hirschhorn, p. 334.

579 The demanding songs of Dorothy Dandridge, in the lead female role, were dubbed by opera's Marilyn Horne.

580 Hirschhorn, p. 342.

581 Filmed on location. Try to obtain the wide screen version. The one compressed for a normal TV screen misses too much of the choreography.

582 Ms. Lucky's most admired film role can be seen in *The Music Man*.

583 Always thoroughly prepared, Sinatra was well known for needing only one take. The double filming was seen as necessary, since it was not known whether the wide-screen version would limit its acceptability in theatres that lacked the specialized CinemaScope 55 equipment. Ironically, most theatres quickly converted their hardware, and this fear proved to be unfounded. In the end, only the wide screen version was shot.

584 Sinatra's version of the *Carousel* "Soliloquy" became a staple of his concert repertoire throughout his career.

585 Hirschhorn, p. 363.

586 Maltin, p. 423.

587 Horschhorn, p. 398.

588 Harburg is best known for his work with Harold Arlen in the film *The Wizard of Oz*.

589 Sennett, p. 332.

590 Hirschhorn, p. 373.

591 You can almost count them on the fingers of one hand.

592 Sennett, p. 68.

593 Hirschhorn, p. 75.

594 Sennett, p. 69.

595 Maltin, p. 501.

596 Flinn, p. 507.

597 Hirschhorn, p. 336.

598 Bordman, p. 680.

599 In the role of gambler Nathan Detroit, Sinatra had little opportunity to display his considerable vocal talent, which in 1955 was at its peak. His only standout solo, "Adelaide," was written for the movie, and was not in the original stage production.

600 Hirschhorn, p. 349.

601 Sennett, p. 319.

602 Hirschhorn, p. 376.

603 Sennett, p. 319.

604 The filming is not static, however. The director used camera angles, close-ups and other techniques to focus attention for dramatic purposes, much as an audience member must do independently in the theatre.

605 Sennett, p. 284.

606 Hirschhorn, p. 354.

607 Maltin, p. 734.

608 Sennett, p. 284.

609 1952, 1956 and 1953, respectively.

610 Unfortunately flawed by a distorted plot, it is the most beautiful version of the three, shot in Technicolor.

611 Hirschhorn, p. 342. The hyphen was omitted from the title this time.

612 Sennett, p. 277.

613 Flinn, p. 511.

614 Hirschhorn, p. 338.

615 Sennett, p. 275.

616 Maltin, p. 796.

617 Only one tune was altered significantly. Most of the verse of the very beautiful "My White Knight" was unaccountably dropped, although the bridge was incorporated into the only new song, "Being in Love."

618 Sennett, p. 337.

619 Nixon dubbed many such parts, notably Natalie Wood's Hispanic-sounding *Maria* in *West Side Story*. She can be seen on screen in the small role of Sister Sophia in *The Sound Of Music*, one of the rare times you can hear her glorious voice, all her own and not in imitation of someone else. She occasionally appears in dramatic (non-singing) roles on television.

620 Sennett, p. 337.

621 Flinn, p. 513.

622 Secrest, *Somewhere For Me*, p. 332.

623 Sennett, p. 287.

624 Maltin, p. 1033.

625 Flinn, p. 514.

626 Sennett, p. 290.

627 Maltin, p. 1033.

628 Hirschhorn, p. 360.

629 Maltin, p. 1033.

630 Sennett, p. 291.

631 Hirschhorn, p. 358.

632 Sennett, p. 291.

633 Maltin, p. 1080.

634 Hirschhorn, p. 365.

635 This film proves that the best adaptations most often feature the original stage actors.

636 Hirschhorn, p. 120.

637 The first sound films date from 1927, just nine years before this production, and many of the difficulties of balance and microphone placement tended to give the songs in movie musicals a distant or garbled texture. Careful attention to overcoming these problems is evident in the 1936 *Show Boat*.

638 Sennett, p. 149.

639 Hirschhorn, p. 120. This is all the more amazing, considering that the director, James Whale, had previously made his mark with the very different *Frankenstein* (1931) and *Bride of Frankenstein* (1935).

640 Sennett, p. 45.

641 Both words and music by Rodgers.

642 Although rarely seen, Nixon is the unbilled voice of many non-singing actresses who have been featured in film musicals.

643 Hirschhorn, p. 362.

644 It was filmed on Kauai in Hawaii.

645 Sennett, p. 286. The film's director, Joshua Logan, later admitted that the colour experiment failed to enhance the atmosphere in any meaningful way, and actually detracted from it.

646 Hirschhorn, p. 263.

647 Sennett, p. 207.

648 Maltin, p. 1303.

649 Flinn, p. 519.

INDEX

Bart, Lionel, 112, 126

Basie, Count, 179

Bartholomae, Philip, 31

Bates, Kathy, 153

Beaumarchais, 14

Beethoven, Ludwig van, 13

Beiderbecke, Bix, 180

Bennett, Robert Russell, 91

Benny, Jack, 70, 182

Bergen, Edgar, 182

Berkeley, Busby, 45, 158

Berlin, Irving, 32, 37, 40, 58, 66, 76, 85,
90, 95-7, 152, 178-9

Berlin Philharmonic, 101

Bernstein, Leonard, 82, 89, 92, 99, 107,
114-8, 126-7, 132, 167, 174, 192

Bizet, Georges, 84, 90, 155, 180

Bloomer, Amelia, 91, 95

Bock, Jerry, 111

Bolton, Guy, 29-32, 42, 67, 71, 170

Bontemps, Arna, 95

Boone, Pat, 167

Borodin, Alexandre, 98, 162

Boublil, Alain, 175, 177, 183, 196

Brando, Marlon, 109, 159-60

Brecht, Bertold, 66, 133

Brice, Fanny, 22, 109, 126, 177, 182

Broderick, Matthew, 163

Brooks, Mel, 197

Brown, Lew, 44, 47

Brynner, Yul, 161, 163

Burlesque, 17-24, 27-9, 35-6, 40, 100,
141, 150, 160, 169-71, 176-7

Burnett, Carol, 150, 152

Burns, George, 176, 182

Burrows, Abe, 86, 109

Burton, Richard, 105-6, 193

C

Cahn, Sammy, 108

Capone, Al, 142

Capote, Truman, 99

Cariou, Len, 130, 167

Caron, Leslie, 106

Carroll, Diahnn, 52, 99

Cervantes, Miguel de, 112

Channing, Carol, 108-9, 126

Chevalier, Maurice, 106

Chicago Times, The, 20

Chodorov, Jerome, 191

Cinemascope, 154-5, 161, 198

Civil War, 8, 16-7, 24

Cohan, George M., 66

Cole, Jack, 159

Colette, 106

Columbia University, 34, 72

Comden, Betty, 44, 98, 114-5, 153, 192-3

Comstock, F. Ray, 29-30

Concept Musical, 88, 93, 169

Constitution, The, 16

Cook, Barbara, 162

Coppola, Francis Ford, 157

Coward, Noel, 99, 102

Crawford, Michael, 158

Crouse, Russel, 78

Cullen, Countee, 95

Curtis Institute, The, 114

D

Dandridge, Dorothy, 198

Da Ponte, Lorenzo, 14

Darby, Ken, 165

Darin, Bobby, 167, 183

Darion, Joe, 112

Davis, Luther, 98

Day, Doris, 164

DeBussy, Claude, 182

Declaration Of Independence, The, 16

Delmar, Harry, 45

De Mille, Agnes, 76, 85-6, 95-6, 101-2, 118,
153, 163-4

Depression, 21-2, 28, 47, 54, 58, 63, 65, 75,

Princess Musicals, 32-40, 42, 43-48, 170, 178

Princess Theatre, 27, 29-32, 40, 67, 71, 176-7, 182

Prokofieff, Serge, 183

Puccini, Giacomo, 13, 146

Q

Quinn, Aileen, 150-1

R

Rachmaninoff, Serge, 183

Radio, 2, 12, 21, 45, 56-7, 70, 101, 176

Raitt, John, 164

Ravel, Maurice, 183

Redgrave, Vanessa, 106

Reiner, Fritz, 114, 192

Remick, Lee, 126-7

Reubens, Paul, 29-30

Revill, Clive, 164

Revue, 17-8, 22-3, 27-30, 32, 35, 39-40, 43-5, 56, 58, 60, 66, 100, 129, 141, 148, 169-71, 177-9, 182

Rice, Tim, 198

Rigg, Diana, 130

Riggs, Lynn, 72-3

Ritchie, Michael, 157

Rivera, Chita, 111, 198

Roaring Twenties, 21, 43, 47, 159

Robbins, Jerome, 86, 97-100, 114, 117-8, 157, 167, 192

Robeson, Paul, 53, 165-6, 181

Rodgers, Mary, 100

Rodgers, Richard, 2, 5, 23, 32, 39, 44-5, 49, 51-2, 54-5, 57-8, 65-76, 79-82, 84-5, 87-92, 95-6, 98, 100-2, 107-9, 111, 121, 124-5, 129, 133, 141-2, 161-4, 166-7, 177, 180, 184-5, 187-8, 201

Romberg, Sigmund, 26, 36, 38, 42, 48, 54-5, 71

Rooney, Mickey, 66

Roosevelt, Eleanor, 150

Roosevelt, Franklin Delano, 66, 150

Root, Lynn, 70

Rose, Billy, 84

Ross, Jerry, 109, 156

Rossini, Gioacchino, 4

Rostand, 110

Runyon, Damon, 109, 159

Russell, Rosalind, 160

S

Saidy, Fred, 82, 86, 95-6

Schmidt, Harvey, 120, 193

Schonberg, Claude-Michel, 175, 177, 183, 196

Schultz, Charles, 192

Schwartz, Arthur, 23, 58, 98

Seurat, Georges, 135

Shakespeare, William, 4, 69-70, 97, 116-7, 180, 184

Shaw, George Bernard, 99, 101-4

Sherwood, Robert E., 97

Shevelove, Burt, 86

Shillinger, Joseph, 61

Shore, Dinah, 184

Shostakovich, Dmitri, 182

Sinatra, Frank, 69, 109, 155, 159-60, 164-5, 183-4, 192, 195, 199

Slavery, 13, 15-7, 33, 50-1

Smith, Betty, 98

Smith, Paul Gerard, 180

Sondheim, Stephen, 5-7, 77-8, 82-4, 88-90, 92-4, 99-100, 109, 113, 116-7, 119, 124, 126-40, 143-4, 146, 158, 160-1, 167, 174, 177, 183, 187, 193, 195-6

Soo, Jack, 158

Spewack, Bella, 97

Spewack, Samuel, 97

St. James Theatre, 126

Steiger, Rod, 163

Stein, Joseph, 99, 111

Steinbeck, John, 91, 187